MAURICE CURTIS

DUBLIN
BE DAMNED!

Discovering a Heroic City.
Surviving a Hidden City.

THE OLD
Dublin
PRESS

First published in 2018 by
Old Dublin Press
Dublin
Ireland

CreateSpace edition   ISBN: 978-1-9996035-3-3
Paperback   ISBN: 978-1-9996035-0-2
eBook – mobi format   ISBN: 978-1-9996035-1-9
eBook – ePub format   ISBN: 978-1-9996035-2-6

Cover image: Courtesy of Dublin City Library and Archive
Cover design by Andrew Brown
Typesetting by Dinky Design

Printed in the EU

Items should be returned on or before the last date shown below. Items not already requested by other borrowers may be renewed in person, in writing or by telephone. To renew, please quote the number on the barcode label. To renew on line a PIN is required. This can be requested at your local library.
Renew online @ **www.dublincitypubliclibraries.ie**
Fines charged for overdue items will include postage incurred in recovery. Damage to or loss of items will be charged to the borrower.

Those inspiring, dedicated and courageous women, past and present in my life, who have had such a profound impact and influence on me.

CONTENTS

ABOUT THE AUTHOR

Maurice Curtis is a well-known Author and Historian. He has written extensively on Irish history and in particular, on Dublin. He is originally from the Rathmines area of the city. He is interested in the dynamics of personal, family and local history and is currently researching identity, ideology, culture and social change in Ireland. He is involved with the Dublin Book Festival and other festivals as well as conducting tours of Dublin. His numerous books have been reviewed in Irish national and local press and other media forms. They include:

Glasnevin in Old Photographs
Temple Bar: A History
The Liberties: A History
The Little Book of Ranelagh
Playing with Skulls: A Dublin Childhood
To Hell or Monto: The Story of Dublin's Most Notorious Districts
Portobello in Old Photographs
Rathfarnham in Old Photographs
Rathgar: A History
Rathmines in Old Photographs
The Liberties in Pictures

1

❦

The Prince and the Prisoner

It all began at Mount Jerome Cemetery. This was where we found, but did not see, Dublin's renowned invisible prince. We happened to come across his final burial place on a visit one Sunday afternoon to one of the city's oldest cemeteries. This extraordinary find posed for us numerous questions and elicited an equal number of answers, but all very questionable.

As children, including our parents, there was six of us in the family. Two adults, four children. Two of us were from our immediate family, myself and my younger sister, the other two were slightly older twin cousins. They had been farmed out to us years previously by an uncle and aunt in Limerick who had twelve children and were at their wit's end trying to cope. It was the custom in those days. For my sister and I, it was an upheaval. Our house smelt of burning turf and noxious farmyard smells for a week afterwards. Not to mention the tiresome fact that the twins quickly seemed to take over the house with their airs and graces and whatnots. 'Up from the bog', I reminded anyone.

We were regular visitors to this 'graveyard', as it was called in our time. Not all together, mind you, but usually in twos or threes and sometimes more. Some people often said to us that it was handy to be living a short stroll – just five minutes – from the graveyard. They said this knowingly, and with a wink. For us, however, it was much handier to be closer to Mountain View Park with its playground, the entrance to which was also just a skip and a jump from our house and opposite the entrance to the graveyard. We would have much preferred to be going there rather than to the other place. When we tried to wink back at these all-knowing individuals, we just couldn't. Our faces, seemingly, were not made for winking.

The word 'cemetery' followed later, a more refined word, some think, and one that did not concentrate one's thoughts on the implications of one's final destiny. There were lots of refined people in the graveyard, mostly in the older part and mostly dead. We visited the graveyard, religiously, every Sunday afternoon, come hail, rain or shine, to the shrine that was our Dad's family's grave. We used to go one way and come back a different route to feed our fascination, or horror, at the mystery, magic and mayhem of where we were. There was something enticingly haunting, ethereal and beautiful about Mount Jerome, whatever the season. We were in a sort of time warp between the past and the future – their end and our future.

In the early years it was usually Dad who brought us. He was a big, happy, hearty man with a genial disposition and lovely silver wavy hair which we were regularly called upon to massage. Mum said that this ensured the hair would keep growing. He wore distinguished looking black-rimmed spectacles (the very height of fashion), carried a leather briefcase when he came home in the evenings and bore himself with an air of confidence, happiness and as someone of consequence. He must have been, as our Mum was always telling us that he knew everyone in town. He had spent many years working in the hotel business and subsequently as a commercial traveller when his health started to give him problems. He was a dab hand at dealing with people, good, bad and small. Of the four of us, I was somewhere in the middle, a situation that suited me just fine. My name is Larry and called after my Dad, Harry. They mixed up the lettering in the birth certificate office, but I didn't mind. But some jackass always had to bring it up. 'Are you sure it was only the lettering that was mixed up?' The sheer cheek!

The graveyard was full of stand-up flat stones, a roll-call of people who were from different times, we believed, people who used the old trams, wore completely different clothing and hurried about as in the old black and white films. It was full and empty at the same time and a place where it was so easy to get lost – maybe forever, particularly since it covered nearly fifty acres. It was divided into the old and new parts. In the old part, near the entrance and surrounding the Gothic Victorian Chapel, were rows of impressively decorated tombstones and monuments. These signalled much affluence, and housed members of the deceased Protestant Ascendancy. Each one stood erect in silence, different from and indifferent to its neighbours and the humbler classes in the far distance. The incumbents of the tombs, vaults and mausoleums were a roll call of the elite and a testimony to the influence, control and monopoly of social, economic and political life by those that practically owned and governed Ireland. Here we saw names such as Roe, Guinness, Findlater, Bustard, Kirk, Hamilton, Drummond, Montgomery and Kincaid, to name a few.

These final resting places had additional features such as angels, dogs or symbols and insignia to denote the interred was a former Freemason, member of the Royal Irish Constabulary, a Huguenot, an artist or architect of some influence, or an orphan of no consequence. Some were cracked and crumbling with weathering and age. Some were covered in a kind of green slime that had accumulated from the overhanging trees. Most were overgrown and unkempt, for now even their mourners had joined them. The faded engravings dedicated to the dead seemed forlorn. Eerie trees leant towards the stones, with branches pointedly reaching out in haphazard fashion, as if in warning to the living or in beseeching forgiveness for those in the earth's embrace who cannot cry out. Crows cawed overhead, circling and swirling above and between the poplars, the yews, the cedars and the cypresses. The damp smell of old stones and moss filled the air, and in places weeds covered the graves of the dead, replacing loved ones who had long since ceased visiting. The labyrinth of narrow paths wove through the maze of graves, often difficult to follow.

In the newer part, our destination, the lines of similar gravestones were mostly of smooth white marble, with new black writing and with a scattering of floral tributes encased in what looked to us like upside-down glass bowls.

When we arrived at Dad's family grave, we spent our time tidying the grave which was enshrouded in the long grass as tall as ourselves and hence most exciting to be hiding in and not doing any such tidying.

One of the main paths leading to the grave was known as the Nun's Walk and ran parallel to the old high grey wall separating the graveyard from the Hospice for the Dying. There was a brick chimney tower on the hospice side which reached towards the sky. Not knowing that it was the laundry chimney we wanted to know how come they needed such a tall chimney? Had it anything to do with the dying people in the hospice? Furthermore, to confuse us even more, there was a ladder on one side going all the way up to the top. 'What is that for?' we wanted to know. 'Why should anyone go climbing up the outside of a chimney?'

'Oh, that's for the wicked in the hospice,' we were informed, 'particularly those who refuse to roll over and die as instructed by their carers'. They have to get out of their beds and climb up the chimney, jump in at the top and then go up in smoke. And,' he added, to make sure we understood, 'like the way the good Lord went up to heaven – in a cloud of smoke, or in His case, in a cloud of clouds.'

We were satisfied with this, more inclined to believe the unbelievable, particularly since the moment of entering Mount Jerome we seemed to be entering another world. One of the first indications of this was the warning just inside the gates: 'If you leave Mount Jerome to go to a local pub, be sure to take your car with you!' We were not sure to whom this was addressed to – presumably the dead, we imagined, since we did not own a car, and very few of our acquaintances did. It had to be a mistake, and the word 'car' should have been 'coffin' was our conclusion. We agreed to bring a marker along with us the next time and rectify the error.

Dad told us that it was the tradition for mourners to go celebrating after a funeral and they often went to pubs. We found this rather strange but his stories about which pubs they went to was even stranger. Besides the local pubs, some of the most popular with the recently bereaved were the Beggar's Bush, the Deadman's Inn in Lucan, the Dropping Well in Milltown, the Morgue in Templeogue and the Gravediggers in Glasnevin. Mourners used to go out of their way to commiserate with each other in these pubs. There was an appropriateness, they felt, in grieving in such establishments rather than in the Sunnybank Inn, Bongo Ryan's, the Brazen Head, the Stag's Head, the Boar's Head, the Hairy Lemon, the Hole in the Wall or the Tuning Fork. And, one dare not even mention Rice's or Bartley Dunne's. All these names carried a particular flippancy or even dubious aspect and lacked the necessary gravitas associated with funerals and the copious consumption of alcohol. The Morgue was thus known because when it was granted a licence in 1848 to serve alcohol one of the stipulations was that it would also serve as an undertaker. This was not unusual as many pubs throughout Ireland then and now often carry out the dual functions. So, if anyone died in tragic circumstances in the wider area, the bodies of the dead would be left in the pub until the coroner was able to examine the body. However, the use of the name, the Morgue, really came into use shortly after the opening of the tramline to Blessington via Mountain View, with the pub serving as a ticket office. Not only that, but the tram tracks were a metre from its entrance. Consequently, some people leaving the pub, in varying degrees of intoxication, were killed by the tram, not only because of its speed, but also its quietness. Conveniently, the bodies would be brought right back into the pub. The deceased customers would have been given a refund, but the publican realised that habits didn't have pockets.

The Gravediggers in Glasnevin is located wall to wall beside the original entrance to the graveyard and derived its name from a long-held tradition. After the opening of a grave and making the usual strenuous and back-breaking preparations for its guest, the gravediggers would go straight towards the nearby pub to wet their whistles. However, they didn't just walk into the pub for their pints.

Instead there was a secret knock on the wall that was shared by the pub with the graveyard. The barman would then pass the stout through the railings to the thirsty workmen, who would drink a toast to the grave's new tenant.

Back in Mount Jerome, along by the Nun's Walk was buried the invisible prince, which utterly confused us children. Dad pointed out a grave to us. 'There's the invisible prince,' he said. We all went 'Where, where, where?' and he burst out laughing. He pointed to a granite vault covered with a limestone slab on the right-hand side to where this 'invisible prince' was buried since the late nineteenth century. The only princes we had heard of were, firstly, the prince and the glass slipper, and secondly, in school, Silken Thomas and the Fighting Prince of Donegal (known as 'Red' Hugh O'Donnell) – the exploits of both of which had enthralled us. With the help of cannon guns, we learnt in school that Silken Thomas had unsuccessfully tried to take Dublin Castle from the occupiers, whilst the Fighting Prince of Donegal escaped from it with the help of tied sheets in the dead of winter. He slipped away on his horse to the hills of Donegal and his friends to plan for future victories.

This invisible prince filled us with questions, particularly the most obvious – how did they get him into his coffin if he was invisible? How did they know if he was still there, and had not flitted off? Yet seemingly someone had buried him, as on his tomb was engraved the words, 'Here Lies Joseph Sheridan Le Fanu, Dublin's Invisible Prince'. It was explained to us that Le Fanu was of French Huguenot descent, and was a famous writer in the late nineteenth century. Dad said that he wrote disquieting ghost stories, to horrify and capture the minds of the readers of his time. We didn't like the sound of that – particularly being captured by a ghost writer. We might end up as ghosts ourselves, flying around in white sheets, going 'Oooh, oooh' and scaring each other to bits.

Huguenots, we were told, were French Protestants that had been forced to flee persecution in France and elsewhere at the end of the seventeenth century. They were welcomed to Dublin by King William of Orange, which Dad found quite amusing since it was he, the reprobate, who had defeated the Catholics of Ireland in battle at the River Boyne in 1689. We had heard of King Billy only recently, having been brought to the Bank of Ireland on College Green on our way to see the Christmas lights in Henry Street. In the bank we saw the enormous carpets on the walls showing pictures of the Battle of the Boyne and the Siege of Derry. We couldn't figure out why they had put the carpets on the walls and not on the floors. The carpets are called 'tapestries', we were told, and were made by a man who had lived on World's End Lane in the very heart of Monto, 'Near where your Uncle Jack lives,' the father whispered to us. We didn't know why he whispered, as if inviting us into a plot.

That building, Dad had said, referring to the bank, was the former Irish Parliament, known as Grattan's Parliament. Just like the Dáil over in Kildare Street where the Taoiseach, Sean Lemass works. 'Him that signs his letters "Is mise le meas",' Dad laughed. Grattan's statue was outside with him pointing despairingly away from his former political home. He looked very regal but somewhat disappointed, as apparently, he had been evicted from the building in 1800.

'Why was he evicted?' we wanted to know. 'Did he not pay his rent?'

'No,' was the reply. 'He wanted the people of Ireland to be fully in charge of the building and everything that went on there, including making laws to run the country, but the greedy powers that be did not want the Irish to run the country as the lords and ladies that owned most of the land knew that it would be them that would be evicted from their lands, since they had robbed the land in the first place. They were like Judas and accepted lots of silver to vote against Mr Grattan, taking control of the building.' Yes, we knew all about Judas and his shocking goings on. 'But,' father whispered again, 'there were no tears shed in Dublin in 1929 when the statue of King Billy was blown up.' The statue of Thomas Davis, whose grave we visited in Mount Jerome, replaced that of King Billy. We liked the water fountain around it. 'What goes around comes around,' he added. Yes, we agreed, being frequent users of the merry-go-round in the playground.

Meanwhile, while we were looking at the grave of the invisible prince, Dad had taken out his pipe from his top pocket. He leant against a bench and tapped its bowl on the side. 'Just making sure it's empty,' he smiled. He slowly lit his pipe. Puff, puff, puff as the smoke was gently exhaled. It wafted, happily, past our noses. He repeated this a number of times and then leant back contentedly on the bench. Everything is well. He had that Walt Disney look to him and I imagined he must have been a film star before he married Mum. Maybe that's why she married him.

'Anyway, to cut a long story short,' he continued, and we gathered around him on the bench, 'Le Fanu was like Kitty the Hare,' and told tales like her banshee stories we read about in *Our Boys* and *Ireland's Own*. We knew all about the strange experiences of Kitty the Hare as she bounded along in her long cloak over the windswept bogs and boreens of Ireland fighting off banshees and headless men on horses. Moreover, we had seen banshees in the film *Darby O'Gill and the Little People* which had the Gaiety Theatre pantomime star, Jimmy O'Dea. We had seen him the previous Christmas singing 'Biddy Mulligan, the Pride of the Coombe' in the pantomime with Maureen Potter, another Gaiety stalwart we loved. Because Jimmy O'Dea was in the film and we knew him, we didn't mind banshees too much. Moreover, in the pantomime he was always going on about 'holding your breath for your porridge' – a feat which we all had tried at home.

But Le Fanu was worse, Dad, bending down, cautioned in a whisper, as 'he was the father of vampires including one called Carmilla.' This, of course, went completely over our heads but he told us that a vampire loved another person's blood and drank it when thirsty, not using a mug or a beaker, but directly from the person's neck! No manners whatsoever. Mum always warned us against drinking directly from the tap.

'Why didn't he drink just water?' asked Minnie, the youngest.

'Because he was just plain greedy,' was the answer. 'He was like the old landlords of Ireland that just sucked the very life out of their tenants by making them pay high rents and never letting them own the land, even though it was theirs in the first place. All blood suckers, every one of them, vampires all!' He said this as his jaws clamped down on his pipe.

We didn't like the sound of that. Banshees just chased people over the bogs and didn't seem to do much except scare the wits out of them, but vampires, they were a different story. However, Cousin Daisy put us wise. '*Empires* is what he is talking about.' She was called Elizabeth. 'Daisy' for short. I wanted to call her 'Lizzie', but she gave me that 'don't you dare!' look. Her outstanding facial feature was the sheer number of freckles on her face which was topped with a mop of frizzy red hair. She and her twin brother looked like they had just stepped off the boat from the Aran Islands or from a John Hinde postcard of children collecting turf in Connemara. When she smiled, which was rarely, her face dimpled, nicely. We called her 'bossy boots' but not to her face. Like her brother, she still spoke, despite her best efforts, with a hint of what we called a 'culchie' accent, even though she had been living with us for years. Going by her appearance, and her brother, we couldn't see any family resemblance with us. 'Red-heads are known to have fiery tempers,' noted Mum. Maybe she was right about our cousin. She always seemed to know what exactly was being said and what was going on. Her eyes were very sharp, sparkling, and had that inquisitorial look that seemed to say 'stop wasting my time.' They were a most striking feature. You wouldn't notice their colour, just that they might eat you up. And she always had all the answers to all the questions and was suspicious of everything, including us. She would find a conspiracy under a bush, but in this case, under a gravestone.

'He is speaking tongue in cheek,' she pointed out, eyeing us. Her lit-up eyes flashed around as she said this in a whisper. She was at times unpredictable as she was equally capable of near hysterical laughing, tittering and sniggering, often erupting into shrieks and being forced to quickly cover her mouth.

'Oh, you mean forked tongue,' chirped in Minnie, an angel on legs.

'Thereabouts,' Daisy said.

The cousins rarely came with us, being 'preoccupied with more sensible and important matters,' according to themselves (which really meant, by my reckoning, constantly reading in Rathmines Library or browsing across the road in the Banba second-hand bookshop). Despite that, we were stuck with our cousins some of the time. Usually they were interesting company anyway and never boring. Minnie had a less sceptical demeanour than Daisy, but often had her arms folded in front of her giving the impression that 'Yes, I'm listening, keep going and I'll decide.' And always full of questions. Dad used to chide her with Cab Calloway's 'Minnie the Moocher' and she liked that. He had us all going around like trainee hunchbacks, singing, 'Hi di hi di hi di ho! Hi di hi di hi di ho. Hey di hey di hey di hey,' and kept us singing till the words got faster and faster and jumbled up and then we all collapsed on the floor laughing our heads off and out of breath.

Cousin Freddy ('you may call me "Frederick", though we didn't), who was a few years older than me, had that Einstein look; you know – the real swot look, with a mop of tousled ginger hair that reminded me of Luke Kelly of The Dubliners. We called him Freddy Freckles, 'Freckles' for short, as, like his sister, he had thousands of freckles competing for space on his sun-burnt rounded face. He took nothing for granted and was always asking questions like Doubting Thomas we had heard about in school. Mum said he was a 'mixed bag' as, some days he would go to the library, but on other occasions he would have much preferred to be up the forbidden Bunner Lane near his school, Synge Street, smoking Sweet Afton and playing cards with his pals. Moreover, he said the grave of the playwright, J.M. Synge, in Mount Jerome, reminded him too much of school. He was sometimes in trouble as he had a propensity for going into people's front gardens on the way home from school and bashing in the heads of the innocent gnomes. Despite that, we were very fond of him and he made life seem very interesting. Minnie and I, however, were happy to go rambling around the ancient moss-covered headstones and vaults, with wide-open eyes and ears, listening to Dad's endless stories. We didn't need to go to Disneyland.

We all agreed that these vampires should give up their old sins and give all that extra blood to Pelican House, the blood bank, which some of us had heard about from the mother, whose name was Annie, a name we all really liked, and who had spent years working in hospitals before she got married. She kept her own medicine cupboard in the kitchen, high up, so we never had to go to the doctor.

To return to Le Fanu. Dad said he had loads of money and for a time was owner of the famous *Dublin Evening Mail* newspaper, later the *Evening Mail*, published from the early nineteenth century onwards from the corner of Parliament Street and Cork Hill, opposite City Hall. Le Fanu died in 1873. This paper, we were told, was Dublin's longest running and continued until the early 1960s. Dad was an avid reader. We happily remembered seeing the comic cartoon characters Jiggs (a former builder's labourer who accidentally became an overnight millionaire) and Maggie (his social climbing wife constantly trying to thwart his efforts to return to his old job and pals) in that paper. The father particularly liked the 'Letters to the Editor' page because, according to him, 'every lunatic in the land was allowed to rant.' He also liked the reports of the sick in Dublin hospitals whereby each person was known only by a number and their relatives would be able to follow their progress, for good or bad.

We were also told that Le Fanu had a huge influence at the time on what was called 'Gothic' or ghost-story writing. Another person who worked for the *Evening Mail*, but decades later, was one Bram Stoker, who had some kind of job going to the theatre and giving his views on the performance. He imitated Le Fanu's writing and wrote the story of Count Dracula, also a vampire. So, this filled us full of questions, as we wanted to hear all about this Dracula chap. We would hear the full story the following week, we were promised.

We waved goodbye to the invisible prince and quickly passed from the Nun's Walk and around by the wall towards the high, not so discreet, green gates that led into the hospice, or from the hospice to the cemetery. This gate with its galvanised covered bars was difficult to see through, except for a small gap near the handles. It was only used at night time and it was to hurry the dead to their graves rather than having to go to the trouble of bringing them all the way around by Hospice Avenue and then up the main road and through the cemetery's main gates. It didn't do to have the dead loitering around for too long, it was felt. Then there would be no need for hearses or mourners' limousines. Just pop the body onto a cart and in through the gates, quick as a flash.

We were highly suspicious of these strange goings-on and suspected that the nuns were covering up something. We were informed that the most likely reason was that the dead did not have the 'means' when they were living to afford themselves a proper burial. Hence, they ended up in second-hand coffins which facilitated a quick turnover but had to be carried out at night away from prying eyes. These coffins might have been purchased from the 'coffin colony' of Cook Street in the Liberties, an area where seventeen coffin makers carried on their lucrative business, with some specialising in 'best second-hand coffins'. This practice started in the eighteenth century when there was a shortage of burial space in the crowded city and often the dead were buried standing up! We thought this quite funny, imagining people dying on their feet, not lying down and being walked to their graves. After a while they were dug up, dumped into the River Liffey, and the coffin used for the next person (presuming they could afford to rent it).

Dad liked to tell us that the 'dying business was a great business to be in as there were always lots of openings and vacancies'. We imagined that no sooner had you turned into a skeleton than you were turfed out for the next tenant. However, we were more interested at the time in exploring the old vaults where, neighbouring children had told us, you could peep in through the door grills and see the coffins piled on top of each other. We hurried on to the family grave, flew through the few prayers, blessed ourselves and off with us back by the Yew Walk to the old part of the cemetery.

A number of vaults and tombs in particular intrigued us. Some were piled high with the dead, shelf upon shelf, from a long, long time ago. Others just had two or three coffins. Vaults were lined along passages side by side, each with their own door, like rows of small terraced cottages, except with no windows. Some of the doors, however, had little window-like grills, so we could peep in. Mausoleums were detached mansion-like structures with impressive architectural features such as pillars and statues adorning them. Some looked like miniature raised temples. Unlike the rows of vaults, these were detached and overlooked their neighbours.

We couldn't peep through the door of the grandiose Cusack memorial along the Hawthorn Walk that looked like a miniature temple on a plinth, but we could with others nearby. Layers of coffins for the entire world to see. What were they doing there? Just waiting for something, it seemed to us. They looked forlorn, all their relations long gone, and probably beside them. Yet to see them so exposed just didn't seem right to us, and certainly macabre. What's the point of being on display? Maybe they saw this just as a waiting room, and it was all 'Oh! A dreadful mistake, how awful!' but they would soon be back with their loved ones again. Maybe it would provide solace to the family back home enjoying their Christmas dinner and knowing that so-and-so is up in Mount Jerome. 'Maybe afterwards we could pop in to see them, to make sure they are still there and wish them a Happy Christmas.' Or so it seemed to us. Yet that class of people wouldn't have been seen dead like that, when alive, we thought. We knew their type from parts of Rathgar. Or maybe they would, as if trying to convince themselves and their loved ones that since they hadn't been buried like the rest of the dead, they were still with us. We could hear them say, 'Who do those awful people think we are? Being buried! Really! How awful!'

One vault, perched on top of a hillock, had a door built into the side of the hill, below it, just in case you had second thoughts. Another vault, along the Low Walk overlooking the River Poddle as it gurgled nearby, had some Latin words, *Fortis et Stabilis*, on the family shield, yet no name, and *per augusta, ad augusta*. Going on the family crest, it might well be of the O'Shaughnessy family, Dad suggested. He, being a man of great knowledge when it came to matters Latin, translated for us as 'through difficulty, to greatness'. 'Never forget that,' he added. We liked that, not the 'difficulty' but the 'greatness'. For us greatness and grandiosity went hand-in-hand. He liked quotes, which he said were better than nuggets of gold. 'If you have a tongue, use it,' he'd say. 'If you have ears, use them. Don't just hear, try and really hear. And if you have eyes, don't just look, see. Because,' he said, 'sometimes you don't actually see what is really there.' It sounded like the game, 'Riddle me this, Riddle me that'. He tried to explain. 'Look down at your feet. What are you looking at?' 'Feet,' we replied. 'Yes, but what else?' 'My shoes have gone all mucky from walking around here,' complained Minnie. 'Very good,' smiled Dad. 'You are seeing not just your feet but something else. Are you buffs able to see anything else?' 'My feet are also beginning to hurt me from all this walking,' piped up Minnie. 'Sorry pet, and yet you are absolutely right. You are looking at your feet not just as feet but as having a purpose – for walking, for running, for playing. Not only that but they are part of your legs and body. You wouldn't be able to get around without them. They are part of the full you that makes you all so perfect.' And we all laughed at being called 'so perfect'.

'Grandiose' was the word for many of the burial sites in this older part of the cemetery. We loved to hear the story of one in particular, that of the Gresham mausoleum near the old chapel. The name Gresham, of course, reminded us of the famous Gresham Hotel in Dublin's O'Connell Street, having heard of it from our father who had spent years working in the hotel business and as Manager of the Savoy Restaurant nearby. He pointed out the pedestal on top of this old burial chamber that supported a bell. There was a chain from it running inside. This was added on the strict instructions of the lady buried inside (presumably before she died, we hoped). She had a dread, as we did, of being buried alive, and she wanted to be able to ring the bell if she woke up, to attract attention. Freckles stuck his oar in just then, a real smarty. 'I guess she was just so used to ringing the bell for service in her hotel.'

'Yes,' Minnie agreed. 'Old habits, you know,' and giggled. I, however, was of the opinion that if I heard a bell ringing over her tomb, I wouldn't go over and ask her 'How are you keeping today, Mrs Gresham?' No, I would run and run!

We thought Mrs Gresham's idea was a great solution and bully for her if she acquired the habit in her hotel. Likewise, we were impressed with the lady in a nearby vault, known as the Weld vault. She was even smarter, we felt, as she had herself buried standing up and stuck to the wall of the vault, covered in plaster. At her feet was her artist's palette ready for work should she come alive again. In her arm was an urn, and we were told that she was holding it to make sure her enemies in the art world did not try to cremate her. Another lady had a similar solution in an adjacent vault. A Mrs Bradley had herself sculpted in stone and put atop her vault when she died. She also kept the empty urn clasped close to her.

However, the tomb which really excited us was just along from the Cusack Memorial and had a howling dog resting on his master's cloak. Apparently, his master was drowned while swimming and the distressed dog pinpointed the exact location on the shoreline where his master, Harvie, had drowned by standing on his cloak, and so rescuers were able to find the body. The family decided to mark this with the carving on the roof of the deceased's vault. Later, the dog was interred in the same vault.

On the opposite side of Hawthorn Walk were the burial plots of the 'Tom Toms' as we called them – Thomas Davis and Thomas Drummond, mid-nineteenth leaders of opposing political movements, who, we were told, were the 'big noises' in their time. Drummond gave his name to the Mount Drummond part of Mountain View. These were Dublin Corporation houses built from the 1930s onwards on the site of former Buckley's Orchard belonging to the Poor Clare nuns, who ran an orphanage and convent just off the main road facing the park. We had therefore heard of the name but not the man. Father pointed to the size of his mausoleum, which, he said, was the biggest monument in the cemetery. 'Even the dead have their vanities,' he said. Not only that, he suggested, but the temple-like monument was also making a statement about the arrogance and power of the British Empire. Not for Drummond the inconspicuous headstone of Thomas Davis.

It was always the way Dad carried himself that impressed us. You could see him thinking ahead yet radiating calm. He glanced through the notebook he always carried, which he called his three 'F's, or 'facts, figures and figments' diary. He licked his index finger before turning a page and smiled at us, and then we heard about Drummond's final resting place. It had a large sarcophagus supported with a massive Portland stone pedestal on top of a granite vault. For us it was as big as any of the two-bedroomed houses called after him on Mount Drummond Avenue. He had been a wealthy man, being the Under Secretary of Ireland from 1835–40. However, the Famine had caught up with him and he succumbed to the fever.

His contemporary, Thomas Davis, was a Young Irelander, an expression which we found quite bizarre – what was a Young Irelander? Were we Young Irelanders? His headstone read 'He served his country and loved his kind' which was fairly similar to Drummond's, which read, 'Ireland, a country which I have loved, which I have faithfully served and for which I believe I have sacrificed my life.' So, both, it seemed, loved, served and died for Ireland. 'But one was English and the other Irish,' was our cry. 'How come both died for the same country, then?'

'Well,' we were advised, 'read closely the other words on Drummond's tomb and tell me what it says.' We rushed back to Drummond's and read, 'I wish to be buried in Ireland, the country of my adoption…' Apparently, he whispered those very words when he was dying in bed. 'So, there is your answer. Like the Normans, he became more Irish than the Irish themselves.' We knew all about Strongbow and the Normans and becoming more Irish than the Irish themselves. What we really wanted to know was what did the Tom Toms actually do? Drummond tried to help the poor and also set up the police force in Dublin because of all the rowdiness during the Great Famine, and Davis tried to bring all the Catholics and Protestants together, just like they are in this graveyard, we were told, nearly side by side, with only a few yards separating them, and having a great chat about the old days. And why not, since they had all the time in the world. No time for airs and graces now. They just had to get on with being dead and put the past behind them.

On the way out, we passed by the Wilde's family grave, just across from the entrance to the Victorian Chapel. 'Here is another invisible man,' we were told, 'by the name of Oscar Wilde.'

'How's that?' we enquired.

'Look at what it says,' and he pointed to an inscription on the headstone: 'Oscar Fingal O'Flahertie Wills Wilde, Poet, Wit and Dramatist 1854–1900.'

'So?' we said in unison.

'His name is here but his body is not, it is in a famous Paris graveyard,' father said. And we wanted to know more about this other invisible man and why he was buried far from home in Paris. 'This is the grave,' said the father, 'that dared to mention his name, Fingal O'Flahertie,' and he explained.

Ah, we soon began to understand, or thought we did. We figured that since Fingal O'Flahertie was Oscar's real name, and he had been found out in England where he had been passing himself off to the high and mighty as one of them, he was exposed as a complete fraud and imposter. They were not very impressed, gave him a good boxing, told him he was a right bowsie and then threw him into Reading Gaol for two years. When he was released he fled to Paris, where he died in shame. The family too were ashamed and did not have his funeral at home in Ireland. Despite that, and blood being thicker than water, they still loved him and therefore included all his names, real and otherwise, on the family's headstone.

Dad called the grave 'holy ground', since the man who was not buried there had suffered for being an imposter. 'That "holy ground" must be the same as the song from the Clancy Brothers,' said Freckles, and didn't he start singing right there and then next to the grave – 'And still I live in hope to see, the Holy Ground once more. Fine girl you are!' He shouted the last line and within a few seconds we joined with him in singing and shouting, much to Dad's bewilderment at what he had started.

When we had finished singing about the Holy Ground, Dad continued trying to explain to the disinterested. Luckily for Fingal too, he said, the French people decided that since they liked his writings so much they didn't mind who or what he was, and consequently gave him a great funeral in their most important cemetery, Père Lachaise. Despite that, there were still some in Paris who were not impressed with Fingal being an imposter and helped themselves to a part of the sculpture that was built over his tomb. After going to all that trouble to steal the pieces, they just used them as paperweights. The French were like that when it came to love. For them it was either love with a passion or hate with a vengeance. With the latter, they specialised in despatching those they hated, not as sliced pans but as batch loaves.

While we were ruminating on batch loaves and the Clancy Brothers, Dad starting rambling on about prophets in their own country, and stuff about gutters and stars, which for us at this late stage was becoming all blah, blah, blah. It was high time to head for Anne's Sweet Shop, beside the park, for our regular ice-cream wafer and broken biscuits. Nothing else mattered.

So, leaving him to hold his breath for his porridge, we went flying down the Main Avenue towards the gates and lots of yummy ice cream. Waving to an on-coming hearse, Freckles grabbed the chain for the closing bell, which was also rung as the hearses glided in silently through the main gates and gave it a good tug. 'Very timely,' said Minnie, as the hearse glided silently past us up the avenue. Bong, bong, bong it boomed, much to our delight but to the consternation of the gate-keeper.

'Come here to me, ye little ruffians, and I'll kill yez,' he roared, as he staggered from his comfortable perch near the waiting room. But we were out the gate. Adler, the ancient car park attendant, mooched around outside, distinguished only because of an old peaked hat on his head. A butt of a cigarette dangled from the side of his mouth and his hands were deep down in the bulging coin-filled pockets of his greasy overcoat. 'Back into your coffin with you,' Freckles shouted at him.

To be described as 'odder than Adler' was either an insult or a compliment depending on the recipient. He liked to tell everyone they 'were looking well' so as to get a tip for minding the car while they visited the cemetery. He even complimented the recently deceased as they were driven through the gates and, for good measure, wished them the compliments of the season at appropriate times. He liked to keep his options open, it was said.

2

⁂

MOTHER BUNGY, THE MISSING HEAD AND MONUMENTS TO THE BRAVE

Mountain View was not always so called. After the defeat of the Vikings at Clontarf in 1014 by King Brian Boru, the residents had had enough of the name Harold as it reminded them of Harold the Viking and his boundary cross near the present-day Century House, which separated his land from that of the Archbishop of Dublin. Harold's land had extended to this marker from the foot of the Dublin Mountains, an area now called Harold's Grange Road. The residents assigned a new name to the area, Conquer Hill, to remind them of the victory over the invaders. Over time, of course, confusion arose over the spelling and because of the sheer number of chestnut trees that grew in the area. Some spelt it the original way; some preferred the 'Conker' way. It was eventually decided that since most people couldn't read or write anyway, it didn't really matter, provided they all pronounced it the same way. It came to pass then that Conker Hill was the accepted name for this unique district.

Conker Hill was very appropriate given its elevated position above the city and the large number of chestnut trees in the vicinity of what is now an enclosed park. For centuries, this was an open common area for grazing sheep, ducks and geese and known as The Green. It was surrounded and dotted with these great trees and a scattering of small houses. In the middle of the seventeenth century, following his victory at the Battle of Rathmines in 1649, Oliver Cromwell sent out one William Petty to map out the area as part of his Down or Petty Survey. In the course of the battle Cromwell's soldiers had noticed with envy the land of nearby Conker Hill.

If ever a person had the most appropriate name to coincide with his nature it was Petty. He was completely dispassionate about Ireland and was just there to do a job for Cromwell, which involved the calculation, confiscation and transfer of ownership of most of the land of Ireland to the victors of the Cromwellian wars in Ireland. As with the rest of the country he wanted to pack the residents of Conker Hill off to Connaught and confiscate their lands. Petty was based in the Crow's Nest on what is now Crow Street, Temple Bar. Cromwell needed lots of money to pay for his wars in Ireland. He repaid his soldiers and those thousands of adventurers who invested in his campaign, with Irish land and property. He infamously said to the Irish after the wars, 'To Hell or Connaught,' and Petty worked out how this was to be achieved. In the process, Cromwell sent 6,000 Irish children of defeated soldiers off to the West Indies as slaves. Some of these were from Conker Hill. When Petty arrived in Conker Hill in 1651, the people working for him were attacked and had their skulls battered and bruised by local residents who used huge prickly chestnuts as weapons. Having had enough, they quickly retreated, saying 'To Hell with this place', ignored Petty's instructions and out of spite reverted to its original name, Mountain View. After Petty left Ireland in the early 1650s, the Irish were left with just 20 per cent of their land. They had been in possession of 60 per cent in 1641.

It was also in Mountain View that the 'bold' Robert Emmet was arrested in 1803 at the young age of twenty-five. He was hiding out in Mrs Palmer's house at the junction of Le Vere Terrace and the main Mountain View Road when that notorious agent of the Crown, Major Sirr, who had shot Lord Edward Fitzgerald when trying to arrest him in 1798, came knocking on the door, demanding the whereabouts of Emmet. Emmet was in the process of escaping via a secret underground passageway that led to the nearby Grand Canal when Sirr managed to capture him. Following his execution on Thomas Street, his head went missing. We were told as children that his missing head was to be found in Mount Jerome, so we spent countless hours looking for it. Minnie thought she had struck gold, but it turned out to be a rotting Halloween turnip head someone had tossed over the wall. Dad was able to quote part of the bold Robert Emmet's speech:

> Let no man write my epitaph; and my tomb remain uninscribed
> and my memory in oblivion until other times and other men
> can do justice to my character. When my country takes her
> place among the nations of the earth, shall my character be
> vindicated, then, and not until then, let my epitaph be written.
> I have done.

We found this all very mysterious as the only 'taph' we had heard about was Pat Taaffe, a famous jockey who had ridden a horse called Arkle which everyone was talking about and saying, 'You should nip into Kilmartin's a put a few quid on him.' Not only that, but here was a man telling people not to put anything on his headstone till the time was right.

'What does all that mean?' I asked, feeling weighed down with all these turnip heads.

'Basically, the young Emmet didn't want his headstone to be inscribed until Ireland was free,' Dad replied. He said it was known as 'The Speech from the Dock' and was one of the most celebrated patriotic speeches of the century, inspiring future generations of nationalists. That's all very fine, I thought, but where is his missing head?

In the early nineteenth century, many aspiring residents regarded the area to be a most suitable location despite the many subversives who seemed to live and congregate there. Over the years some well-to-do folk from the city centre, requiring fresh air and wanting to escape the people flocking to Dublin due to the Great Famine, found in Mountain View an atmosphere conducive to healing and well-being. It was situated on a slightly elevated site above the city, full of little drumlins or hillocks, known as mounts and left by a passing glacier during the Ice Age. The result was place-names deriving inspiration from the local topography such as Mount Pleasant, Mount Drummond, Mount Harold, Mount Tallant, Mount Argus, Mount Jerome and Mountain View. Moreover, in our teen years, we too, derived inspiration. In our case, it was from Mount Anville, Mount Sackville and Mount Rushmore.

It is to be noticed that the area called Marymount differed from other hilly areas which had the 'mount' first. This was because in 1845 the newly arrived to Mountain View gathered for a secret meeting up against the boundary wall with Mount Jerome, where only the dead could hear. Everyone in Mountain View had expected the new convent and hospice complex to be called Mount Our Lady, or Mount Mary, but the good Reverend Mother, being a woman of the world, knew otherwise. 'We don't want to scandalise the Faithful,' she advised. 'They might think we are not nuns at all, just circus performers or, God forbid, bawds disguised as actresses, like in the Smock Alley Theatre.' There, the fierce-looking Mother Bungy was not a nun at all, just a brothel Madam presiding over some of the most notorious bawdy houses in an area called Hell. It was agreed, after much soul-searching, that Mountain View residents must not think that the fiercer-looking Mother Mary Aikenhead, the founder of the convent, was in fact Mother Bungy. Consequently, it was decided that henceforth Marymount would be the new name.

Over the subsequent decades, the locality developed and prospered. The Pym's, well-known Quakers, and the Le Brocquy's did much to provide employment, opening a few factories in the Greenmount part of Mountain View. The businessman and United Irishman, John Keogh, who lived in a mansion in Mount Jerome before it became a cemetery, part-owned a brewery on the corner of Mountain View Road and Greenmount Avenue. More and more nice red-bricked houses were built in the nineteenth century and in 1894, to copper-fasten the district's prosperity and social standing, the former commonage, widely known as 'The Green', was officially opened as a railed and gated park. Residents for years afterwards still called it 'The Green'. All the well-to-do were in attendance at the official opening and the residents were delighted with a very impressive cascading water feature, flower beds, nice mature trees, paths, benches and summer houses.

At southern end of the Green or Mountain View Park as it was now called, and just outside its railings, an ancient chestnut tree was located for hundreds of years and until quite recently. A concrete seat encircled its base and provided much comfort for weary travellers or for the not so weary, but who had plenty of time to discuss matters of some or no importance. This tree was known as the Tree of Knowledge, such was the wisdom that seemed to emanate from those resting there, wisdom that normally didn't reside in those individuals. Over time, it was felt that the tree had certain properties that seemed to transfer to the sitters, thus giving them the appearance and sound of noble elders of the community. These elders, known as the Elder Conkers, in their new-found wisdom were quite happy to adopt the mantle of responsibility thrust upon them. They became poets, politicians and philosophers who at times seemed to be evolving into statues, since the same characters (including one called 'the H') would be seen on the bench all day, every day. They would, of course, be only too happy to join the pantheon of greats that lived in the area. The consensus among them was that they had, unfortunately, left their quills behind. They also agreed that, 'there are those that write, and there are those that speak in volumes' and they preferred to be in the latter category. They puffed on their pipes, leant back against the old chestnut tree and gazed as the trams passed by or the 'human fly,' as the young Lukie was called, scaling the embankment just across from them at no.190.

Any matter put to them was ruminated upon with the help of a number of pipes, called 'doodeens'. Moreover, if someone generously slipped any of the elders a bottle of stout, preferably Stowshus Extra, a satisfactory answer to any problem would be guaranteed.

If you wanted to know the best way to climb up to the Hellfire Club, directly up the steep Montpelier Hill, which was the shortest route, or a gradual circuitous route, the longest, they would advise accordingly, considering all the salient details, your age, height, strength, experience and general attitude. Or if you wanted to know about when the Hurdy Gurdy man, the Dulcimer man or the One-Man Band were last seen in Mountain View, they would know. Likewise, with Jack-the-cockle man, who used to appear in the area on a Saturday evening, guaranteeing fresh cockles for supper. Mad Charley used to walk in his bare feet and loved to dance for a piece of currant cake. The elders would tell about the Dog Woman who owned half a dozen dogs but was deaf as a dead dog. They knew where Canon Brady kept his stuffed hare and why a bald man should have one in the first place. If someone asked about Hell's Lane, they would just point across the road, down from the Geranium House. Enquirers often wanted to know the whereabouts of the Bogey (Police) Barracks. They would reply, 'Which one? The little one or the big one?' And then, after a suitable interlude, they confided: 'Over there, beside the entrance to Mount Jerome.'

Sneaky questions were often directed their way. One such question related to the oldest pub in the area. 'Oh, long gone to some extent,' was the reply. 'And which one had you in mind, now? Was it the seventeenth-century one called the Cat and Bagpipes or the Old Grinding Young?' Someone always wanted to know where the Bird's Nest was, yet not expecting a reply. 'Well, if you look above your head you will definitely find one, but if not is it the Quakers you are interested in, then? Well if so, the answer to your question is that old house next door to Healy's grocers. It was an orphanage for Protestant children until not so long ago. Now, does that satisfy you?' Hen and Chicken Lane, later Mount Drummond Avenue, always came up. The Emmet Dairy at the end of the avenue derived its name from its proximity to the former hiding house of Robert Emmet before he was captured. Numerous discussions continued as to whether or not this was Mrs Palmer's house or the smaller one around the corner. The whereabouts of Robert Emmet's missing head was a frequent question and as many possible solutions were offered as one required.

They liked telling people to 'go to Hell' when enquiries were made of O'Connor's Jewellers on Hell's Lane, overlooking the park. They could also tell you the flow of the Swan and the Poddle rivers underneath Mountain View, where and whether they were culverted and where the Stone Boat that never sank, which divided the flow of the Poddle, was located. Likewise, they knew who was murdered from Armstrong Street during the Civil War and where he was murdered. If you asked 'Where's he buried?' you would be told, 'He's with O'Leary in the grave,' in Glasnevin Cemetery.

That the most famous bagpipe player in all Ireland lived in the area did not bother them at all. 'Leave it to Rowsome' is all they would say. If you wanted to know if Casimir Road was so-called after Countess Markievicz's husband or Father Casimir from Mount Argus, they would know. Someone might ask for the whereabouts of the Little Tin Church and you would be directed to the Rosary Church. And if you were looking for 'a good Samaritan' they would point you to the stained-glass window of the big church beside the entrance to Mount Jerome.

They liked quizzing one with a puzzle of their own. 'Tell us,' they would begin. 'What famous individuals lived only about one hundred yards from each other, as the crow flies, and at the same time, just up the road there? And we'll give you a hint,' said they encouragingly. 'They each won a Nobel Prize!' And they pointed with their doodeens to the top end of Mountain View, beyond the church. And if you were still perplexed, they added: 'Both of them wanted to flee the area!' They laughed heartily at this. 'One sang "Take me up to Monto", while the other sang "I will arise and go now …"' They would never tell you it was Joyce and Yeats – you were left to figure it out yourself.

Subversion therefore was never far away from Mountain View. Revolutionary ideas continued to flourish and a prominent reminder is visible as one approaches the park and the fork in the road. Right side for Mount Jerome, straight through the park for the Tree of

Knowledge at the opposite end of the park and both ways bring you to the village proper at the southern end of the park. At the fork and marking the junction there is a finely sculpted High Cross. One is greeted by this fine grey carved monument of Celtic design. When one looks closer, one notes that it is an actual memorial to the good people in the area, from the 4th Brigade of the IRA, who fought and helped win the War of Independence against the might of the British Empire, that empire on which the sun was always supposed to shine. To this day, comely maidens are regularly seen dancing at this crossroads on many a warm summer's evening.

In the early twentieth century Mountain View was a staunchly nationalist area but in a constituency that was 90 per cent unionist. It was surrounded by Rathgar, Terenure, Rathmines and Portobello, all unionist with just a smattering of nationalists. But that was more than enough, particularly since there was a long tradition of rebellion. Providentially, many aspects of the 1916 Rising were planned and engineered from Mountain View, not from Mount Jerome or from Countess Markievicz's house on nearby Leinster Road. The authorities were constantly watching her house in the light of all the strange comings and goings and the sound of guns being tested in her back garden. However, the authorities did not realise that the innocuous looking house on Mountain View Road, overlooking the park, and facing the entrance to Mount Jerome, was the very hotbed of political activity and planning. This was the one with the huge pots of lovely red geraniums, visible behind lace curtains, decorating the front ground-floor windows. This old house, impossible to miss, had become the very epicentre for the real planning of the 1916 Rising thanks to the 4th Brigade of the Old IRA. Volunteers, meanwhile, used to train up the road in the grounds of Larkfield House with Eammon Ceannt, Commandant of the brigade, thanks to Joseph Mary Plunkett, the owner of the house.

The House of Geraniums, as it was known, was called upon and not for the first time either. Over one hundred years previously, in the crucial years prior and after 1798, when John Keogh's house in Mount Jerome was under surveillance, meetings were held on the opposite side of the Green in this house. Upstairs, in a back bedroom, there was a secret small alcove, hidden in the thick wall and used as a hiding place for valuable documents. And it was here, it was rumoured, that Robert Emmet's head was placed after the 1803 Rising.

Coincidentally, this house was picked by Padraig Pearse on his way home to St Enda's in Rathfarnham. He was sitting on the number 16 tram as it trundled along the Mountain View Road with the park to his right and the 1750s house to his left. He noticed that the blood-red geraniums never withered or died, no matter what the season, and were always shining forth, bringing hope and good cheer to passers-by like himself. Being a poet as well, he pondered on this phenomenon and something seemed to seep into his subconscious. He realised the message the geraniums were sending out to him, day in, day out, and took great heart as a consequence. This terrible beauty, this apparent contradiction, finally inspired him to coin the expression 'blood sacrifice' that was needed for Ireland to become an independent nation. Such was the hope he derived from this realisation that in 1915 he was able to give his famous graveside oration for the bold Fenian man, Jeremiah O'Donovan Rossa, in Glasnevin Cemetery. His use of the term 'blood sacrifice' inspired tens of thousands of Irishmen and Irishwomen to rise up in 1916 and throw off the shackles of foreign domination.

On that fateful morning, at the beginning of the Easter Rising, Patrick Pearse and his men visited Mount Argus Church in Mountain View. Following the visit to the church, the fifty-two men caught the number 16 tram, not too far from the Hospice for the Dying. They bought their one-way tickets and began their journey towards the General Post Office (GPO) and into the pages of Irish revolutionary history.

To this day, the House of Geraniums stands as a beacon that reminds us of those brave souls that gave us the freedom to achieve greater freedom. The red geraniums continue to decorate the windows. Besides their beauty and decorative value, they symbolise that unquenchable, passionate and unique spirit of the people of Mountain View.

As children, we marvelled at the sight of the veterans of 1916 and the War of Independence proudly marching along the main road, down towards the city centre and the GPO, for their commemorations. They were real stand-up-straight walkers, shoulders thrown back with a look of defiance, seriousness and a sense of achievement. Another regular event for us was the sight of the Irish Army Band marching in the opposite direction from Cathal Brugha Barracks at Portobello to Mount Argus Church. We'd rush out of the house on hearing the banging of the drums.

In recognition of the huge importance Mountain View played in the fight for Irish Independence a number of events took place over the following decades. In 1938 the Robert Emmet bronze bust and plaque was unveiled on Clanbrassil Bridge, renamed the Robert Emmet Bridge. The 'shaking hand of Dublin', the renowned Alfie Byrne, ten times Lord Mayor of Dublin, was the only person the residents would allow to perform the unveiling. They were not in the least perturbed by his shaking hand. 'Sure, don't we all like a drop of the craythur,' they said, and they all rushed forward to shake his hand. Some had the dubious motive of wanting to check for themselves how bad was his shake and if he was capable of standing still on the brow of the hill for the unveiling of the plaque. There were even fears that he might topple over into the Grand Canal below. They might have to report back that it doesn't do to have an absolute drunk as Lord Mayor.

There was further confusion in 1954 when President Seán T. O'Kelly unveiled the High Cross. He was given a huge welcome, most unexpected he felt, and asked his aide-de-camp afterwards about it. 'Not to worry, President, didn't some of them think you were the spitting image of Jimmy O'Dea, and could well be him! They have a great appreciation for Mr O'Dea, as well as yourself, of course. They love him as "Biddy Mulligan, the pride of the Coombe".'

'Thank Heaven's for Rathgar,' sighed the President. 'At least they have only three blind windows.' And away with him singing to himself:

Dublin Be Damned!

There are some quite decent suburbs, I am sure,

O Rathmines is not so bad or Terenure,

In Dartry they are almost civilized,

O we've heard of spots like Inchicore,

but really don't know where they are,

For, thank heavens, we are living in Rathgar.

3

Hawkers, Whiffs and Sticky Fingers

So, we hailed from Mountain View. What about Dad? He hailed from the Liberties, regarded by the locals as the oldest part of Dublin and home to 'the real Dubs'. For us it was the home of Spud Murphy and some drunk called Arthur Guinness. Dad was from a family of twelve, most of who were farmed out to relations as children and then banished to England when they grew up. They were like thousands of others forced to emigrate from Ireland in the 1950s.

Emigration is too kind of a word for the reality. Even 'exported' or 'deported' did not adequately explain the horrible upheaval and heart-breaking severance they were forced to endure. Mothers of Ireland, who had nurtured their children into their teens, had them wrenched from their arms by the very establishment that insisted on mothers having as many children as possible! It was as if they were bred for export – 'To Hell or to Kilburn' or Cricklewood or anywhere else. There they found some solace in Irish dancehalls such as the Galtymore, the National or the Gresham. Those forced to leave the country were whipped onto freight trains and shunted to the ports. Then they were stamped and processed and herded onto the cattle boats bound for Holyhead. Passengers had to endure the further indignity of being second-class, with the cattle having the better berths below the slatted decking. As with the cattle, the exporters made money, since the emigrants sent 'remittances' to help alleviate the hardship of those that remained left behind. 'Calved and carved for an English table,' Dad used to say.

Dad often regaled us about stories of playing football in his bare feet with his pals from Cromwell's Quarters, Murdering Lane and Cutthroat Lane, all around the Ceannt Fort and Mount Brown area of the Liberties. Sometimes, the lads played against other teams, including from the Barn, Cow Parlour, the Ranch, Adam & Eve's, Dung Hill and the Back of the Pipes. In the Summer, the teams would meet up in the Fifteen Acres. He went to the Model School, off Thomas Street. Around the corner, on Pim Street, he liked helping the coopers make the casks for Guinness's brewery. He said that at one time there were up to 300 coopers making wooden barrels or casks. This was before the advent of the iron silver-coloured barrels we have today.

Dad had a wide variety of likes and activities. He was a great hill-walker and had climbed mountains from as low as the Hellfire Club on Montpelier Hill in the Dublin Mountains to the heights in the Wicklow and Kerry Mountains and even as far as Mount Snowdon in Wales. He loved participating in musicals, pantomimes and, in particular, Russian and Georgian dancing. He was quite an expert at the Cossack variety with him squatting down and his legs and feet shooting out back and forth in front of him. He would go, 'Hi hi hi di hi hi …' He also loved swimming in the River Liffey, it being literally on his doorstep. All he had to do was run down in his bare feet, over the wall, down the ladder and over and back to the various quays. During the summer, he went out to the 40 Foot Gentlemen's Bathing Place in Sandycove and many a time he was thrown up on the rocks. When he went into the hotel business, he trained in the Royal Hibernian in Dawson Street. He continued to play snooker and billiards in the nearby hall in Andrew Street. After his training, he was sent to Switzerland and then to the

Shannon School of Hotel Management. When he finished, he worked in the Moira Hotel just off Dame Street and other top Dublin hotels and restaurants. He also bought himself a red sports car, and this was during the Second World War. Later he opened a new restaurant at Dublin Airport. This became hugely popular as a result of increasing interest in air travel, which was still limited to the prosperous. Many of the restaurants' customers just went to dine, view the planes and see who was coming and going. So, he enjoyed the good life.

On a previous visit to Mount Jerome we discovered the vault of Arthur Guinness the Second and Dad suggested that we might visit the home of the brewery some time. At least ten of the Guinness family were buried in Mount Jerome. The name suggested to Dad a visit to the Liberties, 'the home of the black stuff'. We were delighted to hear mention of 'the black stuff', though ours was different to his. However, he surprised us by asking one summer morning, 'Who would like some Gur cake?' This was our kind of black stuff. Moreover, he didn't say, 'Let's go the Liberties.' No, he didn't operate that way. It was always us who ended up agreeing to go somewhere. 'What's that?' we asked politely, but just making absolutely sure. 'Very black cake the colour of the stout and really tasty with lots of fruit and a sugary pastry layer on top. It's what all the folks in the Liberties eat!' Talk about a helter-skelter. We must have run around in circles. So, off to the Liberties with us. We had no idea what or where they were, except that Dad grew up there and played football in his bare feet and liked to jump into the River Liffey.

We got off the bus opposite John's Lane Church, 'run by the Augustinians for nearly one thousand years' we were informed. 'They must be very old,' pointed out Minnie. And of course, we were dragged in there to light a candle and look at the Harry Clarke stained-glass windows full of shocking reds and blues and all sorts of strange colours. Near these windows up towards the sanctuary were a few glass cases on the walls full of what appeared to be thrown-away jewellery. The story went that people over the years had donated gold and silver to the church for favours asked of the saints. A real Aladdin's Cave, we thought, and locked securely. Dad told us that Mum had given her engagement ring to the church following an 'incident' on the farm. When she had been holidaying down in County Laois with Dad just after their engagement, they stayed on Mum's family farm. When she was helping with the washing up, she took off her new sparkling ring, wrapped it in tissue and left it on a mantelpiece. A sister came along tidying up and threw the paper into the roaring fire. There was absolute consternation with everyone running around looking for Mum's ring. The following morning, they raked it out of the ashes but it was all shrivelled and blackened. They decided to give it to John's Lane Church, where it joined the rest of the donated jewellery in glass cases around the altar to Our Lady of Good Counsel. 'Yes, all very sad,' we went. However, just as Dad was going to explain the 'lovely reds and blues" of the Harry Clarke windows we, having restless hearts, had decided that one more stained-glass window was one too many. Dad understood, to a point.

We groaned when we backtracked towards two churches stuck together — the two St Audoen's. We didn't wasn't to visit any more churches, we told Dad, but he said in a funny voice that 'this was our lucky day' and left it at that. We knew all about 'Lucky Bags' and had hopes.

One of the old buildings looked like it was half buried in the grounds of the surrounding park and old walls of Dublin. The other was a more recent huge Catholic church of the mid-nineteenth century. Beside them on High Street, Dad pointed to a wall plaque with the name 'Napper Tandy' commemorated on it. We all liked that name. 'Napper MacCrossan. How does that sound?' asked Freckles. 'It suits you just perfectly,' replied Daisy. 'You are always napping from what I hear.' Before matters deteriorated Dad pointed out that our friend Napper Tandy was one of the United Irishmen who planned the rebellion of 1798.

Near to the entrance of the older church we found the Lucky Stone of Dublin perched up against a wall in a tiny passageway, which Dad said was a late ninth-century grave slab adorned with a Greek-style cross. This stood outside the tower of St Audoen's for centuries and was rumoured to have a supernatural guardian because, despite being removed a number of times, it has always returned to its rightful place. In 1308 a marble cistern was erected in Cornmarket to provide the citizens of Dublin with their first public water supply (beer was hitherto deemed safer to drink). The Lucky Stone was set up beside the cistern so that all who drank the water might have luck. Local merchants believed that success in business depended largely on making a daily visit to touch the stone. In 1826 people from outside Dublin stole the stone. However, during the theft, the stone became heavier and heavier until the horse collapsed under the weight. The thieves dumped the stone on waste ground. Later, when workmen attempted to smash it, the stone moaned and rolled. It was eventually brought back to its rightful place and has not moved since the 1860s. 'What do we have to do to get lucky?' asked Minnie. 'Do we have to kiss it like the Blarney Stone?' 'Ah, no, pet. Just touch it or, even better, give it a good kick!' This suited us all just fine and we ran out with sore toes but happy to be filled with luck.

'Where did the name "Liberties" come from?' Freckles wanted to know as we walked towards Thomas Street. Dad filled us in. Around the time of the Normans and in return for not giving the King too much trouble, the people in this part of Dublin around Thomas Street, which was outside the old walled city of Dublin, were allowed to pay less taxes and run their own affairs. We thought that was a good arrangement. The Liberties folk always held their heads high as a result, Dad added. No one was going to take any liberties with them, for sure! We decided to walk up the street with noses high up in the air, just to look like good Liberties folk!

Next door to the Clock Pub on Thomas Street was a big gateway, aligned with two black steel bollards. That was a former entrance to the world-famous Power's Distillery. The only reminder, Dad pointed out, was the letter 'P' over a former corner entrance. 'Maybe that was the toilet?' laughed Minnie. Around the corner on the main street, the words Private Residence were emblazoned on the brass plate of the front door of No. 109. 'Letters' was inscribed on the brass letterbox. The lettering was important as it signified the social standing of the former residents of the house on what was a prosperous street at the heart of Dublin's commercial life. Dad said that there was an old saying in the Liberties that 'one side was the sunny side, the other side the money side.' We tried to figure out which was which with Freckles strongly advising that first we had to find out in which direction the North Pole lay. We left him looking for the North Pole as we headed along the west road.

One thing that struck us was the cacophony of varying sounds of Thomas Street, coming particularly from the stallholders selling their merchandise. Dad said that Thomas Street, like Moore Street and Camden Street, was one of a few areas in Dublin where hawkers were legally entitled to have stalls on the main street. We strolled past the hawkers and their stalls stretched in a line in front of the Carpet Mills, Manning's Bakery, Baker's Pub and near the corner with Meath Street.

The stallholders all seemed to be shouting and roaring in different languages. I heard one of the hawkers hollering at some dubious-looking customer, 'Janey Mac! Here you! Gerrup owa dah! Keep your maulers off the merchandise.'

And another one, 'Thanks, Mai, that's a darlin' cup of cha.'

'A me aul segosha, not a bother,' came from the donor of the tea.

'And how's that jewel and darlin' daughter of yours these day, Lily?' and on they chatted.

Behind us we heard the shout of 'Lock hard, Jem, lock hard! Fair play! Fair play!' A brewery lorry was reversing outside Baker's Pub.

'What language are they speaking?' Freckles asked, him being from somewhere beyond the Aran Islands.

'Liberties-speak,' was the reply. 'That's the reason why they always say, "Ye know wha' I mean?" or "Ye know, like," after each sentence. They are very polite that way. This is the real Dublin. These people have been here for hundreds of years, or forever, according to themselves.' Dad said he remembered Father Cullen, who was based across the road in John's Lane Church in the 1940s and '50s, calling the characters of the Liberties 'God's aristocrats'. He also said he remembered the large number of traders and hawkers with their own distinctive costumes and cries: the strawberry girl calling, 'Ripe strawberries, ripe strawberries,' or another calling, 'Dublin Bay

Herrins,' and 'Old rags, any old rags, take money for your old rags, any hare skins or rabbit skins...' People used to love eating rabbits in those days, Dad said.

Some of the hawkers looked like they had been there a long time indeed. Minnie nudged me. 'Hey, look at your man there, helping himself to some apples, look...' Before she could utter further, an almighty shriek erupted from the sharp-eyed stallholder: 'Here you, give up yer auld sins outa dat,' her ire directed at the unknown shifty sinner. 'Come here to me, will ye! If I get me hands on ye, I'll brain ye, I'm telling ye. I'll kill ye, so I will!' 'Ah, leave him be,' said her companion. 'Sure, couldn't you strain the cabbage with his head?'

Then there were the unforgettable smells. The brewery at the end of Thomas Street or the butchers' and bakers' aromas wafting out, it seemed, just for our noses. Dad quoted the Liberties saying that 'a blind man could find his way around Dublin because of the smells.' 'There are half a dozen strong competing smells in the Liberties,' said Dad. The 'Player's Please' smell coming from the cigarette factory on the not-too-far away South Circular Road was one. Another was the making of fig rolls in Jacob's biscuit factory over on Bishop Street.

Dad said that in spite of all the competing smells, there were just a few that people never forget. 'Firstly,' he said, 'living in the Liberties would not be the same without O'Keefe's the Knackers.'

'The who?' we queried, not believing our ears at Dad's language. There were certain words that we never used at home. The 'f' word and the 'k' word, for instance.

'Well, your noses wouldn't believe it either,' said he, reading our minds. 'The waft of dead animal carcasses at O'Keefe's, the animal slaughter yard on Mill Street near Newmarket Square, straight south from here as the crow flies, would put you off your beef forever.' Most people just called it 'Keef's' and its foul smell permeated the whole area. 'On good days,' said Dad, 'the pleasing aromas from the Guinness Brewery overcame the putrid smells from Keef's. So, you were better off living in the Liberties only part-time!'

Freckles was dying to know more about Keef's. 'What were they doing with all those dead animals?'

'Well, in actual fact Keef's were known as "renderers",' Dad said. They specialised in buying dead animals, particularly horses, and crushing the bones to make fertiliser. The dead animals were placed in a huge vat of boiling water which would strip the flesh from the bone. The bones would then be ground down to a finer material. The rendering plant worked like a giant kitchen with the boiling process going on morning, noon and night, with the smells wafting through the air. The ground outside Keef's would be littered with dead animals, entrails, skulls and all the bits and pieces. In summer, some of the men would work outside with the dead animals, taking them apart. 'Many a time I saw chaps having their cups of tea and sandwiches and happily working away! It was also a regular sight to see a local lad playing football in Newmarket Square having to wade through all that to retrieve his ball! Locals had got used to the smell for years, often (with more hope than fact) seeing it as useful for keeping down disease! Despite the whiff, the fertiliser was highly regarded by Irish manufacturers as the best and cheapest.'

Luckily for us, on that particular day the aroma from the brewery soothed our noses. Dad said we were there on a great day as we were smelling the combined aroma of coffee and chocolate and freshly baked bread, whereas on other days the smell might not be so nice, 'like a maturing cheese,' he said. 'You mean mouldy old cheese,' we laughed. 'How come there are different smells from the brewery?' we wanted to know. He explained that the smells derived from the two main Guinness-making processes of roasting the barley, then boiling the wort and hops and mashing the malt with water. 'Boiling and mashing,' they used to say. Dad seemed to revel in the whiff. 'It is an intrinsic part of the Liberties,' and he inhaled deeply. 'When I was going to the Model School, it was really strong, especially during the summer months, and it does bring back some happy memories.' Well, thanks to the Lucky Stone, we were enjoying the Guinness aroma and not the Keef's one coming our way.

Dad said there was awful rivalry between the brewery and a big local distiller called Roe's. In fact, such was their rivalry that they competed with each other to try to impress the Dublin folk how kind they were. Guinness poured money into St Patrick's Cathedral for renovation purposes and Roe's Distillery did the same for Christ Church Cathedral. The people then called the first 'the brewer's church', and the latter 'the distiller's church'.

We were dying to hear more about this so we went into Manning's Bakery, as we knew we would sooner rather than later. 'That's all a body needs,' said Dad, 'Gur cake and a coal fire.' Once seated, he bought us huge slabs of Gur cake, with sugar sprinkled all over the top, and tea. That is, all of us except Daisy, who said to the waitress, 'I think I would prefer an éclair, and bring over a napkin as you're at it, please.' She's some éclair herself, I thought. We liked the homely atmosphere of Manning's, which appeared to be a family business. The lady looking after us said it started off baking home-made bread in a grocery shop. The aroma of freshly baked bread and buns wafting out from the back kitchen practically carried us away. And the window was just full of delights. Gur cake, tipsy cake, doughnuts, cream cakes, éclairs, jam tarts, fruit cakes and meringues. All sitting there, smiling at us. Waiting patiently to be eaten.

'These sticky buns remind me of a notorious chancer known as Sticky Fingers Brabazon,' said Dad, interrupting our reverie. 'He is buried up the road there underneath St Catherine's Church where the bold Robert Emmet met his maker. Let me tell you about the man with the sticky fingers. Nobody even knows that one of the most infamous men in Irish history, Henry VIII's right-hand man in Ireland, the one that threw the nuns and monks out of their convents and monasteries, lies here in the heart of the Liberties.'

'Why was he called "sticky fingers"?' Minnie wanted to know.

'Because he was sticking his fat fingers into other people's land and money, when he was supposed to be doing his job for Henry VIII! He was the King's Treasurer here in Ireland and supposed to be minding his money for him. See, his fingers became real sticky from using all the money as his own personal loot.'

Dad continued. 'In 1886 there were three major distilleries in the Liberties: John Powers John's Lane Distillery, George Roe Distillery, Thomas Street (the largest distillery in Europe in 1887) and W. Jameson of Marrowbone Lane. They (along with the other Jameson's in Bow Street) were part of what was known as "the Golden Triangle", such was their importance.' We liked the sound of the golden triangle.

'Let's get back to the rivalry between Roe's and the brewery,' said Dad as we happily munched away in Manning's. 'The distillery had its beginning in 1757, when Peter Roe bought a small distillery on Thomas Street. Two years later, Arthur Guinness set up his famous St James' Gate Brewery across the street. Given that they were close neighbours, and that they shared the complementary callings of producing a fine whiskey and a fine stout, one would have assumed that they shared admiration for one another. Apparently, that was not so. Over the years, generations of the Guinness family considered their stout to be the "nurse of the people" while they considered whiskey to be the "curse of the people".'

While Dad was talking, we could just about see the windmill of the former distillery. The striking green copper-clad onion dome is topped by a figure of St Patrick carrying a mitre and a crozier. Dad told us that the windmill was twelve storeys high. It was the tallest Smock Windmill in Europe at the time of its construction and was built years before the distillery opened. It belonged to a corn mill that had previously occupied the site. The windmill contained huge stones that could grind 1,500 barrels of grain a day. Dad pointed to the base of the tower and an old pear tree. 'It's a sight to behold in the springtime,' he said, 'with masses of blossoms and it still grows pears in abundance.'

'What happened in the end?' we wanted to know.

Smiling, Dad said that despite the enmity and competition, the Guinness's and Roe's eventually got together again – this time in Mount Jerome cemetery, where their respective tombs lie within a few yards of each other along the winding Guinness Walk.

'Let's drink to their good health,' said Freckles, draining his mug of tea. He never gives up!

Just then we heard a banging and bumping sound coming from the front of a pub across from Manning's. Guinness workers were delivering barrels to the pub via a trapdoor in the ground. The silver-coloured barrels were bounced from the lorry onto some kind of hard cushion and from there rolled to the cellar hatch. Then they were dropped down where a cellar-man looked after them. Dad said that those kinds of barrels were only a very recent change as for hundreds of years the stout was stored in wooden barrels known as casks. Those who made and repaired the casks or barrels were known as 'coopers'. Some coopers were specially appointed as 'smellers' to weed out any foul-smelling casks for treatment in the cask repair shop. We thought that working as a 'smeller' was a most unusual kind of job and Dad said that it might take years to develop a good nose since there were so many different and competing kinds of smells in the Liberties. 'Go over to O'Keefe's the Knackers for some kind of strange smells,' he chuckled.

Dad also explained why the black stuff was often called 'stout' or 'porter'. 'Stout' originally referred to a beer's strength, but eventually the meaning shifted toward body and colour, and in this case a black beer. Arthur Guinness started selling it in 1778 and called it 'porter'. The name 'porter' came from porters in the Billingsgate Markets in London who liked the taste of the product. 'To this day, porter or stout mean the same thing so when a customer asks for a pint of stout or a pint of porter they mean the same drink. Guinness has also been referred to as "the black stuff" and as a "Pint of Plain".' Freckles said that if people get so confused over different names for a pint of Guinness even before they start to drink, it's no wonder they are totally confused when they finish their drink!

We finished our Gur cake and Dad suggested we stroll back along Thomas Street for another kind of smell. He pointed to C. Seezer Pork Butcher's, who were in business since 1900. 'Nip in there for a quick look at what his sign says.' We peeped in and there was a sign in the shop saying that Charles Seezer, the pork butcher, was a 'humane killer'. We screeched and ran out.

We liked the old Carpet Mills shop with carpets hanging from the rafters everywhere. They also had a funny sign: 'Our Products are being Walked on Every Day' and we did just that. In we charged, leaving Dad to do some of his hotel business work in Manning's.

Dublin Be Damned!

Carpets everywhere in sight from Killybegs to Curragh, from Navan to Youghal and more. Oh, we tested them all right and would be still testing them till we heard a roar which suggested we disappear as fast as our legs could carry us.

4

CHASTISING CHILDREN AND
HELL FOR LEATHER

Besides all the day trips with Dad, whether it be to Mount Jerome or the Liberties, the Botanic Gardens or the Phoenix Park, St Stephen's Green or Sandymount Strand, we also had a great time growing up at home and in Mountain View itself. As very young children we availed of the fine 100-foot-long L-shaped garden that stretched down to the back of Marymount School.

A timber-framed glasshouse was at the bottom of the garden containing a vine struggling to grow. We also had a pear tree, a plum tree, cooking apple and eating apple trees in a line from the top of the garden to the end. The pear tree in spring, with its abundance of snow-white blossoms, was, Mum used to laugh, 'the apple of my eye'. We had to compete for the fine big pears, as half the time they were eaten away by greedy birds or swarms of bees. We were left with the squashed remains and sometimes given no choice in the matter, as they often fell on your head. We spent a lot of time chasing the birds away. We used to do this by throwing anything, including our shoes, into the tall tree to scare them off.

Perched beside the enormous trunk of the pear tree, wizened with jagged pieces of brown bark, was a big children's iron swing, painted green. It was an ideal location as the tree was mushroom-like with the leaves and branches high up. Dad had assembled and erected it for us. This swing was one of the best investments he made for us children and we spent innumerable happy hours every day all year around on it. One of our favourite pastimes was swinging as high as possible and using our feet to try and touch any of the low-hanging branches. We also loved jumping off the swing when it was in full motion and at a height to see how far from it we landed. When we bounced on to the grass we usually ended up having to run down the garden to slow down!

We made wigwams in the garden, had bonfires with the leaves from the trees, played all sorts of imaginary games such as shop, marbles, conkers with chestnuts, climbed the trees and walls, playing chase and 'Ring-a-ring-a Rosie', which went:

> Ring-a-ring-a-Rosie,
>
> A pocket full of posies,
>
> Atishoo, atishoo we all fall down.
>
> Down in the bottom of the deep blue sea,
>
> Catching fishes in the deep blue sea,
>
> Ashes in the water, ashes in the sea,
>
> We all jump up – one, two, three.

The garden walls were lined with fruit bushes – mainly gooseberry and blackberry. We used the glasshouse for planting rhubarb, lettuce and potatoes. We were delighted with the bumper crop of potatoes we had every year – twenty or so, that lasted us for a week. Seeing ourselves as part of the farming community we had to check for potato blight every so often. We dug up the growing potatoes and if there was even the slightest hint of the Great Famine we applied copious quantities of disinfectant.

Mum loved the garden and had her favourite flowers and plants. Geraniums were her favourites, followed by roses, daffodils alternating with tulips, sweet pea, golden iris, Michaelmas daisies, gladioli, marigolds and fuchsia. She had fuchsia scattered all over the garden and in pots on the kitchen windowsills. *Deora Dé* she called them in Irish, 'Tears of God', and the drooping pink, red and purple flowers with a hint of white indeed seemed like they were about to weep. When we were very young, we did much damage to her joys, finding delight in knocking the heads off the poor innocent flowers. I suppose this was a break from knocking each other's heads about. Separated from the garden by a large wall was a yard containing a coal shed, an outside toilet, and two larger sheds, one full of geraniums and the other Daddy's tool shed.

We carved 'Welcome home mother' on the garden path when Mum was in hospital with an appendix. Well, she got a nice welcome home indeed as within a few short days she had to extricate chewing gum from Minnie's fluffy hair. Minnie and I were throwing gum at each other, hoping it would stick and it stuck alright. Mum was none too pleased. We were all pleased, however, to be helping Mum with the pages of Green Shield Stamps that she got with her shopping. We loved licking the stamps and sticking them on to the pages of the book. When the book was filled, we sent it off and received boxes of Jacob's Cream Crackers a few weeks later.

At around two o'clock in the afternoon we ran in from the garden and listened to children's storytelling time on the wireless. We loved this and the plummy BBC voices. Afterwards we might have our hair washed by Mum, always using a sachet of Loxene shampoo, which was a greenish colour. Then we might help ourselves to bread and butter slices covered in sugar or home-made jam. Sometimes we used to help ourselves to the setting jelly and then added water. Once we added milk accidentally and liked the settled milk jelly the next day.

'Where are your manners?' she would ask, to which we quickly responded, 'In the garden robbing the orchard!' She would tell us not to say 'what' but 'pardon' when we are being spoken to. Or, 'elbows in or you'll fly away' at the table. Mind you, when walking down crowded Henry Street, she would say the opposite, 'elbows out.' It's surprising we didn't fly away, having to practice all that. In order to help improve our personal development we were given copies of a little book, *Courtesy for Boys and Girls*. We found this very helpful as we practiced the opposite to what was advised. Instead of raising our hats to an adult as we passed by, we pulled our hats down over our eyes. Instead of saluting as if we were in the army, we bowed or said 'How', Indian-fashion.

Back from hospital, Mum was extremely busy, and some of us were sent off for a few weeks to Madonna House in Foxrock while she recuperated. This was run by the Sisters of Charity. While in a playpen, the nuns tried to give me food I found most distasteful and so refused to eat. On the last occasion, I scrunched up my tiny little fist and then swung it up and under the plate the nun was holding. It flew out of her hand, with the contents mostly landing on her. She grabbed me up like I was Golly, my cuddly little Golliwog teddy, and shook me so fiercely that I could feel and hear my bones and teeth rattling. Even Golly was all shook-up but managed to keep smiling. Finally, her rage dissipated, she dumped me back down. And so, for three weeks, I was left to die. I didn't mind as I preferred that to eating their muck. Eventually I returned home and struggled in the hall door all bony and half dead. I remember being on Mum's lap by the fire having warm milk laced with honey in the hope I would survive. This was followed by tiny pieces of egg. Leaping flames caressed my wan cheeks. I knew then I would be all right. I smiled down at the picture of Winston Churchill emblazoned across the front page of the newspaper strewn on the floor. I also knew that he would understand when I gave him the two fingers.

When I had sufficiently recovered, I was sent to Marymount School at the age of four. I was barely in the door and assigned to what is now called Junior Infants, but then called Low Babies, when I perpetrated a dastardly act – the unmentionable. Despite warnings from the Sister to the class not to do what I did, well, nature just took over, and I did a poo in my pants, right there in the classroom. Naturally enough, I told no one, but the splat was out of the bum and the whiff was soon out as well. In a burst of energy, the nun rushed over and hauled me out of my seat. Just a quick snatch. Not very difficult as I, being only four years of age, weighed about the same as a two-stone bag of potatoes. But unlike the potatoes, I was not a dead weight. Up and over her shoulder I went, waving my little hands at the rest of the boys and girls below. Suddenly, she flung me across the room towards the swivel blackboard. I hurtled at some speed, but, despite my predicament, I meant to finish what I had started. I did so and this expulsion probably saved my bacon if not my bum. I hit the blackboard, slid down its chalky black surface and landed with an audible splat on something soft. I had finished what I started. The blackboard spun around over my head as I ducked to avoid a whack. I was left to my own devices until lunchtime. I squelched home by myself, which luckily was only a short distance for a short-taken lad.

My legs were soon back running and jumping and I started to learn Irish dancing in school with Miss O'Carroll. I thought the 'One, two, three and back again' was an absolute gas altogether. 'Keep those arms right beside you!' she kept roaring at me. 'Don't even move them,' she went. I never heard such nonsense in my whole life. It was as if she imagined my poor arms were going to run off by themselves. How do you go about minding your arms? Do you give your hands the job of holding your arms? Do you put them in handcuffs or something? I found whatever it was she wanted me to do very difficult. I carried on regardless with my arms remaining attached to my body without any help or restraint on my part. Moreover, they went flying about in rhythm with my dancing legs. Up and around, sideways and every way. It felt wonderful. It was like conducting an orchestra while cycling a bicycle. I felt I was ready to take off into flight! Miss O'Carroll would have none of it, however. She wanted something completely different. Something along the lines of doing the Hanged Man's Hornpipe with the arms tied.

Despite that I enjoyed those early days in school. Everything was very exciting and new. I even marvelled at the silver-coloured iron staircase we had to climb every day to our classroom. When the painter came to do a job on it I was mesmerised to see something being painted silver. It looked so different and so shiny. I was so used to dark browns and dull colours in our neighbourhood. At home it wasn't too bad as we had lilac pink and light green on some of the walls. Some of the neighbours looked askance and frowned when we painted the hall door a nice cheerful green.

A roll of cellotape fascinated me as I had never seen one before. I had to have it and I did acquire it much to the consternation of the rightful owner. I told him to zip it! There were many other distractions and opportunities, of course. We were forbidden to climb the chestnut trees in the field beside the veranda where our classes were located. Well, when you have trees and children, they go arm in branch and branch in hand. Up we went, and down came Sr Magdalen's walking stick on the backs of our legs and bums. Not to worry, we still had currant buns and jam sambos on Wednesdays and Fridays respectively and white bread sambos for the other days. They were delivered in big silver boxes to the school every day. These were washed down with a small bottle of milk. Sometimes, and bearing in mind the needs of my siblings, I stuffed mountains of currant buns up my jumper and brought them home as 'leftovers'. Eventually I was told to bring them right back, so I squashed them back up my jumper again. Some of the other children complained to the nun about the buns turning into pancakes.

Up the avenue from the school was the main entrance to the Hospice for the Dying, the grounds of which backed on to our garden. It was known to the young locals as 'the Hosser'. You might be one of the lucky ones invited to spend your last days in its grand surroundings. From your lying down position in the ambulance, clasping your naggin of whiskey under the blanket, and thanking God that you shoved a second one down your sock, you were able to peer upwards and outwards from the ambulance window. The driver turned off the Mountain View Road and up a long steep and winding avenue. Just as he drove through the gates you would see an arc over the main entrance gates with the words Hospice for the Dying emblazoned in gold on a black background. You immediately knew then, before you even settled in, that the inevitable outcome of your visit would be that you were bound to end up playing with skulls. There was no mention of the 'living', with the implication that you were not really living at all. Or even dead for that matter. You were in an in-between zone – not this world or the next.

Despite that, the kind people, the nuns who ran this institution, would ensure that you stayed dying as long as possible, not the worst option. Comforting too, to know that the food came from their own farm which surrounded the hospice. No shops for them, with all that processed stuff. Here the chain of command was straight from field to food. They appreciated 'organic' and 'natural produce' before the words were even invented. This, of course, ensured that you were very well when dying and you would have no complaints whatsoever, at least about the food, when you died. Nobody died hungry, for sure. Well, not since the Famine times anyway. And even then, if the starving hordes did go hungry due to the shortage of potatoes, the Reverend Mother reminded her listeners that they were surrounded by fish, so consequently – 'let them eat chowder, seafood chowder. None of our nice floury potatoes for those Soupers and Quakers. They're for our dying!'

We used to sneak into the mortuary, or 'the morgue' as we called it, and see loads of stone-cold bodies lying on the marble mattresses with marble pillows. The big towering hospice laundry chimney was located behind it and up against the cemetery wall. In we tippy-toed and over to the nearest body. We lifted the coins on the eyes just to check that they had really gone. Minnie rearranged flowers around the mattresses, candles too, moving them here and there, putting some order into the place. She fixed the habits or the rosary beads of the deceased and tidied the coffins. She liked to change names around on the various corpses, 'just for the variety,' she giggled. Sometimes she popped in a few bull's eyes or acid drops in case the deceased got hungry and then could suck on the sweets. Or she tied thread to the deceased's finger and hid in a corner and when relatives visited their nearest and dearest, she would tug gently on the thread and the finger would wag at the visitor. On then to the next body. We lifted a coin and the eye winked up at us. We blinked, then gulped and were down the Hospice Avenue with shrieks and shouts that must have woken the rest of the dead. We rushed into the house. 'Serves you right going around disturbing the poor souls trying to have a decent rest for themselves,' remonstrated Mum. We left it at that but it took us a while before we went back exploring around the Hosser.

Primary school seems like a blur. Certain teachers stood out, though, particularly the friendly, pipe-smoking and trilby-wearing Mr O'Brien, known as 'Bushy eyebrows'. Then there was the young Mr Freeman. He introduced us every Friday afternoon to the magical world of Tom Sawyer and Huckleberry Finn. Our lives would never be the same again. It was as if everything we had learnt up till then was only a preparation for this new world we were intent upon inhabiting.

Halloween was a happy time also and we sang, 'Apples are nice, nuts are better, please Sir, give us no ecker.' We liked the *Our Boys* magazine with the stories and tales of magic and mystery. We relished stories about Kitty the Hare, mostly ghost stories and others from a long gone Gaelic past. We also liked the mystery, adventure, exploring, Western and detective stories and followed the exploits of the perennial young, mischievous schoolboy called 'Murphy', who was always trying to do one better than his elders.

During recreation time we played football and chased each other all over the school yard. We also chatted about the TV programmes such as *The Virginian*, *The Fugitive* and *The Man from U.N.C.L.E.*, or *Tolka Row*. Not that I had seen any of these programmes since we didn't have a TV. Despite that I played along and joined all the cowboys and spies infiltrating the school. Each one of us insisted he was the real secret agent, Napoleon Solo, and ran around the school, hiding here and darting there, and sneaking about everywhere with our hand shaped like a gun. We also thought we were Maxwell Smart from *Get Smart*. We loved singing 'We all live in dirty margarine', our take on the Beatles' *Yellow Submarine*.

Punishment via the Leather was the only drawback in those early schooldays. I always found it intriguing that it was somebody's job to make these Leathers. They were masterclasses in craftsmanship and detail. They consisted of a few layers of the very best black leather welded together with precision stitching and finely shaped, nearly artistically. The purchasers must have attended classes to learn how to use them to maximum effect, that is, to develop a swinging technique to inflict the most pain on hand, wrist and bottom. Many times, I saw some of the 'hardest' lads in the class reduced to tears with bruises, welts and red, torn skin to match.

I found it particularly galling when, having helped a Brother carry home bundles of copies to be corrected, the next day he turned on me and give me six whacks of the Leather. I recall we had been tasked with writing a small half-page essay as homework. Homework was called 'ecker' or 'exercise'. The subject was, 'The most favourite thing in the world I would like.' I wrote about getting lots of sleep since I had to share a bunkbed with Freckles smelly feet poking around, which did not exactly guarantee me a decent night's sleep. However, after having spent hours writing the half-page essay and giving it to the Brother, I was called up in front of the class. Little was said except, 'Hold out your hand!' Whack, whack, whack went the Leather with ferocious and deliberate force. The intention being to beat out whatever hell was in me. It didn't work and the hell stayed in me. I was absolutely horrified, not to mention having very sore red palms. I could not understand why I was being whacked and equally how I could be so whacked by one professing to be a 'Christian' Brother. Having mulled over the matter at length, I undertook a three-fold revenge. Firstly, I lost interest in Christianity. I decided to become a Pagan and vowed to make further enquiries about joining up. Consequently, I no longer brought in flowers to help decorate the May altar in the classroom. Secondly, I told the Brother that he would have to find someone else to help him carry home the copies. Thirdly, I devised a way to beat the effects of the Leather, a discovery I felt should have been patented. This discovery, which I called 'Getting the Upper Hand', involved raising one's outstretched hand higher and higher just before the punishment was exacted so that the perpetrator would have great difficulty bringing his full force upon your hand. He would have to stand on his tippy-toes! And, if he told you to lower your hand, all you had to do was lower it as low as possible which made his job equally problematic! I told all the lads this and it worked, particularly since the Brother in question, known as Brother Plum, was of small stature, and so we quickly got the upper hand.

We also had an alternative plan in case that one didn't work – we would drive him mad! We had noticed that whenever he would start to Leather the life out of us, he had a habit of sticking his tongue out of the side of his mouth – presumably to give him some kind of grip while he whacked us. We initiated a tongues-out campaign at irregular intervals in the class. He would walk in and find us all sitting there working away, with our tongues sticking out of the sides of our mouths. He didn't say anything and neither did we. We couldn't anyway with our tongues sticking out. We did this for a few weeks and eventually he disappeared forever from our classroom.

Word about our upper hand technique for evading the Leather quickly spread throughout the school and then the country. We could beat the Brothers at their own game. The easy solution was widely welcomed, culminating with the Irish government reluctantly admitting defeat and finally abolishing corporal punishment.

5

'Lugs', the Liberties and the Little Drummer Boy

We were regular visitors to the Liberties over the years. One of the many characters we had heard of but never met was one 'Lugs' Branigan, 'a legend on legs', as Dad said. We had gone along with Dad as he was giving a big order for cakes to Manning's Bakery and when we heard that name we kindly suggested we would accompany him. Just as we were leaving the bakery, a loud booming voice hollered from across the street. It was the infamous Sergeant Jim Branigan, an old friend of Dad's from their childhood days and known in Dublin as 'Lugs' Branigan. 'He was born and bred in the Liberties, up on James's Street,' said Dad. 'He and I used to swim in the Liffey together and play football in our bare feet up in School Street. He's a great boxer also. Speaking of which, many the time we boxed the fox together in some of the orchards out beyond the Grand Canal, am I right Jim?' and the two of them roared laughing.

Sergeant Branigan was walking his old beat on this particular day, and he knew everyone. 'Any messing he'll give you a choice between a good box in the ears or a day in court! So, behave!' Dad said. We were in awe of this towering figure that seemed to us to be ten feet high. He looked like a strong, fearless bull ready to lunge at us and we momentarily stepped back, terrified. His face was bashed in, full of lines and scars. His ears seemed to be huge abnormal additions at each side of his turnip-shaped head. 'Lugs' suggested to me to come along and learn boxing in the National Stadium on the South Circular Road. I certainly didn't relish boxing with him and his big cauliflower ears. How would I look walking around with a squashed face and being called 'Mugs' MacCrossan instead of Larry? I said I would look forward to going a few rounds with him. 'That's the spirit!' he said and gave me a little dig which nearly put me across the road.

Dad said Sergeant Branigan was involved in sorting out the Animal Gangs. 'Like the Teddy Boys or the Mods. Hard men with soft centres!' Dad laughed. 'Particularly when they ran up against Sergeant Branigan.'

'Why were they always fighting?' queried Freckles, who had kindly blessed us with his presence on this sojourn.

'Well if you had to live in the tenements they lived in you'd be fighting all the time, I'm sure,' answered 'Lugs'. He said some of the worst tenements in Dublin were to be found in the Liberties. Often you had a family of twelve sharing one big room in an old run-down house with dirt and cobwebs everywhere and having to use a shared toilet out the back somewhere. There was lots of fighting and he was on call all the time to sort out problems in families – it was a feature of life in the Liberties. 'Lugs' said, 'What do you expect when you have poverty, half-starved children with no shoes and rags for clothing, no work but money for drink.' Husbands beat up wives, gangs tormented communities. The so-called Animal Gangs of the 1930s and '40s were not just from the Liberties, but they fought pitched battles in Baldoyle and Tolka Park regularly with similar Animal Gangs from inner-city areas around Gardiner Street and Sheriff Street and also from the north side of the city.

'Lugs' told us the story behind the gangs. The term 'Animal Gangs' came to the public's attention in 1934 in the newspapers following court cases and referred to a gang in Corporation Street in Monto who had emerged out of the printer's strikes of that year and were mainly street newsvendors, a hugely important occupation for poverty-stricken communities. The term then came to be applied to any gang causing trouble in those decades. Despite that, 'Lugs' said that some of the communities remembered a couple of the gangs as some class of Robin Hood figures who protected the poor, while others remembered them as brutal thugs whose nickname reflected their savagery. Some of the north inner-city gangs were young dockers who carried large hooks that they used during their work. Other weapons included blades hidden in peaked caps or in potatoes!

'Lugs' told us that he had first-hand experience dealing with the gangs. Some of the criminals he arrested were no angels either, Dad pointed out, citing one famous court case. He said it involved a notorious incident when a criminal bit him on the bottom during an arrest. Sergeant Branigan told the Judge that the arrested 'was worse than the Balubas. At least they cook you first.'

'Why was he called "Lugs"?' Daisy wanted to know. Dad said he got his nickname 'Lugs' early in life due to his cauliflower-like ears acquired while boxing.

'Lugs' and Dad chatted on the corner of Meath Street and, having had our fill in Manning's, we were happy to listen to their reminiscences. 'Lugs' mentioned the old 'toss schools' which he was ordered to break up. We wanted to know what kind of schools these were. 'Let me show ye,' said 'Lugs'. He dug deep into his enormous baggy trousers and brought out a handful of pennies. 'Come with me,' and around the corner we trooped into a lane called Molyneux Yard with loads of horses and manure and hay and enough smells to cause any farmer to lick his lips and rub his hands with glee. He gave each of us a penny. 'Now,' he went. 'Look closely at your pennies. Check the heads and harps signs. What you have to do is to throw the penny to the base of that wall there and guess which side of the coin the penny will land on. Heads you win, harps you lose. That's the game. Will it be heads or harps?'

We flung our coins towards the wall but not before guessing which side we hoped would be facing up when landed. The coins landed and we rushed forward. Freckles and Daisy were delighted as their harp guesses turned up. Minnie and I were not so lucky. 'That now,' said 'Lugs', 'is a game of pitch and toss. It seems very easy and nice but in the old days, serious money was wagered on the toss of the coins. You'd see stacks of silver coins on the ground being gambled on the toss. Lots of men lost their shirts on these games. Nearly worse than cards. Men used to play for hours and there were often fights. There were also a few sharpers who used to play with fixed pennies. They had the same face on both sides! This was done by placing two pennies on top of each other, say on a railway track. The train would come along and squash them together to look like one coin but with two harps or two heads. One of the worst of these toss schools was hidden away behind Kevin Street and we were called many times to break it up.'

He then asked us a question which made me blush. 'Do you lads ever scut?' Scutting was grabbing hold of the back of a lorry or a battery-run Johnson Mooney & O'Brien bread van and jumping on for a free lift, or 'scut', and then jumping back off again when the vehicle slowed down. We did it a few times but mainly on borrowed bikes. We would cycle really fast alongside the bread van and then grab hold of the backdoor hinge and the van would do the rest of the pulling work with us flying along beside it. If you happened to jump on to the back of a lorry for a free lift you could land yourself in difficulties when it was slowing down. Quite dangerous when jumping off. Even worse if it didn't slow down for then you would end up ten or so miles out in the country.

'Of course not, Sergeant Branigan!'

'And do you ever swing on lamp posts? That's very dangerous as you might meet a car coming towards you as you swing out onto the road.'

'No, Sergeant Branigan.' By the sound of us we were walking saints. I didn't mention, of course, the time I took a shortcut under a long, articulated truck that was stopped at some traffic lights near Sally's Bridge coming from school. Freckles reported me to Mum the minute we came home and there was absolute war in the house that evening. I had the last laugh, however, playing pitch and toss in Molyneux Yard. While Dad and 'Lugs' were chatting away, the rest of us continued playing the game. Freckles was getting all cocky, having a run of wins. He flicked his coin towards the wall. It bounced off it and quickly rolled into a big dollop of horse dung. Completely unretrievable, greedy Freckles rushed forward hoping to grab it. Too late and he followed the penny in with his foot and the soft plop and his screech of annoyance could be heard for miles. Dad dragged him out and brought him to a pile of hay and told him to scrape it off. The rest of us were hiding our laughter. Freckles came back with a sour puss on him, as he always did when he was feeling mean. He knuckled me in the lower back ribs. Not very nice and it hurt badly. Dad intervened and said he would give us both 'a foot in the pants' if we didn't stop the messing. I'm glad he intervened as Freckles had really bony hands, whereas mine were more suitable to playing the piano, according to my aunt over in Grosvenor Avenue. She never tired of trying to encourage me to learn the piano. She said I must have blue blood in me, whatever that meant, whenever she looked at my hands.

Well, we certainly enjoyed meeting Sergeant Branigan and before we parted he said he would let us in on a little secret, all about knocking on doors! We of course knew all about secret knocks on doors, having devoured every one of Enid Blyton's Famous Five and Secret Seven books, not to mention *The Secret of Spiggy Holes*. We listened anyway. The law of the land stipulated that pubs were to be closed at certain times of the day, called the Holy Hour, and also on certain days, including Good Friday and Christmas Day. Well, certain characters had great difficulty in abstaining at those times and on those days, according to the Sergeant. Sometimes it was more the fact that drink was just suddenly and completely unavailable to them. But there was a certain attractiveness in trying to access out-of-bounds drink. The subterfuge element added to the spice of enjoyment. Bear in mind that there were very few off licenses in Dublin in those days, so if you wanted a pint, the pub was the only place to get it.

During these forbidden days or hours, the pub was locked up with blinds drawn. Nobody there. Or so it seemed. In actual fact, certain pubs known to locals would be a hive of activity but unbeknownst to ordinary passers-by. There wouldn't be a sound to be heard or a light to be seen. Yet the serious pint drinkers were happily inside and sitting on their favourite bar stools, saying 'Same again, Pat!' How did this work? Secret knocking, not just any kind of knocking but a knocking code which went 'rat tat tat,' then pause, then 'rat tat' – a three and two code or a four and one combination, or other variations. The barman would know the exact code as would the customers. 'My job,' said 'Lugs', 'was to check out pubs, see if there was any illicit drinking going on and put an end to it. Once I knew the code – which I managed to acquire through various means known only to myself – you should have seen the faces of them when we caught them drinking. They leapt up like monkeys in the zoo and jumped this way and that to escape the forces of the law. Men you would think hadn't an ounce of energy in them suddenly found legs and spurted out of the place. Ah, it was funny just to watch them!'

Just before it was time to part from Sergeant Branigan, he brought us over to a small playground near the yard. 'Did you ever play "rings"?' he asked. 'Try this.' He pointed at a three-square-foot board pinned to a wall and dotted with about twelve hooks. 'Here's what you do.' He whisked out a bundle of two-inch-wide black rubber rings from his pocket. 'You have to throw these rings at the board and see how many you can latch on to the hooks. That's all. Very straight-forward.' It was not, as there was a particular way of holding the ring to be thrown. Your fingers had to circle the ring and hold it standing straight in your hand so you could look through it and only then should you lob it towards the board. Off with us then and we had a great game amongst ourselves for half an hour or so while the grown-ups chatted. Minnie went off skipping and playing ball with some school pals near Michael Mallin Flats. We could hear them as they sang:

> Queenio, queenio, who's got the ball?
>
> Is she big or is she small?
>
> Is she fat or is she thin?
>
> Or, is she like a rolling pin.

Dublin Be Damned!

We had barely said goodbye to 'Lugs' when who should come out of the pub just across at the corner but a scraggly-haired, rough-looking chap carrying a guitar case as battered looking as himself. 'Hiya Harry,' he went. 'What has ye down in this neck of the woods?'

'Ah, just showing the buffs where I learnt my trade!'

'I won't ask what that trade was,' laughed the gravelly voiced man. Dad introduced us and said he knew our musician friend from the hotel business. 'This is Mr Furey who plays ballads and folk music, just like the Dubliners. He's from around here.' There was an awful amount of folk music going on in those days, going by what Mr Furey had to say. And across the road was the church where he and his wife got married. 'Every time I look across to John's Lane I start crying,' he joked. We wondered why he was crying. 'Don't forget, lads and lassies, this is where the Dubliners also have their roots. Sure, didn't the man himself, Barney McKenna, although known as "Banjo Barney of Donnycarney", originally came from here, the Coombe.'

Before he could proceed, didn't Minnie get a word in. 'Aren't we all from the Coombe, Mr Furey? Most of my friends in school were born there.'

'I guess we all are, love,' he replied. 'Barney came back to the Liberties and served part of his musical apprenticeship at the Pipers Club further along the street there, and it was there that he and future fellow member of the group, John Sheahan, met as teenagers in the 1950s. And I'll tell ye this for nothing,' added Mr Furey, 'them bagpipe players, the Chieftains, also have roots in the Liberties. Sure, didn't Tommy Potts' family come from the Coombe at the bottom of Meath Street? Number 6 the Coombe I think his house was. So there!'

'I'm not finished, yet,' he went on. 'Did you know that the 1916 leader Eammon Ceannt, who used to train with the Irish Volunteers up in your neck of the woods, was a member of the Dublin Piper's Club that held their practice sessions in a house opposite the old windmill up there in Thomas Street. He was a skilled piper. And I'll let you go with this one: you kids must love that Christmas song, "The Little Drummer Boy". Am I right? Well, one of Ceannt's fellow commandants in the Rising, Michael Mallin, was known as "the little drummer boy" as a child, such was his talent. He was born and raised just across from John's Lane Church. What did he do when he wasn't much older than yourselves? He joined the English army and went off to India as a little drummer boy. There he was marching at the head of the army as they went into battle!'

We loved the Christmas song he was talking about and just then, Minnie started singing 'Rum, pum, pum, pum, I played my drum for him, Pa rum pump um pum, me and my drum...' 'Yes, the little drummer boy had no gifts to bring to the king so he played his drum instead, isn't that right Mr Furey?'

'Spot on,' he replied.

'Why did he come home to Ireland?' asked Freckles.

'He wanted to fight for Ireland,' said Mr Furey. 'That was the gift of the little Irish drummer boy to Ireland. He gave his life so that we could enjoy the freedom we have today!'

Still humming the 'Little Drummer Boy' to myself, I thought of what Minnie had said about everyone seeming to have come from the Coombe and the Liberties. 'Hold on! So do I! Well, well! Isn't that why good old Dad is showing us around? Janey Mac, me shirt is black! Aah, me aul segosha!'

Mr Furey told Dad that some of the older residents still recalled hearing the sounds of the great tenors Enrico Caruso and Count John McCormack, and the arias from the great operettas, wafting out the tenement windows on Francis Street, Meath Street or the Coombe. Others recalled the singer and accordion player Paddy Aldrith, fondly known as 'Paddy All Right!'

Our poor little legs were worn out at this stage. Minnie said she just wanted to lie down on the ground and sleep. 'Let's go for a little bag of chips before we go home,' suggested Dad. We popped into Burdock's near our bus stop. 'Burdock's has been selling chips since 1913,' said Dad. Freckles, smarty pants as usual, went, 'Let's hope they don't serve us chips made in 1913!' Burdock's was opposite St Werburgh's Church. 'That's where two mortal enemies are buried,' said Dad while we were waiting for our chips. 'Lord Edward Fitzgerald and the notorious Major Sirr, who arrested him in 1798, right after the

Rebellion.' However, by that stage we had lost interest, particularly when our eyes caught sight of a wall song:

> In the year nine hundred and eighty-eight,
>
> As everyone must know,
>
> The Vikings came to Dublin,
>
> 'Cos, they had nowhere else to go,
>
> They landed on Wood Quay, where they all jumped off their ships,
>
> And legged it to Burdocks,
>
> For a little bag of chips.

To use a Liberties expression 'we were bunched' as we headed for home on the bus. Still, we found the energy to happily munch on our fish and chips with lots of vinegar. We also managed to sing *Molly Malone* on the bus.

6

❧

THE BULL RING, THE TIVOLI AND 'KILL OR KURE'

It was a dry, brisk spring morning when we were back in the Liberties. Dad needed to do some business in the markets so we were dragged along. Meath Street was bustling as we arrived. With its shops and markets, it was a hive of activity and an absolute delight to our senses. Here we saw long-established business such as Larkin Brothers, Dunne's and Tony Martin's Butchers', and O'Neill's Fish and Poultry – all thriving. We saw butchers bent over, hauling carcasses to and fro, and enjoyed the aroma of freshly baked batch loaves wafting down the street from St Catherine's Bakery. It was the only place in Ireland where one could get a sliced Turnover Loaf. You could still buy Tipsy cakes/Russian slices and Gur cakes here. In we went, me first in the queue – you bet. This time, we agreed, we would stock up on food before we traipsed around.

Other shops we noticed were Fusco's Chippers, the Bull Ring, the Liberty and Molly Malone Markets and Bazaars, as well as the many pubs, hairdressers, chemists, and various other exotic shops. As if we didn't have enough of the street hawkers on Thomas Street, there were more on Meath Street. There they were again with their tried and trusted calls for us to buy, jostling for our attention.

Dad waved to 'a great' Gaelic and soccer footballer called Kevin Moran and then stopped to say hello to Jack Roche of Roche's Grocers on Meath Street. 'Nice to see you back Harry; I'm still chopping the cabbages and the turnips. See! We could consider ourselves not so much a shop, but more a way of life,' he said, looking at us. 'So, come in and browse.' He was some chancer, I thought. What on earth would we be doing browsing among old cabbage leaves, turnips and the like? The whiff of parsnips ran us out of the place.

'We'll see you over in the Bull Ring,' we shouted to Dad, and belted over to see the bulls. Years after our visit to Meath Street, people of the Liberties still remember when Taoiseach Bertie Ahern brought Russia's Mikhail Gorbachev there during the course of a visit to Dublin. From what we heard, he was there for the opening of a Russian shop. We felt that things must be really bad in Russia if he had to come to Dublin and set up a business here. When he arrived, he walked the length of Meath Street, looking for suitable premises, or so we imagined. He popped into a butcher's shop and afterwards one local woman exclaimed about the chops in the window, 'They'll have to call them Gorbychops now!' Another excited onlooker called him the 'man with the map on his head', because of the birthmark on his forehead.

When Jack Roche met the Russian president, he handed him a bowl of fruit with the two landmark words *glasnost* and *perestroika* emblazoned on top and with a handwritten note thanking him for his work in Russia. It was something he just did on the spur of the moment. And as he approached the president, he could sense the heightened alert in the attitude and the body language of the security guards, in case there was a bomb hidden amongst the cabbages! That's what the Liberties was all about – always expect the unexpected.

On the subject of heads, we ended up in St Catherine's Church across from the bakery, where Dad showed us a not-so-well known monument that commemorated a War of Independence patriot. 'Few who visit this church,' Dad said, 'are aware that they are being silently observed from above by a young lad who was executed during the War of Independence that followed the 1916 Rising.'

'Where? Where?' we clamoured.

According to Dad, when the church was being renovated in the 1920s a decision was made to place facial impressions of the country's litany of saints at the base of each of the plaster ribs extending up to the ceiling. They were all there, including St Patrick and St Brigid. Yet when it came to St Kevin of Glendalough they were, seemingly, unable to find a suitable image of the man to put up on the wall. Kevin Barry's father was from Pimlico, where he had a dairy shop. The parish priest of St Catherine's knew Kevin's father and had Republican sympathies. This facilitated the placing of Kevin Barry's image in the church. Fortunately, there had been a death mask of Kevin after his execution, which provided a suitable compromise. He was the one without the beard.

Dad then brought us around the corner to Francis Street, full of old three- and four-storey houses, and with more pubs in it than shops. He reminisced about Harry Sive's rag-a-bone and clothing merchant, who had his business in the area for many years, reflecting on the poverty-stricken times and circumstances many of the residents lived in not so long ago. This was a tenement-filled street with hundreds of families, huckster shops, nine pubs and all sorts of businesses: the Myra Bakery with its penny cakes loved by the locals sold in their thousands; Johnny Ray's ice-cream parlour renowned throughout Dublin; the popular Joyce's Bakery likewise used to have great queues for pancakes on Shrove (Pancake) Tuesday for years.

We trooped into the Iveagh Markets, where we never saw so many hawkers selling second-hand clothes in our lives! Mountains and mountains of old clothes everywhere, nearly reaching the high glass ceilings. Hawkers were sitting around smoking and chatting. Customers were poking here and there and trying on all sorts of garb. Minnie and I ran up a hill of clothes and nearly got lost in them. 'Get yerself down outa dat, yang wans, or we'll have to dig yez out!' screeched a hawker. We had fun anyway, trying on hats and scarves and all sorts of rags and what-nots.

On the front of the market we liked the carved heads high up over the entrance, each with a different expression. The facial expressions on some of these extraordinary heads were well worth a closer look. Some were happy, some sad, some really tired and some laughing their heads off. The large bearded grinning face was reputed to represent Lord Iveagh of the Guinness family, who built the place and lots else including the Iveagh Flats, St Patrick's Park and the Bayno play centre for children and famous for its chocolate drink and currant buns. The heads were supposed to represent the various trading nations of the world. Dad said that there used to be a washhouse at the back of the Iveagh Markets used by local people who brought their washing there. It looked to us like they left most of it behind.

Across the road from the Iveagh, we saw the cinema Dad used to visit as a boy. The Tivoli was known as 'the Tivo' by the locals. With pride in his voice, he recalled its opening night in 1934 with the screening of *Cockeyed Cavaliers*. For Dad, and for so many of his generation, the Tivo and cinemas in general were more than a picture house – they were universities where they learned all about the Blue Nile and the White Nile, about Stanley and Livingstone and 'things we never learned in school'. He said it was like being led by the Pied Piper of Hamelin; 'We just followed the call to the cinema as often as we could and when we went in and sat down, it felt to us as if we were all in wishing chairs, our dreams coming true right there in front of us.'

The official opening of the 1,700-seater Tivoli cinema was just a few days before Christmas, Dad remembered, so it was a really exciting time. The opening honours were performed by local councillor Patrick Medlar, a former undertaker with Medlar & Claffey of Thomas Street. If you were heard to have a serious cough, you'd be assailed by the phrase 'Medlar's gotcha!' He was a strange character indeed and had a glass panel inserted in his own coffin so that his face could be seen when the coffin was closed. Some locals were afraid to look in just in case he looked back. 'Others looked in to make sure he wouldn't be coming back,' laughed Dad.

Dublin Be Damned!

Sitting on the steps of the Tivo, Dad told us about another famous institution on Francis Street, at No. 3, beside the markets. This was Mushatt's Chemist, known for 'either curing you or killing you!' We were somewhat alarmed by the sound of that. Harold Mushatt was the 'Kill or Cure' chemist who operated the family business. If you were sick or needed a cure Mushatt's was the place (and in most cases the only place) to go in the first half of the twentieth century. Because they made up their own medicines, they became known as the 'fellas with the cures' or you were told, 'go to Mushatt's for cures'. Dad also recalled Daddy Nagle, in Meath Street and who was another popular chemist. He was known as the 'Lucky Man' because of similar healing renown. With their mixtures and preparations, these two seemed to cure all the ills of the poor of the area. 'You could say that they were modern-day witch doctors,' laughed Dad.

They sold all their preparations over the counter and, because many of the local people couldn't afford a doctor, they often brought with them their own Baby Power bottle (a small Irish whiskey bottle) for a penny- or tuppence-worth of the various mixtures – camphorated oil for a child's cough or iodine if they had a cut. It was a big part of the business, whole families coming into the shop complaining of various ailments – stomach trouble or skin rash, toothache or scabies – but no matter what the complaint, they had a mixture for them. They sold their own brand of remedies, labelled 'KK'. KK Foot Paste, for example, was for 'corns, welts, callouses and bunions – no need to use dangerous razors, knife blades or burning acids.' It was claimed that KK really stood for 'Kill or Kure'. After hearing about all this 'kill or kure' business, we were very glad to have McCaul's Chemist down the road from us in Mountain View.

Just as we were walking towards St Nicholas of Myra Church, Dad uttered his famous words, 'Did you know…?' as was often his custom. He said that the man who introduced the national flag, the Tricolour, to Ireland was a Huguenot silk-weaver who lived in Francis Street in the nineteenth century. He was called Edward Hollywood, born in 1814, and years later became a member of the nationalist independence movement, the Young Irelanders. In 1848, he travelled to Paris as part of a three-man delegation (with Thomas Meagher and Smith O'Brien) to pass a message of congratulations from Ireland to the new French government. He was inspired by the French Tricolour to weave an Irish equivalent. He returned to Ireland with a flag based on France's red, white and blue emblem, given to him by the French government. His republican tricolour – featuring green to represent the Gaelic tradition, orange to represent the followers of William of Orange, and white to represent peace between them – was later adopted as the flag of the Irish Republic in 1916 and by the Irish Free State which succeeded it in 1922.

'Thanks, Dad,' I said, 'you are certainly flying the flag today' and we hurried along. We were anxious to visit the church on Francis Street, not to pray or anything else but to hear about its link with Good Saint Nick – Santa Claus! There are fascinating treasures to be seen both outside and inside this beautiful church, with its connotations of Santa Claus. St Nicholas of Myra, a bishop of the third to fourth century, from a town in Turkey, is depicted on a stained-glass window in the church. Three golden bags and an anchor lie at his feet. The golden bags are a reference to Santa Claus carrying his sacks of presents for children, we were told. 'Goodbye, good Saint Nick. Don't forget to call to our house next Christmas,' said Minnie to the window. At this stage we felt it was time for us to be on our travels – not to Santa's Grotto at the North Pole, but home to Mountain View.

7

SAMMY SALMON AND SMELLY FEET

After having seen and been in so many shops in the Liberties, you would imagine we'd had enough of them. But not so! The number of shops in Mountain View did not defeat us whatsoever and we regarded it as an Aladdin's Cave on our doorstep. There were butchers, drapers, shoemakers, bakeries, bicycle shops, grocers, sweet shops, a post office, chemists, hardware shops, pubs and everything besides. By the middle decades of the twentieth century Mountain View was a thriving and contented village, with shops stretching from the bridge to the Kenilworth cinema and beyond.

Starting at the bridge over the Grand Canal, we had the Salmon Barber. Even before we entered this establishment we had our suspicions, particularly with the barber's name, Samuel Salmon, known to all as Sammy. He looked like Elvis's older brother with his jet-black, oil-polished hair. His name was a complete distraction, reminding us of the salmon leap, the Grand Canal, the zoo, going up to the River Dodder or eating fish on Fridays. How could a man be called after a fish? Despite this ongoing quandary, we were despatched there regularly for our 'short back and sides, please'. The briskish barber used to whisk out a plank when it came to our turn. Across the armrests of the chair it rested and up we'd climb to admire ourselves in the mirror. Meanwhile, with a quick flick of his wrist, he bedecked us with a magic white cloak tied gently at our necks. Oh, we felt important! We liked the feel of the shortened hair at the nape of our necks after the visit. It felt bristly, sharp, rigid and tough. Like ourselves.

Next door was Delaney's cycle shop, 'mending bikes since 1917', and, going on the time we sometimes had to wait, it seemed to us as if they were still mending bikes from that time. In fact, nothing had changed since the old days. The bare floorboards were oil saturated to slippery and dirty black with little gaps and cracks between them. We liked that as we were able to peer down into the basement, full or old oil lamps or bicycles awaiting repair since 1917. Maybe some were uncollected by the long-deceased customers who had abandoned all hope of dying in the saddle. There they were, High Nellies, Penny Farthings and the old trusty Raleigh's, all lined up, going nowhere. Peeping down was always the first thing we did when we went into the shop. It felt dangerous, as if we were on a precipice looking down into the chasm. While waiting for our bikes, we also spent a lot of time looking at ourselves in the huge old mirror inside the door.

There were many grocery shops along the main road as this was the time when self-service supermarkets were only starting to emerge. Consequently, we had Sweeny's at the Bridge and Sweeney's across around the corner from our house. The same family ran both and we distinguished them by adding 'at the Bridge'. One of the family used to partake in the famous Liffey Swim and we were always in awe of him. We had many favourite shops. The Beehive newsagents, down past the hospice, and Ma Ryan's across the road, doubling as the local post office. Ma Ryan's was the best sweet shop around and we went in there every day to be served by two sisters, both known as Ma Ryan. That they both shared the same name didn't bother us as we were never served by both at the same time and we never could tell the difference anyway. They were two stout elderly ladies and as I become older I felt sorry for them having waddle away from their nice warm kitchen behind the shop just to come out and sell me Clipso Bars, Rolo, bags of toffee chocolates, Bull's Eyes, Aniseed (Nancy) balls, Gobstoppers or Acid Drops. All were served in little white bags and perfect for carrying. Sometimes we bought lemon curd pies called Lemmy Jammy's. We loved the tang.

Just past St Mary's orphanage was Mulcahy's shop, famous for being the centre of much gossip, particularly about us. Despite that, it had an orange football in the window which I longed for and eventually bought after endless saving and doing odd jobs. It was my first football and burst after a few hard kicks.

There were many shops in the village itself including Cooney's, Healy's and Gowran's, all family grocers. Gowran's also had a separate pork butcher next door to a general butcher, Farren's. Farren's on a Sunday morning had chickens barbecuing in big glass cookers. We used to go along and loiter outside, just for the sheer pleasure of the succulent aroma wafting out. We never got to taste them. Next door was P.J. Kilmartin's bookmakers, a real den of iniquity for the local corner boys and long-retired corner boys. They had 'Turf Accountants' beside the name, which totally confused us as we couldn't establish a link between bogs and bookies. Marguerite's, next door, was a ladies' drapery shop which I had the misfortune to visit regularly. Not to buy anything, but to call for a pal of mine, known as Four Eyes. Whenever I called in, ever second day in fact, and doubtlessly much to the annoyance of Mrs Marguerite, I was suddenly enveloped in women's tops, cardigans, wool, needles, skirts, vests and sundry unmentionables. Customers would eye me up and down with great suspicion. 'Is Four Eyes in?' I would ask, and tension in the shop would subside until my next visit. Another of the lads lived above and behind The Magnet newsagents. The Magnet was true to its name and regularly drew us in. It was owned by a small, fat, genial man called Fred Hand. We just needed sweets and comics and always seemed to call in when he was making himself a fry in the kitchen. Next door was Concannon's bakery. This was famous for its 'Cannon' or rock buns, and much else besides. The son was one of the lads, too. His Dad was known as 'Mr Bun'. Next door was Murdock's hardware, where Freckles used to get his nails and paint.

Paddy Walsh's bicycle shop was perched in an ancient building on the corner, facing the Tree of Knowledge. It's a wonder that the local lads didn't give that man grey hair. In fact, his hair was always black and smart-looking. Not surprising, since he was also a renowned dancer. We pestered that man with repairs. I had a cheap old yellow-coloured bicycle I had found in the church grounds and which I was given after no one claimed it within six months. It was a right crock but I loved it, being my first bike. However, it needed lots of work to make it roadworthy. To make matters worse for poor Paddy, since I was also having lots of 'slow punctures', I was in to him every second asking to have my tyres pumped. I had no pump. He was a very kind and patient man. He had to be when it came to dealing with RTÉ's Mike Murphy, who played a 'candid camera' trick on him. Murphy went in looking for a free bike and tested the patience of the poor man. When he died, his headstone had a bicycle carved on it in remembrance of a great character.

Killeen's motorbike shop was a few doors from Mount Jerome and was where dreams were made. We loved sitting up on the BSA's (for 'bloody sore arse' we used to joke) and the Triumph's. Such was our desire to 'try out' one that I 'borrowed' a Garelli from a neighbour's garage and took it for a 'trial run' into town. This was only a moped and the engine started with the help of fierce pedalling. I was stuck in the one gear since I didn't know exactly how to drive it. Consequently, there was much noise and smoke belching from it. It didn't matter to me in the slightest as I hurtled down the road at 20 miles per hour towards Emmet Bridge. I suddenly saw myself as Evel Knievel jumping the Grand Canyon. I slowed as I approached the rise for the brow of the bridge. The opposite site was invisible. Quickly, I revved the engine and the bike took off up the hill and shot up and over the Grand Canyon-like bridge, landing on the cobble-stoned opposite side with a bounce and away with me towards town, my hair happily blowing in the wind. A bored-looking Garda on duty outside the Department of Foreign Affairs stopped me at St Stephen's Green. He was extremely understanding as I had no licence, insurance or anything! 'Just return it as quickly as possible,' he directed and I shot off, still stuck in the same gear, leaving him covered in a cloud of soot and smoke.

Beside Killeen's was a shoemaker, where we were regularly had our shoes 'soled and heeled'. I needed to go in there frequently, since I seldom had decent brakes on my bike. Often times a few of the lads would go for a cycle up the Dublin Mountains, or maybe to visit the notorious Hellfire Club at the top of Montpelier Hill. Later, we liked to tear down, non-stop, from the bottom of that hill to the Yellow House Pub at Rathfarnham. I used my shoes as brakes all the way down. 'Burning rubber' we called it.

There were three chemist shops in Mountain View – McCaul's on the corner of Greenmount Avenue, Walsh's nearly opposite the church, and O'Dea's at the major junction for Rathgar Avenue. McCaul's was the one we used the most, mainly for sugar barley if we were sick. Its distinctive shopfront consisted of large panes of glass surrounded by chromium-plated steel. We loved the white weighing scales at the entrance. This was an old-fashioned type where you stood up on a platform and inserted a coin in a tiny slot above the face which stretched five feet up from the platform. We managed to weigh four of us for the price of one by easing the second person onto the platform while the first person was easing him or herself off it, and so on.

Anne's shop, beside Paddy Walsh's bicycle shop, was useful for just two items as far as we were concerned – broken biscuits, popular because they were very cheap. If they had no broken biscuits, one had to buy a small packet containing about five biscuits. However, the ice-cream wafers were the biggest attraction, with a large one for 6*d* and a half for 3*d*. These would last us forever, particularly the bigger one, as it was nearly impossible to bite on it. Our mouths just weren't big enough, so we had to make do with licking it all the way around.

O'Hanlon's further up the village was an alcoholic's paradise. We bypassed Deveney's off-license right next door, which was an emporium of colourful bottles of gin, brandy, whiskey and vodka on out-of-reach shelves which could only be accessed with a ladder. It was even better than a pub, having a selection of every possible concoction from the far ends of the earth. As well as being a grocery shop. O'Hanlon's was our frequent destination as it sold ginger ale, which we had read about in our Enid Blyton books. We were under the distinct impression that because it had 'ale' on the label then it meant just that. So much so that we felt obliged to sneak into this tiny grocery-cum-sweet shop and mumble our requests for ginger ale, with us looking really suspicious, gazing about us, ready to be told they don't serve underage drinkers. Having acquired the contraband goods, we darted up the lanes nearby, Fitzpatrick's Cottages or Ryan's Cottages, and swigged away to our heart's content. Having had our fill we naturally enough belched, as is the required custom in most licensed premises. If we also indulged in Russian slices, also known as Tipsy cake, bought from The Pixie shop just over Emmet Bridge, then we were in real trouble. This small square of sugar-saturated cake, made from the bakery's leftovers all squashed together, and topped with a slab of pink icing, was, we believed, much more potent than Christmas trifle. When we earned pocket money from doing odd jobs, we bought the Tipsy cake and rushed up to O'Hanlon's for the ginger ale. What a mixture! Within fifteen minutes we emerged from the surrounding lanes transformed into the village drunks, barely able to find our way home.

Some of the factories in Mountain View were very kind to us as children. Bossenet's had a jam factory at the bottom of St Mary's Avenue, around the corner from our house. All we had to do here was collect jam jars, bring them in and – lo and behold – we got free pots of jam in return.

However, it was the excitement surrounding the Tayto crisp factory on Tivoli Avenue that really caught our imaginations. This factory had been there for about ten years. Joe 'Spud' Murphy, from Thomas Street in the Liberties, had founded the company. The name 'Tayto' had come about because his son, as a very young child, was unable to pronounce 'potato' and called it 'tato'. So, by adding the letter 'y' Tayto was born in the early 1950s in the Liberties. The opening of another factory in Mountain View was an indicator of its growing popularity. The flavoursome variety of 'cheese and onion' was developed just around the time certain small individuals in Mountain View tried to enhance the crisps' flavour. Barrels of crisps were left outside the factory entrance to cool down, or so we thought. We used to creep up so the staff wouldn't see us and then plunge our grasping hands into a barrel. This kept us supplied with crisps for years until one of the lads decided that the flavour needed enhancing. Conkers was his name and he had the first and last brainwave in his entire life. He suggested climbing into the barrel and jumping and dancing on the crisps, 'like they do in wine-growing countries'. 'They do it to bring out the flavour,' he told us, sounding very knowledgeable for once. The only wine we were used to drinking was the altar wine and we agreed that its flavour could be improved. Maybe it just needed more jumping on. So, we helped him to climb in. 'Oh, you headcase,' went a despairing Redser. He was so-called because of his bright red bulbous cheeks, which made him look like a trumpet player. 'Take off your shoes first,' he ordered. Out climbed Conkers with great difficulty, took off his shoes and back in with him, jumping away like a monkey. He reached down into the barrel and pulled up a handful of crisps. 'Now try these.' We did and noticed a slightly different taste from the usual. Even the aroma had changed. We all recognised it – Conkers' smelly feet – and immediately spat the crisps back into the barrel. Just then a loud roar came from within the factory. 'Quick,' shouted Young Banjaxed, 'it's Spud Murphy! Scarper!' He came, he saw, and we ran, leaving Conkers stuck in the barrel. That's what friends were for we, we believed, a lesson we had learnt from a very early age.

Of course, we didn't limit ourselves to crisps, as we were within strolling distance of a sweet factory, Clarnico Murray's, where we soon became well-known faces, always willing to help out. This factory, known as St Pancras Works, had been on Mount Tallant Avenue since the 1920s. Naturally enough, and as expected, our kind offers were sometimes turned down, the utter disappointment on our faces only being allayed with bags of Iced Caramels, Macaroons and Maple

Brazils. After much persuasion (or pestering) we did manage to run errands, getting the papers, pints of milk, and packets of cigarettes or tea. Following this coup, we acquired the status of being connoisseurs on Mint Creams, Choc Mint Creams, Wine Gums and Liquorice All Sorts.

At the opposite end of Mountain View, near the bridge, was the Greenmount factory complex with two big factories – the Greenmount Oil Company and the Greenmount and Boyne Linen Company. What was particularly memorable about this complex was the Second World War air-raid siren that used to go off ominously every day. The siren, known as 'the hooter', didn't go off suddenly but gradually, building up to a high wailing sound and then slowly quietening down. We constantly expected to see German bombers overhead at any time. Its purpose was to remind the workers of their starting times in the morning (eight o'clock), breaks and lunchtimes, and finishing time at six in the evening. We found it handy for returning to school after our lunch as it went off at half past one. We were caught out a few times, not hearing it, as we fought our way along the Grand Canal to school.

8

Bang Bang and the Monarch
of the Liberties

D ad called us 'nothing but a shower of chancers'. Well, wasn't that nice on that fine spring morning and us going about our business, helping out in the house, playing in the garden, and supposedly doing some tidying in our rooms. 'I'll prove it to you, as well,' he continued, talking to nobody in particular. We knew however, it was for our ears. So, after much ado about everything, it was off down to the 54A bus stop with us, along by the hospice wall. We were going to *Gulliver's Travel's* land, we were informed, just as the bus pulled alongside. 'What country is that in?' Minnie wanted to know. 'An imaginary country but full of real rascally people,' came the quick reply and she still looked puzzled.

As the bus passed down Clanbrassil Street and Leonard's Corner we passed a shop, Kilbride's, with three brass balls hanging over the entrance. 'Why are all those golden balls over the entrance?' asked Minnie. She was curious on that day, indeed.

'I hope you never have to go in there,' Dad said with a frown.

'That's where you go when you have no money left and the bank won't look at you. They give you a miserable few bob for a loan if you give them your confirmation suit, dress or even your watch. If you want to get your property back you then pay them back, with interest. But most times people can't afford to pay back the loan and so the pawnbroker sells your goods at a great profit,' he said, pointing to the window display.

'But why do they have three shiny balls?' Minnie persisted, thinking of Good Saint Nick in Francis Street with his three sacks at his feet.

'I believe it is the symbol of those in the moneylending business, particularly pawnbrokers, as that is what that business is – moneylending. They are similar to banks or credit unions in that they lend you money, but it's usually only small amounts given to the hard-up folks.' He said it was the family crest of the famous Medici family in Florence, Italy, long ago. 'They were well-known bankers and moneylenders. One of their workers had a fight with a bully and bashed him on the head using three bags full of stones. The Medici's were so impressed that they used the symbol of three bags or balls on their family crest. Since then when people see the sign they know it's all about moneylending. I well remember,' he continued, 'when there were hundreds of pawnbrokers all over the city of Dublin, such was the poverty ever since the 1913 Dublin Lockout. That was when so many lost their jobs for going on strike for better working conditions. Oh, they were hard times, indeed!'

The bus trundled on and we soon saw the outline of St Patrick's Cathedral in the distance. Just as the bus pulled out from a bus stop, we heard a commotion below deck. 'Bang! Bang!' went an old crusty voice. 'Bang! Bang!'

'Yippee!' shouted Minnie and we all rushed to the back of the bus and peered down the stairs. 'It's good old Bang Bang.' And she was right. There he was, this old tramp, standing on the platform, wobbling and hanging on to the bar with one hand, while the other held this enormous key, like one to open an old castle door. He was using it as a gun, pointing to all and sundry and shouting 'Bang! Bang!' Minnie was delighted when he pointed up at her and shouted. She fell back with a cry: 'I'm shot! Please help me!'

This part of Dublin was on the edge of the Liberties and all sorts of characters seemed to appear on approaching this magical area. Johnny Forty Coats – we had seen many times when we were coming from the Iveagh Baths. He was a friendly sort of chap who was laden down with many layers of clothing no matter what the weather was like. Stoney Pockets was another, with his pockets full with all sorts of stones. Zozimus was a character from long ago; he was known as 'the blind bard of the Liberties' who used to live at Faddle Alley near Fumbally Lane. He had an astounding memory and made his living reciting poems. He would stand on a corner and shout to one and all: 'Ye sons and daughters of Erin, gather around poor Zozimus, yer friend. Listen boys, until yez hear, my charming song so dear.' He had a terrible fear of being buried alive and of his body been stolen, so he confided in his friend, Stoney, and begged him to make sure the 'Sack-em-Ups' (as the grave-robbers were called) did not take him. He wrote a poem on his fears:

> Oh Stoney, Stoney, don't let them Sack-em-Ups get me,
>
> Send round the hat and buy me a grave.

In those days, Dad said, Bully's Acre in Kilmainham was the local cemetery for the poor and bodies would be squashed into every available space. However, unlike today, the depth between the corpse and the grass above was not an issue, which meant that shaking hands with the dead was a frequent occurrence, particularly for a wager. Body-snatchers would hover around funerals, waiting for the departure of the mourners before pouncing on the barely dead and shunting them off to Trinity College for dissection. 'Zozimus's fears were well-founded,' Dad added.

Dad rhymed off a few more names. 'Despite being called Bang Bang by everyone, the chap used to call himself Lord Dudley. Then there was Damn the Weather, who roamed around the Liberties in the 1940s and '50s frightening people to death with his curses. Other famous characters included Hairy Lemon and Oney, the funeral-goer who loved following hearses. He often walked in front of the mourners and always knew the way! Also, Peg-the-Man and the irrepressible Cantering Jack, a busking fiddler and dancer in odd boots who followed carriages for miles until paid by the passengers to go away! Then there was Bird Flanagan, President Keeley, Tie-Me-Up, Lino, All Parcels, Shell Shock Joe, Bugler Dunne, Jumbo No Toes, Mad Mary and Jack the Tumbler. Not forgetting Fat Mary, the prima donna of Dublin's streets, and Dusty Lawlor. We loved the crazy names. 'Each of these characters has a story to tell, you can be guaranteed of that,' said Dad.

'Enough for now,' he said, 'as here we are at the "four gates of hell".' This startled us but Dad allayed our fears, pointing out that it was because of the four pubs, one on each corner. The priests gave them that name to discourage people from going there. 'Just up Dean Street there, is Fallon's Capstan Bar,' pointed out Dad. 'One of the longest arms in the world once belonged to a man that once owned that pub. There was once a terrible fire beside the pub, with flames running down the street because all the whisky caught fire.' Oh, we thought that was funny, but we wanted to hear about the longest arm in the world. We were then told all about a legendary boxer, Dan Donnelly, in the early nineteenth century. He fought at a time when boxing was of the bare-knuckles variety and bouts had no time limits. No nice soft boxing gloves in those days. He took part in three major fights, winning each of them. They said at the time that he owed his success to the fact that he was so tall, nearly seven feet, and with a reach that no other boxer could match. Donnelly became the proprietor of a succession of four Dublin pubs, all of them unprofitable. 'Dan was a fine boxer but a poor publican,' Dad said. Fallon's Capstan Bar was the only one to have survived those great boxing days.

We neared our bus stop. Standing on the platform as the bus slowed, Dad said, looking at Bang Bang in the distance behind us, 'If it weren't for the insane, we'd be all mad.' I nodded in agreement, not wishing to join a long queue of millions clamouring and banging on the doors of Grangegorman, trying to get in.

We arrived at St Patrick's Cathedral and hopped off the bus. 'We can walk the rest of the way,' Dad said, and we groaned.

'All the way up that steep hill?' moaned Minnie, she of the little legs.

'Don't worry,' he comforted, 'there is a great playground hidden behind these shrubs and we'll pop in afterwards. But I want to show you a cage first.' Our eyes lit up and we de-waxed our ears. 'But first, look right behind you – there, up at that plaque on the wall. What does it say?' Up our eyes gazed and we read: Patrick Joseph McCall (1861–1919) composer and musician best remembered for his epic ballad of the Rebellion of 1798, 'Boolavogue', born in this house. Dad said that he was also the author of 'Kelly the Boy from Killanne', 'The Lowlands Low', 'The Boys of Wexford' and 'Follow Me Up to Carlow'. 'Let's hear a bar of "Boolavogue" as we head over towards Jonathan Swift's home.' Away with us in full gusto, 'A Boolavogue, a Boolavogue, as the sun was setting…' We got louder and louder as we approached the entrance to the cathedral.

'Have you finished that book, Freddy, the one you got from Rathmines Library – what was it called?'

'You mean *Gulliver's Travels*?' was the reply.

'That's the one. Well, the man who wrote it lived right here,' said Dad, pointing towards the cathedral. '" Pen mightier than the sword," they said of him. He was the man that wrote, "Tell us what the pile contains, many a head that holds no brains." Now here's a brainteaser for you lot. What pile was he referring to? And here's a hint – carpets!'

We mulled and mused and suddenly little Minnie came out with it. 'It's the big roundy house near the Meeting of the Waters man, and, and, and, it has enormous shaggy pile carpets hanging on the walls instead of on the floor. Weren't they the silly billies to do that?' and she laughed and laughed. We all clapped at Minnie's enthusiasm.

'By the way,' said Dad, 'our friend Swift was known as the "Monarch of the Liberties" because he fought for the good people who lived through some very hard times.' There were lots of linen and silk factories in the area and the English government tried to do away with Irish exports because they were so good, but Swift fought back, writing loads of secret anonymous letters called *Drapier's Letters* which proved that the pen was mightier than the sword.'

'How come?' we wanted to know.

'Well, the Irish had been fighting the English for hundreds of years without much success but along came Swift who had no army, only a pen and a sharp wit, and he did much to frighten off the English government by laughing at them in his pamphlets. It worked and the English were forced to back down and leave the factories in the Liberties alone, so people were able to go back to work.'

'But what exactly did he say that shocked the English?' Daisy wanted to know.

'Oh, just for the poor to fatten and then sell their little one-year-old babies as nice tasty meat to rich families,' Dad explained, as if this was just a routine matter and he had not a care in the world. 'Swift wrote this in a pamphlet called *A Modest Proposal.*' We couldn't believe our ears at what Dad had come out with and him all calm and collected. 'Oh, he was just being sarcastic, but it worked! Now, let's ramble in to see the man himself, and his grave which is not too far from that of the richest man in Ireland!'

'What about the chancers you mentioned this morning, Uncle?' went Freckles.

'All in good time, young man. Fasten your seatbelts!'

Dad brought us around to the back of the cathedral and showed us a door with a small hole in it. 'Now put your hand through that,' he told us. Why should we, we wanted to know, not being in any hurry to lose our hands. 'Please do,' he insisted. He disappeared suddenly and we heard his voice again in the distance. 'Go ahead and I will join you in a minute.'

Freckles, being the bravest, thrust his arm in. 'Ouch!' he went, as his hand was grasped and tugged. He withdrew his arm, but minus the hand. We stared in shock. 'Fooled you,' laughed Freckles, as his missing hand resurfaced from his sleeve. Dad reappeared. 'Well done, Freddy, you are a true chancer and you just proved it!' The rest of us followed suit and shook hands through the hole in the door with Dad. Then he told us the full story.

The origin of the story lay in a famous incident during a feud at the end of the fifteenth century between two prominent Irish families, the Ormond's and the Kildare Fitzgerald's of Silken Thomas fame. At one point, a nephew of the Earl of Ormond, 'Black James' as he was known, took refuge with his followers in the chapter house (this is where the cathedral staff lived). After a while, Gerald Fitzgerald, the Earl of Kildare, came to realise that the feud was nonsense and tried to make peace. In order to prove that no villainy was intended and that his wish for reconciliation was genuine, he cut a hole in the door and thrust his arm through to shake hands. In doing this, of course, he was placing himself at the mercy of those inside, who could easily have cut it off. He need not have worried: Black James grasped his hand warmly and his peace overtures were accepted. 'This is where the phrase "to chance your arm" comes from,' Dad said, 'and you buffs have just proved to me what a shower of chancers you are! Am I right? Now look over there at Swift's monument and then we'll have a quick gander at Mr Boyle before we visit the cage!'

Having had a good look at the grim-faced Swift who, Minnie said, 'seemed to have his nose out of joint,' the colourful Boyle Monument was the complete opposite. It was huge, nearly twenty feet high and ten feet wide, showing family members kneeling, and the contrast with the Swift monument couldn't have been more obvious. Swift's was circular, quite small for someone who had made such an impression – really just a bust of his head and shoulders. The huge and colourful Boyle Monument was erected in 1632 as the family tomb of one Richard Boyle, the richest man in Ireland and England at the time of his death in 1643. Such was his ruthlessness in acquiring property that Oliver Cromwell said he was inspired by him and wished he was still alive when Cromwell initiated his 'To Hell or Connaught' policy in the 1650s. Boyle was corrupt and unscrupulous, like 'Sticky Fingers' Brabazon of one hundred years previously in the sixteenth century. He grasped every opportunity to amass a fortune at other's expense and loss. He built Cork House (he was the Earl of Cork) on Cork Hill, Dublin, which later became the Royal Exchange and is now the site of City Hall. That was his town house. His country house was Lismore Castle in County Waterford. 'Interestingly,' said Dad, 'his son was even more famous and for a completely different reason. Does anyone know who and why? I will give you a hint – Boyle's Law.'

Freckles, of course, being a real teacher's lick in school, piped up in a grand voice, 'I do seem to recollect in the course of my studying chemistry in school, that a certain individual by the name of Robert Boyle was called the "father of modern chemistry". Am I right, kind sir?' Oh, I felt like giving him a right good kick for himself!

There were many other monuments in St Patrick's including the first president of Ireland, Douglas Hyde, and the Duke of Schomberg, William of Orange's second-in-command, who was killed at the Battle of the Boyne. The famous blind harpist, Tourlough O'Carolan, is also celebrated there.

We left St Patrick's by a side entrance leading to St Patrick's Close, a winding cobblestoned street linking Patrick Street to Kevin Street. 'This has to be the most romantic street in Dublin,' said Dad, gazing at the curved line of cherry blossom trees straddling both sides all the way around the side of the cathedral. 'This is where your Mum and I passed many an enchanted evening,' he mused. The figure of Sir Benjamin Lee Guinness, the benefactor for the church's restoration, was relaxing on a plinth between the entrance and the cemetery. In his hands he held a scroll containing the plans for its restoration. Opposite the entrance was the Cathedral Choir school, founded in 1432.

Further along the road is an old disused graveyard containing a number of interesting gravestones. The graveyard, the castellated battlements on the curving grey walls, the old grammar school, was reminiscent of a different era. We were lucky, Dad said, to have come on a spring day as the tree-lined road was particularly picturesque with the pink blossoms cascading and creating a bower effect. Dad called the scene 'a jewel in the Liberties crown'. We wouldn't have described it as a 'jewel' but it reminded us of an old Sunday Matinée film we had seen on Telefís Éireann, starring Fred Astaire and Judy Garland, *Easter Parade*. It was certainly quite magical. There was a black door on the curving wall with the words 'The Vicarage' barely visible. A bigger building next door, with the entrance on Kevin Street, was the Deanery where Dean Jonathan Swift lived for thirty years in the early eighteenth century. We took in the scene sitting on the edge of an old granite horse trough. Then it was time to see the oldest public library in Ireland, known as Marsh's, which was through a gate in the grey wall and up a flight of steps.

The inside of the library had changed very little since 1701. We didn't know that, but the librarian, who looked like he had been there since then, told us so. It had a strange atmosphere, heavy with the scent of leather and age. Walking in the door felt like stepping back in time. The interior had dark oak bookcases standing in the same place since it was built. Many of the books were still kept on the same shelves they had been placed in the eighteenth century. The oak bookcases had carved and lettered gables topped by a bishop's mitre. However, what really intrigued us were the three wired alcoves or cages where, we were told, readers were locked in with rare books. We had to try them out!

'Why do you have cages here?' asked Minnie.

'Books were very expensive then,' said the librarian, 'and the ones on the lower shelves were chained to a rod so that they could not be stolen. If you wanted to read one of the most valuable ones, you had to go into one of those cages where you would be locked in.' He allowed us to try out the cages and kindly gave us some ancient books to look through, full of old Latin words which the others could not make head nor tail of. Of course, having a smattering of altar boy Latin, I came to the rescue and managed to convey, after much effort, the meaning of certain words. 'What does it say?' asked Minnie.

'Quite straightforward,' I went and mulled over what I was going to read.

'Go on, hurry up and tell us,' they urged.

'Okay,' I went. 'Let me see. This is very difficult, but I will do my very best. Ah yes, I understand now. Listen.' I read very slowly. 'Please lower your voices as you are in a library.' By the time the penny dropped I was out of the cage.

The cobblestoned street which complemented the castellated walls brought us out onto Kevin Street, with the old horse trough at the corner, and behind it the former Archbishop of Dublin's palace, St

Sepulchre's. It is now a Garda Station, the oldest and only one in the country with both red and blue lanterns hanging outside. The lanterns illustrate the old police force and the newer one – An Garda Siochána – the past and present.

Across the road from the horse trough was an old abandoned graveyard, known, according to Dad, as the 'Cabbage Garden' as it was where Cromwell's soldiers planted cabbage when they were in Dublin in the 1650s. It was said that no one had seen or eaten cabbage before, but from then onwards the Irish loved cabbage and 'cabbage, bacon and spuds' was a very popular dietary mix for generations.

Around the corner from Kevin Street Garda Station was the famous Dublin Bird Market, which has been held on Bride Street/Peter Street for over a hundred years. We didn't see it on this occasion but Dad brought us back one Sunday morning when the market was in full swing with birds singing all around us. As well as the adults selling birds we also saw a number of children (including a barefoot girl) carrying birdcages and looking for buyers. Dad said we were part of an old Dublin tradition of bringing children to enjoy the bird market. Here we saw what Dad called 'bird fanciers' gathering at the corner of Peter Street near the old Jacob's biscuit factory, where they hung their cages containing canaries, budgies, parrots, pigeons, finches, love birds and other exotic species from Africa and far off countries. Dad said to keep our eyes wide open when looking at the birds as some 'local' birds, according to hearsay, were often painted and sold as exotic birds. But he doubted that very much, saying all you had to do was look at them and listen to their lovely singing to know they had just arrived into Ireland. Freckles chipped in. 'Ah sure, you'd know where they come just by listening to their accents – if they sing with a Dublin accent they are not foreign, despite appearances, right!' We just ignored him.

We found that the sound of the sweet singing birds on that Sunday morning against the backdrop of the cathedral bells of St Patrick's made for a fascinating and memorable harmony.

9

⸎

THE POPE AND THE PETROL BOMBER

I was six years old when my parents decided that I had the makings of an altar boy. Maybe because I overheard them saying that I could recite my prayers backwards, I don't know. I even tried to recite them backwards but stopped at Amen.

Off I went with my freshly ironed white surplus and black soutane folded carefully in a Roche's Stores plastic carrier bag. I was delighted with myself, swinging and flinging it up into the air as I skipped along through the park on the way to the church. I was somewhat overwhelmed by it all when I arrived, however, when I discovered that I had to learn how to serve Mass and many other ceremonies. But not for long, as I was soon enjoying myself as an actor in part of a great show.

I had joined at the beginning of the year but within a few weeks it was discovered that I was unsuited for the new role, being only six rather than the minimum age of seven. I was just shy of that age by a few months. It was expected that I would have made my

First Confession and First Holy Communion. I had done neither and was therefore on the verge of being regarded as a complete pagan, if not already one. I, in the meantime, had enjoyed all these theatrical activities, such as carrying big heavy holy books, passing glasses of wine around, lighting and blowing out candles, burning incense and charcoal, bowing, kneeling and gadding around in a strange black and white two-piece costume. If it weren't for the many other lads also wearing these flowing garments, which to me looked like dresses West of Ireland women wore years ago, I would have taken early retirement anyway.

However, without my having gone through the required rites of passage before ascending to the altar, a schism between Ireland and Rome was inevitable. I was quickly rushed off the altar for fear of widespread contamination. Luckily, a major doctrinal, liturgical and schismatic crisis in the Catholic Church in Ireland was averted when the priests contacted Rome for advice on the matter. The Pope listened, looked at all the issues involved, called in his Cardinals, and eventually issued a special letter or solemn Papal Bull on the matter, called *Minor Matters*. Basically, I would have to resign, go through the various relevant rites of passage and then return, much sanctified, to resume my saintly duties. This I did and was back on the altar a few months later just after my seventh birthday and with my halo intact.

I quickly grasped all the essentials of the altar life and within no time I was 'altar boy of the year', for which I received a guinea book token presented to me at the altar boys' Christmas party.

However, my head was soon becoming uneasy from wearing such a heavy crown and I abdicated in favour of Redser, an altar boy with bulging red cheeks and who was much more ambitious than I in such matters. Within a short time, I was cast amidst the commoner altar boys and the slippery slope became inevitable. There was a tradition among the older lads of playing cards and drinking altar wine in the sacristy while waiting to perform their duties. I was soon inducted into their milieu. On one occasion after such activities the lads went swinging the thurible, a deep silver bowl full of smouldering charcoal, held up with four long chains attached to a handle, and staggered out on to sanctuary in front of the altar. They had difficulty kneeling down and two of them fell asleep. Saying that, Young Banjaxed had no such difficulty since he was always falling asleep on the altar. Many times, we had to support him between two of us. He was able therefore to have a good sleep while kneeling. Myles Furlong was assigned the task of nudging him awake when the Mass was over.

On this particular occasion, enormous clouds of smoke billowed here, there and everywhere from the thurible. They had put too much incense onto the charcoal. The priest then added more incense. A huge fiery sizzle shot up. The more we swung the thurible the more smoke billowed out. Then the hymn singing started. *Tantum ergo sacramentum*… we never sang with such gusto. There was much swaying around the altar with candles dripping wax everywhere. One of the boys started tittering, the wine taking its toll. The priest quickly turned around – 'Off!'

He was Canon Brady, an elderly and severe priest, probably explained by the fact that he had a metal plate in his head. Seemingly, he was a chaplain in the Second World War and had sustained injuries. He was inclined to turn around on the altar and reprimand us for chatting. Usually there would have been six of us serving Mass, three on each side of the altar. We didn't see ourselves as silent statues for fear people might start praying in front of us. So, we chatted amongst ourselves about Cassius Clay beating Sonny Liston, the Small Faces singing about feeding buns to the ducks and getting 'high' in 'Itchycoo Park', Lester Piggott and his run of winners, how much we made at the wedding the previous Saturday, and what was the likelihood of making money at a forthcoming funeral. Not very likely was the consensus, but we did agree to feed buns to the ducks in Mountain View Park and get 'high'. We asked another altar boy, Little Bun, if his Dad, who owned Concannon's Bakery, could spare us some mouldy auld dough for buns.

Just then didn't the Canon turn around and mutter something about not talking. We thought that a complete liberty altogether, and us having to put up with his incessant windbreakers. Even the candles swayed when he let off. Moreover, we were doing our very best to act like Holy Joes, but it was very difficult to keep it up, particularly since our natural inclination was towards being Dickey Devils. We had a lot to put up with. Others, the living or the dead, must have got wind of him, as he was buried on a corner site of Mount Jerome cemetery known as Tottenham Corner, with no graves anywhere near him.

Father Purcell was tops. He said Mass in ten minutes and was the most popular priest in the parish. Father Meade was an altogether different proposition. He had a stammer and if he caught us chatting amongst ourselves on the altar, the whole church would hear him. His voice went up and down – quietly at first and then a sudden rush of roaring words – 'SHUTTHEBLOODYTALKINGWILLYEZ!' His sermons were even worse. The congregation only heard half of what he was saying; '…and youse a… a… a… go… to HELL!' – with the word 'hell' coming out like a rocket. The congregation were terrified as they expected him to suddenly jump out of the pulpit and rush down and attack them. Even those that had fallen asleep were quickly rehabilitated.

It was a wonderfully unreal world we inhabited. What with the dressing up, bowing, genuflecting, crossing ourselves, thumping our tummies, and burning candles, charcoal and incense. It was also absolute fun and laughter. We knew nothing of the symbolism, ritual and imagery that lay behind this imaginary world that was our reality. In our surplus and soutane, we looked and felt like participants in a black and white minstrel show. Consequently, we acted accordingly; we threw ourselves into the great game of charades and all the ceremonies and processions.

We had no interest whatsoever in what was being said and what we were supposed to be doing. Because there were so many of us, nearly sixty, fighting invariably broke out either in the sacristy or on the rare occasion on the altar, with much shoving and pushing. Our older cousin, Freckles, was involved in one such fight, years before my time, and had his head put through a plaster partition in the sacristy, while waiting to serve Mass. Fighting always involved Roches Stores, H. Williams, Five Star or similar supermarket bags. Most altar boys carried their altar gear in these bags. They were fantastic for swinging at each other's heads. So fantastic that on one occasion the flung bag went right out through the sacristy door when the target ducked. The only problem was that the speed of the bag ensured that the bag didn't suddenly stop when it passed the door. No, it kept going, straight to the altar, and whacked the priest saying Mass. We just disappeared *en masse*. Luckily for us the priest was a young easy-going chap called Father Browne, who just carried on and took not a blind bit of notice. He was a very popular priest in the parish.

Half the time it was like being backstage and organising a performance. We had non-stop activities and duties to carry out. Rolling out carpets, altar linen, lighting the big six candles known as 'the six tops'. Lighting these involved holding a ten-foot-long candle lighter with a lighted taper attached. You needed steady hands as the top half was inclined to sway. Other activities involved preparing charcoal, gowns, various pieces of attire, bells, chairs, cruets with the water and wine, positioning of holy books and all the altar paraphernalia. And you also had to listen to complaints about 'running around on the altar' from 'shockin' holy old biddies', as one new entrant described them. The Sodalities, the Confraternities, the Missions, the Retreats, weddings, baptisms and funerals, were also great opportunities for mayhem and mischief. We could never fathom why funeral-goers had a strange habit of leaving bulging envelopes of money on top of coffins. Conkers decided one evening to open a coffin and pile all the envelopes in on top of the corpse. 'Who said you can't take it with you?' was his view.

'Where are the envelopes left for the priest?' the Sacristan wanted to know.

'Mount Jerome!' he heard in response.

With sixty of us running all over the church in our black and white outfits like a huge team of mad footballers, weaving this way and that, shouting at each other, we felt that we were the most important people in this endless pageantry. The wonderful thing is that despite being there, nobody actually noticed us, which was even better. So, we would sometimes sit down behind the altar, play cards or snakes and ladders, or have a quick pull on a cigarette butt. Our smoke blended with the candle smoke. Maybe we might have a read of one of our comics stashed away in a back pocket. Marbles too sometimes, particularly for the younger boys, to keep them busy, while we, the older ones, bowed and scraped as in 'Yes, Father. No, Father. At once, Father. Most certainly, Father. Leave it to us, Father. No problem, Odlum. You just relax there, take the weight off your feet, have a glass of Kelly's best altar wine, and we'll do the rest, even say Mass for you. Don't worry, we know it backwards.'

We also undertook lots of well-paying jobs for the church. One of these involved delivering Christmas and Easter Dues envelopes into the houses in the parish. We were told on no account deliver to the Jews on Westfield Road, which had a large concentration of members living there. This confused us no end as we didn't know what on earth the priest was saying about no dues for the Jews. So, we delivered to all the houses, ignoring the complaints of our Jewish brethren. We just waved, called out 'Heil' real friendly-like, gently closed the garden gates, and carried on.

Another job which featured in our good works was collecting the altar breads, as the Holy Communion was called, from the nuns in the enclosed convent on Mount Tallant Avenue – the Sisters of Perpetual Indulgences. We pressed a bell beside a large curved hatch. We didn't see them and vice versa. We just heard a few words, like 'Praise the Lord' or whatever and we replied 'Amen' or 'Praise to you, Sister.' The next moment, a revolving polished hardwood drum with a large opening to one side would swivel around towards us to show the inside of a large wooden barrel. We popped in the empty boxes and the barrel would revolve around 180 degrees to the nun's side. Five minutes later the nun would return with full boxes. She would then repeat the swivel-barrel routine and off we'd go, praising every deity as we went.

This was an enviable job, well paid and much sought after by lesser qualified but equally ambitious altar boys. Two boys asked Billy, the sacristan, for a chance to do the job. Being of an amiable disposition and always going around whistling, even on the altar, he referred them to us. Some of them were quite persuasive, even threatening to use parental influence. However, we were not mean-spirited so agreed for them to have a trial go at 20 per cent of the normal rate. We told them to follow the precise rules – don't speak to the nuns, just follow the instructions. Off went the two lads carrying their empty boxes. They arrived at the convent, rang the bell and the barrel swivelled towards them with the open side ready and waiting. What did they do? They climbed into the barrel, with some difficulty, totally squashed and with the equally squashed boxes. With even more difficulty, the nun managed to turn the barrel back around to her side. She was greeted with bashed boxes, boys and bums. She fainted, hitting the floor with a thud. We continued our weekly visitation to the convent much to the delight of the Reverend Mother. She was very happy not to see us again and vice versa. Being in charge of the altar boys Mass Roster, we appointed the pair to serve the 7.30 weekday Mass for the following week. Weddings, funerals, baptisms and any duty that involved money-changing-hands we confined to ourselves, given our seniority and as a point of principle.

We, that is, Redser, Four Eyes, Doc, Cotton-head, Morty, Paddy Purple, John Jo, Brenno, Markie, Nobby and I, were in charge of the Easter ceremonies. Young Banjaxed was not, as we knew he would invariably fall asleep. Father Browne took pity on him one day and we overheard him saying to the Canon in the sacristy, 'That young lad always looks banjaxed.' We never knew his name and so Young Banjaxed he became. Seemingly, there were ten in his family, living in a small terraced house on Mount Drummond.

The organising for the lighting of the Paschal Candle in the darkened church porch via a small charcoal fire was part of our responsibilities. Once this was done the lights came on and we were to proceed up the aisle. However, we interpreted this responsibility to mean organising a bonfire. On this occasion, because of the wind, we decided to use petrol on the reluctant fire to ensure that it would definitely light for the priest, who could then use the flames to light the big Easter candle. For a drop of petrol, we had sent an altar boy called Gary Barry next door to Doherty's Garage, where he worked part-time on the petrol pumps. He returned with a full gallon can, enough for one hundred bonfires. We applied the petrol to the charcoal, with much splashing, added bits of twigs and balls of paper. We then felt ready for the evening's ceremonies.

When the proceedings started that evening in the dark porch, the priest struck a match to start the little fire. Out shot an enormous flame, taking everyone, including ourselves, unawares. We all leapt back as one. The copper Old IRA plaque in the corner glistened in the flames. The painting of Matt Talbot became illuminated, with his gazing hopefully upwards. A pious member of the congregation quickly rushed forward with a fire extinguisher and sprayed us all with white foam. 'Begone Satan!' he roared at the invisible devil. We ran around like miniature snowmen. One of the altar boys, known as Barrel Boy, because of his girth, charged up the aisle, 'Fire! Fire! Jayzus's house is on fire!' which was quickly followed by a flurry and scurry from the crowd. The priest sought for calm. The proceedings had to be temporarily halted. He wanted to know who was responsible for this outrage. We reluctantly pointed fingers at the petrol bomber. 'You should be up on the barricades in Northern Ireland,' he hissed at the miscreant. Brenno and Markie sniggered at the back of the snow-boys. The trainee arsonist was summarily dismissed from further duties and spent the rest of his altar boy career confined to the sacristy polishing our shoes. And rightly so, we thought, with him having a very bad influence on us.

Ringing the church bell kept us equally busy and fit. Every so often, particularly when the Sacristan was on holidays, we, as seniors and totally responsible lads, were asked to ring the church bell for Mass, the Angelus or various other ceremonials. Redser, Four Eyes and I literally jumped at the opportunity. We had to, since this 100-foot rope reached up to a five-ton bell, miles up in the belfry. The part we held, the end of the rope, was a knot bigger than a football, great for gripping on or sitting on with the help of the other two lads. You would be hoisted up onto this knot, and then grip the rope. Once aboard you would be grabbed by the other two lads who would start pulling and pushing up and down and eventually you would be moving on the bells' steam. Up fifteen feet in the air you went and back down again. Oh! What a thrill. The bell room itself had a twenty-foot high ceiling with the rope swinging through a rounded hole in it. You had to be very careful not to go up too high when swinging up and down as otherwise you would end up with a permanent halo imprint on your head.

The time arrived for us to get the punters into Mass. They were known as the 'pay, pray and obey' brigade. We had to give the bell rope many really hard tugs before we got a sound from the bell high above us. At first the sound was boom, bang, clang – real loud and so out of kilter with the usual ringing that half the populace came running to the church wondering if the nuclear holocaust had happened. Yes, this was the reaction, since only recently the Irish Government had dispatched a nuclear fallout booklet to every household in the country. This was not too many years after the stand-off between Kennedy and Khrushchev over Cuba. A false alarm, however, we advised and blamed an ESB power failure. We were going on the hope that since people, well used to electric doorbells, would also assume that their local church bell was rung with the press of a button. We weren't too far wrong, as that came into practice a generation later. Luckily for us it was the era of non-stop power strikes, milkmen strikes, farmers' protests, bus strikes, bin men strikes, breadmen strikes, gasmen strikes, oil strikes and even gun-runners strikes. Later commentators described this time in Ireland as the 'Stricken Era' because there were more people on strike than actually working. Anyway, after some practice we got into the stride and could ring very well to give a nice melodic peal to remind the Faithful in the area to take their time and that they had at least fifteen minutes before start-off.

I developed a liking for altar wine from the age of six, although the taste was an acquired one. Furthermore, it greatly encouraged my vocation to become a priest. This latter vocation, however, I realised would involve me having to undergo rigorous practice and training. So, every so often I would go into the priests' sacristy, borrow their garb, including a black biretta with its fluffy tuft at the peak, and wander around the church grounds reading the Office (in fact the *Pit and the Pendulum* or the *Travels of Marco Polo*). Every so often I would briefly raise my biretta to those who saluted me. This became rather tiresome after a while and I quickly learnt that just barely raising a hand was enough for the Faithful. I must have been the smallest priest in the country.

This caper would of course have been an impossible feat today, but in those days, back in the late 1960s and early '70s, Mountain View had five priests, in addition to the many Missionary priests' home on holidays, and visiting priests giving Retreats and Missions, there were all sorts of Devotions, confraternities, sodalities and processions. So, it would not have been unusual to see a pygmy priest rambling around in the milieu. Many parishioners still talked about the 1932 Eucharistic Congress in Dublin, when it seemed that every lunatic bishop, priest and cardinal in the world descended on the city attired in every conceivable kind of garb ranging from turbans to Apache Indian headdresses. There were also thousands of parishioners, always coming and going, so the church was a place of mayhem most of the time. In my case I had an advantage with my altar boy gear, so it was easy to make the transition. All I had to do was to add a bit of charcoal dust from the sacristy to my face here and there, stick a black square hat with a little bobble onto my head, and there I was, unrecognisable, even to myself. One parishioner enquired where I was from and I replied 'Pygmalion' off the top of my head.

'Where's that, may I ask, Father?' she enquired in a real nosey voice.

'Oh, it's somewhere over near Greece,' I replied, and that shut her up. She probably didn't know where Greece was. I had heard of that place from Dad on one of our trips to Mount Jerome. He said the Shaw family were the owners of the land in the 1830s and were responsible for setting up the Dublin Cemeteries Company and using the 47 acres of land for a cemetery. The well-to-do of southside Dublin didn't think it was appropriate to be traipsing all the way over to Glasnevin cemetery or anywhere else for that matter. They just wanted to stay right where they were. The Shaw family lived in Terenure and owned land around the house known as Shaw's Wood. Years later this was turned into a great park which we regularly visited. Subsequently, it was bought by Dublin Corporation who called it Bushy Park. Anyway,

Dublin Be Damned!

I don't know how or why Dad mentioned Pygmalion except that there was some connection between that place and the Shaw family of Portobello, Terenure and Mount Jerome.

Next, of course, I had to go into the Confession box and practice being a priest there. I mainly heard Confession during the evenings, when it was quite dark in the church. I enjoyed sitting on the nice comfortable cushion as opposed to kneeling on a hard, wooden step, which the penitents had to endure. Then I gently pushed across the grill, muttering any old words in Latin, which I had plenty of, from being an altar boy and also learning some in school. I might say, for instance, *'et cum spiritu tuo'* ('and also with you'), or *'Bellum, bellum, bellum, belli, belli, bello'* ('war, war, war,' etc.) and nod for the penitent to proceed. Usually, however, I opened the grill and muttered, 'Go ahead, sinner, I'm listening!' I forgave everyone their sins, although to my mind I had never heard such atrocious sins in all my years. I was appalled. I said to myself that Mountain View is a right den of iniquity, everyone who came in was a right sinner, with potential wife murderers, thieves, drunks, swindlers, gamblers, wife beaters and wife swappers, and everybody having affairs or wanting to have affairs. There was nearly nothing I hadn't heard nor forgiven and later I checked my hair to see if it was going grey. I told some of these to forget all about eternal damnation; throw a few coins in the poor box on the way out and take a good brisk walk up to the Hellfire Club.

I was surprised at the number of readers of 'dirty magazines' in the parish. I had never heard of half the names of some of the disgraceful magazines with names such as *Mickey Maid*, *Call Me Anytime Jane* and *Bronco Betsy*. I told them to desist from reading any more of such magazines and find a good book in Rathmines Library. A few of the perpetual sinners kept telling me the same story week in week out. I had enough of these unrepentant sinners and told them that as penance they were to bundle the magazines up when finished with and send them off to the African Missions, in the hope that the missionaries might find some solace and a reminder of home. Well, someone had to listen and give sound advice. I gave plenty more of that, including telling robbers and the like not to be too hard on themselves. 'God is good,' I'd say and sent them off, telling them to light a few candles on the way out to St Jude, Patron Saint for Hopeless Cases. No penance from me. No muttering through reams of prayers.

Although saying that, I did take particular umbrage with one sinner, who worked in a local pub and liked to water down the whiskey and put slops back into the barrels down in the cellar. Now, of recent, there were rumours circulating in the village about the increase in the number of sober drunks to be seen. Moreover, the bona fide houses, where the law encouraged one to drink morning, noon and night without harassment, such as the Dropping Well, were witnessing an increase in business, to the chagrin of local establishments. I peered through the grill and recognised the reprobate with the darting, ferret eyes and streaks of greasy hair plastered atop a bald skull. Yes! It was he who had refused to serve drink to some of the older lads. In fact, I was so incensed, that I quickly took off the purple stole, donned my biretta and grabbed the Parish Priest's blackthorn stick that was beside me in the confessional. Quick as a flash, I was out of the confessional, pulled the hare-baiter and miscreant out of the adjoining box where he was kneeling, whacked him on the backs of his legs and chased him out of the church. 'You're barred!' I roared after him. 'You're barred!' I was determined to take my new role as a 'man of the cloth' very seriously.

On one occasion I had to deal with a distraught husband who said he had fallen out with his wife over a silly quiz. He had been asked the colour of his wife's nightie on the night of their honeymoon. He replied that she was wearing a transparent nightie. She responded saying that she wasn't wearing anything at all. 'Like the Emperor's new clothes?' I suggested. He didn't answer, so I said that is what happens in love – nobody really cares what someone is or is not wearing because they only have eyes for you. 'Go home and tell her just what I said,' I advised him. He seemed pleased with that. 'Oh, by the way, do either of you wear glasses? It mightn't be any harm to get your eyes seen to as well. You never know. Were the lights turned on or off? Were either of you under the influence?' However, he seemed to have gone by this stage and the next sinner was coming in. I could see myself getting used to this new job. 'Move over Dear Frankie,' I thought!

Of course, when it came to penance, I had to make exceptions, in particular listening to the shocking sins of the many boys in the parish who queued outside. What with robbing orchards, cogging their homework, regularly sneaking out of the house, and reading in bed by torchlight when they should have been asleep – the list went on. I was delighted to hear the sins of some of the local lads and insisted these ruffians hand over everything in their pockets, including cash. I put one hand holding a collection plate out through the curtain as the boy was leaving – he popped everything into it. This worked for months, until I got bored and had made enough loot. Moreover, by then I had a feeling that I was losing my vocation.

I was in a very difficult situation, particularly serving at weddings. I was falling in love with every bride I met. The only person that got so near to the bride's face was the priest, the groom and myself. The priest gave her Communion, the groom kissed her after the exchange of rings, and I had the honour of holding a gold-plated plate, held by a handle, called a 'paten', near her face, in case the Communion host fell. I held this under her chin and I took my time gazing at her loveliness and into her deep eyes, pools of darkness and promise. Then she closed her eyes for a few seconds, and I could bask in such beauty. Well, we hard-pressed altar boys had to have our perks, and that was one of the many. If I regarded the groom as a rival, I made sure he felt the paten nudging and bumping his freshly shaven neck.

We liked when Missionary priests came home in the summers. This provided us with lots of opportunities, but mainly to make money. They invariably gave us a half crown after serving Mass. Then we would rush across the road to O'Beirne's newsagents shop, with its tongue-twisting twin sisters, and buy an Armada paperback for 2s 6d. Sometimes we engaged in deep philosophical conversations with these missionaries over a glass of altar wine in the sacristy. I remember discussing how many angels would fit on top of a pin, and issues relating to predestination. I forget the answers, but it didn't matter as the wine was a good year. I told them anyway to forget about the angels on the pin as it all depended on their size. Moreover,

I said, 'What is far more important, and this you need to know, Your Eminence, is the effect a tiny pin can have when you stick it into someone's bum! This way you can turn little angels into little devils, see?' Thus, with one quick jab, I put an end to centuries of fruitless theological speculation.

On another occasion two visiting missionaries were saying Mass on different side altars at the same time. I had no choice but to do likewise, going back and forth to help out with both simultaneously. I knew this was an opportunity not to be missed and I was right, as both remunerated me very well.

I never forgot the Latin which I had learnt off and which was necessary for serving at Mass. I saw myself as an expert, in fact, and even developed a learning technique for the trainees. I would tell them to give an English version of the Latin – 'there is a rat in the GPO' which translates as *Secut erat, im principio*. I also liked the *mea culpa, mea culpa, mea maxima culpa* part with its up and down rat-tat-tat sound. I knew what it meant because I had to whack my tummy reciting each part. I presumed it was to release trapped wind and I had plenty of that, what with Macari's batter burgers or pickled with Farren's spice burgers, the first of their kind in Dublin.

I couldn't believe what happened next, though. No sooner had I become an expert than I was told to forget it, as the Pope had said there was no need for altar boys to learn Latin anymore. Everything was not lost, however, as I soon became a rarity among altar boys. Visiting priests home from the missions or wherever often asked for a Latin lad to serve them at Mass. Yours truly was happy to oblige, particularly since I was well rewarded for my knowledge. But Latin was not the only language that gave me trouble. I had a similar experience with Irish, which I loved in school. I loved learning and mastering the old Gaelic script. I felt that I was like one of the monks that wrote the Book of Kells we had seen with Dad in Trinity College Library. We all oohed and aaahed at the lovely and intricate colours and writing style of the old monks. So, I was not happy when told to forget all that old Gaelic style of writing. From now on we were to use the English script.

Dublin Be Damned!

But that was not the end of my conundrum. I also had to abandon my German! My growing expertise in that language was inspired by the Swastika Laundry, based in Ballsbridge but which had a branch located to the left of Mount Jerome cemetery and on Mount Argus Road. The tall chimney stack was emblazoned with a big black and white swastika which could be seen for miles. The laundry had been in Ireland since 1912; it was not a German company, but founded by a Leitrim man, John Brittain, one of the pioneers of the laundry business in Ireland. He used the symbol on his battery-driven vans since the sign was an ancient symbol of good luck and a sign of peace originating from the Sanskrit in India. The laundry vans were painted in red with a black swastika on a white background. Many of these vans were to be seen in Dublin until the 1980s. They were a regular feature in Mountain View in my young days. The vans, combined with my voracious reading of English comics such as the *Hotspur*, *Victor*, *Hornet*, and the *Hurricane* with their Second World War cartoon stories, helped encourage my love for the language. So, myself and two other pals, Redser and Four Eyes, went around addressing each other as 'Heil Hitler', 'Heil Hesse' or 'Heil Himmler', and using such words as *'achtung,' 'jawohl, herr major,' 'mein herr,' 'mein kampf', 'seig heil,' 'ja,' 'nein,' 'himmel hoch'* and *'schweinhund.'* We had picked up the last from a Norman Wisdom film, *The Square Peg*, which roughly translates as 'pig dog' and we knew plenty of those! We didn't really know what most of these words actually meant, but luckily it was never a problem and we carried on regardless. We were greatly disappointed when the laundry closed down and we had to revert to our own names.

There was another downside to those challenging times. Lent involved us children getting out of our warm beds to attend St Mary's Convent down the road for 7.30 a.m. Mass every morning before breakfast. We also had to give up sweets and biscuits. The only positive aspect was thinking of the poor orphan girls up in the choir balcony behind us in the convent chapel. In particular, one of them, a girl called Bernie, with her wishful and expectant eyes. This sustained me and helped me carry my cross down the road at such an ungodly hour.

10

STRONGBOW, THE PILLAR AND 'DUBLIN CAN BE HEAVEN'

We had long heard about Strongbow's tomb in Christ Church Cathedral and knew that someday Dad would bring us to see it. 'How about looking at some mice playing the organ near Strongbow's tomb?' he teased. It was the middle of a sunny weekday morning by the time we departed for the cathedral. When we got off the 54A, Dad brought us the few yards to the top of St Michael's Hill, just before it hurtles down under the arch to Winetavern Street. 'Here you are, at Idler's Corner,' he told us. 'This is where all the corner boys stood around long ago. If you were seen here, passers-by immediately knew you were up to no good, and hurried along.'

'Maybe, then, we should do the same!' urged the boy with us who looked like Luke Kelly.

Our first port of call in the cathedral was the crypt to see the old punishment stocks used long ago across the road from the cathedral. Christ Church Place, as it is called now, was then known as Skinner's Row because of all the leather works doing business in the vicinity.

It was also the location for The Tholsel, a forerunner to City Hall, and where all the Aldermen gathered to discuss the running of the city and draw up rules and regulations. And if you were inclined to disobey some of these rules, then you might end up in the stocks being pelted by the mob.

The crypt was enormous with vaulted ceilings and shadowy caverns. It hadn't changed for one thousand years, we were told. Dating from the late twelfth and possibly eleventh century, it was not only one of the largest medieval crypts in either the UK or Ireland but also the oldest structure in Dublin. On the day we visited we saw a forest of heavy rough-stone pillars, which carried the weight of the cathedral and central tower. It is not quite clear what it was used for initially but it is reported from as far back as the fourteenth century that it was used as a warehouse to store French wine. In the seventeenth century it was divided up and rented out as shops and taverns, and quickly achieved a notorious reputation as one of the taverns was called 'Hell'.

Freckles popped his legs into the stocks and Daisy then slammed down a piece of timber with a handle which locked his legs in place. He hadn't bargained for that! 'Here, take that,' she laughed and threw some popcorn at him.

'How about a rotten egg or tomatoes,' came a voice from the gloom and a minister of the cloth appeared, laden down with all kinds of stuff to throw at the bold and the bad.

Poor Freckles looked horrified. 'Let me outa here!' he hollered.

'Not on your life,' we replied, laughing.

'Thanks very much, Vicar, and yes, we'll take all these!' Much to Freckle's consternation we backed away from the stocks and stood in a line, ready to fire at him. The look on his face would have sunk a thousand ships, that's for sure. We started firing and with him trying to duck. Wham! Whap! But no splat! We were throwing dummies but Freckles didn't know it until they landed on him. It was well worth it as we lifted the much-relieved villain from the stocks. 'You were lucky,' said the guide. 'In those days they threw anything at the miscreant, but usually rotten fruit and vegetables.'

We loved the huge and atmospheric old crypt full of darkened corners, arches, caverns and hidden doors. Later we saw the mummified remains of a cat and a mouse, presumably in a chase, but ending up stuck in old organ pipes. They were stuck there since the 1860s. Dad said that 'Egypt may have Tutankhamen but Dublin has Tom and Gerry!'

Back upstairs, we saw the tomb of Strongbow who we had heard so much about in school. The tomb had a figure of a knight resting on top, holding a shield and dressed for battle. His hands are joined and his legs crossed. Minnie thought he must be cold all right, what with no blankets to cover him.

He was a Norman knight who had come to Ireland when the wretched Dermot MacMurrough had invited him to make war on his enemies. Strongbow came and helped and then married MacMurrough's daughter, Aoife, and later became King of Leinster. 'The Irish spent hundreds of years trying to evict the Normans ever since,' said Dad. 'And we had to wait until the "Spy in the Castle" helped Michael Collins get rid of them. Isn't it strange,' he mused, 'Red Hugh O'Donnell, your "fighting prince of Donegal", wanted to escape from Dublin Castle, whereas our spy friend, David Neligan, wanted to stay there! He was working as a secret agent for Michael Collins, finding out vital information which helped win the fight for freedom. Last question,' he went. 'Do you know where the "spy in the Castle" is buried?' We didn't but had a good guess. 'Mount Jerome!' Dad was lost for words.

We said goodbye to the cathedral and walked down Lord Edward Street and Cork Hill. Pausing for a minute, Dad pointed to the building facing the side of City Hall. 'That's the Rates Office,' he said. 'Rates are another tax we pay every year for the privilege of living in a house. Eammon Ceannt, one of the leaders of the 1916 Rising, worked there for many years. Many years before that it was a bank. From here to Trinity College is full of banks and insurance companies, making lots of money.' The banks along each side of the street ahead of us, he said, were 'very decorative inside and were mostly designed to look like Venetian palaces.' Minnie was somewhat confused at this 'Venetian' thinking of 'venetian blinds', till Daisy pointed out to her that Dad meant 'Venice'.

'Wow!' we exclaimed, being able to see through the windows of the former Munster Bank opposite the Olympia Theatre, where we had seen a pantomime the previous Christmas.

'This one beside us here leading into Dublin Castle was once known as Newcomen's Bank, after the owner's name. Do you remember we talked about all the Judases in Grattan's Parliament long ago? Well, he was one of those bucks who got his thirty pieces of silver to sell Ireland around 1800. Well with all his filthy loot, what did he do?'

'He put it in the bank to make more money,' said Freckles.

'Nearly there. With the loot, he opened up his own bank, right here in front of us. It was a small building, only half the size it is now. He extended it and if you look up at the garlands you will see different colours, the old and the new. However,' went on Dad, taking out his pipe, 'like Judas, his greed backfired. Didn't the bank collapse? No, not the building, you silly billy! He ran out of money because he lent people money who were unable to repay it. He was too greedy, you see. He didn't have enough money in the safe in the basement, so when the people whose money he had lent out came looking for their money back, he said, "Sorry, it's all gone". Well, if your money was gone from the Post Office, would you be happy?'

'No way! What happened then?' asked Minnie.

'Like Judas, he realised his mistake too late.'

'And did he do away with himself like Judas?' she posited.

'I'm afraid so,' said Dad. 'By the way, do you remember us mentioning and the "invisible prince" and Dracula when we visited Mount Jerome? Well Le Fanu and Bram Stoker, who wrote those kinds of stories, both worked across the road there, in that red-bricked building opposite Tarlo's. That's where the *Evening Mail* was published, and where those two buckos worked for a while.' The building looked forlorn, with the *Evening Mail* sign still high up over the front corner entrance. Jiggs and Maggie, the invisible prince and Dracula, all sprang to mind. We looked and sighed, remembering the mischievous Jiggs always trying to outfox Maggie and us looking for the invisible prince.

Ah, Dad was cute, we could see. We had no interest in seeing old ruins of houses in Temple Bar so he opted to pointing in all sorts of directions from outside City Hall. 'This is where Dublin really started,' he said. 'Around Wood Quay and just to the left at the bottom of Parliament Street.' He pointed down to the old ruins of Isolde's Tower, the last remaining defensive tower of the old wall of Dublin. 'Over there is the Royal Exchange Hotel where I did some of my training years ago,' he said. 'It was called after this building, now the City Hall, but built for the merchants of Dublin to conduct their business and was called the Royal Exchange.' Next door to the hotel was an ancient-looking shop, all black board and shutters swinging on the front and the name Read's over the display window. 'Do you want to see the largest penknife in the world and scissors that could trim a fly's whiskers?' Now he was talking and we trooped into Read's.

'This is Dublin's oldest shop,' Dad said, on entering the dark, musty premises. We fully believed him, looking around. It seemed to have some of that old-world charm, like Dickens' *Old Curiosity Shop*. Dad introduced us all to Mr Read himself, busy behind an old counter. 'Welcome to my family's business,' he went. 'We have been here since the 1760s, with all the original display cases, drawers and counters.'

Freckles whispered to me, 'He looks as old as the shop itself.'

Mr Read said that the famous furniture maker Thomas Chippendale supplied the shop's beautiful display cabinets. He told us that the area around his shop was renowned for many years for some of the country's finest craftsmen, jewellers, silversmiths, goldsmiths, engravers, mirror makers, embroiders, lace makers, printers, publishers and bookbinders. That was 'Dublin's Golden Age' at the end of the eighteenth century, he added, when all the fine buildings and squares were built and laid out, including the Four Courts, the Custom House and the Bank of Ireland on College Green. He said the wealthy landed folk had buckets of money to throw away thanks to all the rents they were pulling in every week from their tenants. He said that 'this shop fulfilled the needs of all the classes of Dublin people. For some, it was the purchase of an expensive sword, like the one you are looking at, or a medical instrument, and for others, simple items of table cutlery.'

'Alternatively,' and he smiled at us, 'maybe one needed the world's smallest pair of working scissors, small enough to trim a fly's whiskers!' Much to our astonishment he gently lifted from one of the cabinets a tiny pair of scissors that measured a quarter of an inch. Only Minnie's little fingers were able to use it, much to her delight. 'Go over there and try it out on some of the stuffed flies,' he said, pointing to an open glass case. With the help of a magnifying glass, Minnie was able to trim the fly's whiskers. 'Nice job! Didn't I know yez didn't believe me! Am I right?' laughed Mr Read. He also showed us the world's largest penknife with 576 blades, which was somewhat heavier. We asked Freckles to count the blades but Mr Read said we needed to be careful handling so many sharp knives so close together.

We liked the swords bearing Read's name. These were Irish-made swords and imports were not required for years. According to Mr Read, the shop catered for the needs of the gentry and army by making magnificent crafted swords. We had great difficulty even lifting one of the swords yet it was amazing to see such a dangerous weapon so close up. The 1780s and '90s were decades when Read's' swords were highly regarded and sought after in an era when duelling was at its most feverish. In the eighteenth century, when duelling was considered an indispensable part of a young man's education, and the two questions he was asked by the family of a prospective wife was 'Who was his family?' and 'Did he ever blaze (duel)?' The duel proved the young man's bravery as well as cementing relationships with one's opponent, if he survived. But it was also crucially about personal honour and public reputation. There were a number of duelling clubs to train young men in the finer points.

Mr Read also told us that in those 'Golden Age' years people took out their swords (or pistols) for all sorts of provocations. Richard Daly, manager of the Theatre Royal on Crow Street, fought nineteen duels in two years – three with swords and sixteen with pistols. Even prominent people fought duels. Daniel O'Connell, who we knew as the 'Great Liberator' and whose statue was on O'Connell Street, also had no hesitation when it came to a duel and his last was in 1815, with both parties using pistols (each with a notch indicating previous kills). 'Sounds very like the Wild West here in Dublin,' said Freckles, remembering the quiet of his family's farm in Limerick.

Mr Read nodded. 'You are absolutely right, son. Dublin was very much wild in those days. I heard someone once say that it was a city of extremes – of poverty and wealth! That's how this shop made its money in those days. Making swords for other people to go to the blazes, as they called it then.' He laughed and we all started shouting at each other, 'Go to blazes!'

We were surprised to hear about Daniel O'Connell and Henry Grattan going to blazes. In his last duel, O'Connell met John D'Esterre, a member of Dublin Corporation who had claimed O'Connell insulted him in the course of Corporation business. D'Esterre was known to be a crack shot, but to no avail as O'Connell shot him in the groin and he died two days later. Henry Grattan was also prepared to support his arguments with a pistol. He fought Lord Earlsfort and the Chancellor of the Exchequer, Isaac Corry. The duel with Corry was over the latter's support for the proposed Act of Union legislation. Grattan managed to wound Corry in the arm. Duels were often fought in the fields near Merrion Square or in the courtyard of Lucas's Coffee House on Cork Hill. Patrons of the coffee house used to observe the laws of honour and the proceedings from the windows above the courtyard, and often laid wagers on the possible outcome. Most duels there did not end with fatalities but at least two did. Newspapers at the time often complained of stray bullets, a particular danger for passers-by. Visitors to Dublin were advised to avoid any disagreeable encounters. Consequently, the Phoenix Park became a popular location. 'So,' went Mr Read, 'when you are walking around this part of Dublin, keep looking over your shoulder for a stray bullet! However, by then it could be too late! More important, be nice to everyone – otherwise you might end up going to blazes!'

After leaving Reads, Dad brought us around the corner to an old Huguenot house on Eustace Street, opposite the Quaker Meeting House. We liked the name Quakers and it conjured up for us images of people going around shaking with fright all the time. We had great fun indeed in the old house. We felt like the Hardy Boys, the Secret Seven or Famous Five as we went around tapping on the old brown wooden panels looking for secret doors. We couldn't believe our luck as we found a secret door in the sitting room on the first floor. It had nearly invisible hinges and we could see the old walls behind it. It was only a small door, probably used for hiding things, but a person wouldn't be able to hide in it. We didn't mind that in the least as we loved the spooky atmosphere of the house, which Dad said dated from around the 1730s. There was also a secret passage in the basement which led from the house underground and down to the River Liffey. If anyone was trying to escape from the soldiers or the police, he said, they would have used this passage and a boat would have been waiting for them to whisk them away! Wow! What an adventure.

Leaving the panelled house, Dad pointed to a plaque on the wall next to the Commercial Buildings just beyond one of those insurance palaces on the corner of Fownes Street and Dame Street, which he had been talking about earlier. 'That was a pirates' den,' he laughed. The plaque commemorates the Ouzel Galley Society. The name derived from a ship called the *Ouzel*, which, under the command of Captain Eoghan Masey, disappeared at sea in 1695 yet turned up five years later. Having been presumed lost at sea, insurance money had been paid out to the owners, Messrs Ferris, Twigg and Cash, after much debate. We laughed at the name 'Twigg' and 'Cash'. However, when the *Ouzel* galley sailed into Dublin port in 1700, the initial jubilation turned to consternation. The galley had been captured by pirates in the Mediterranean, under the leadership of a notorious pirate called Algerine, but after a few years the captain and crew, with the pirates' loot and the original cargo, managed to escape.

The question then arose, Dad said, as to who owned the ship and the contents? We tried to figure this one out. The owners had been compensated so they could not claim it and the insurers had contracted to insure it, and so they too had no claim on it. It was finally agreed by all parties, including Dublin Corporation, that the money would be used for charitable purposes, including any poverty-stricken merchants in Dublin who had fallen on hard times. Moreover, the saga motivated the Dublin merchants to form a society for the future sorting out of similar business disputes. The Ouzel Galley Society was its name and the organisation later evolved into the Dublin Chamber of Commerce.

Before we went to catch the bus for O'Connell Street to climb Nelson's Pillar, Dad asked one last question. 'I have some business to do in Jury's Hotel and I shouldn't be more than fifteen minutes. In the meantime, I would like you buffs to undertake a "Riddle me this, Riddle me that" puzzle.' We liked the sound of that. 'Quickly,' he said, pointing to Minnie and myself, 'I want you two to nip up there and look carefully at the shape of the building from the outside,' and pointing back to the City Hall, he continued, 'and then tell me its shape. But not yet. Freddy and Daisy will nip inside the building and also look at the shape and then come out and tell me. Quick as a flash and I will see you all outside Jury's shortly.'

Off we flew up Dame Street and waved to the 'Why Go Bald' smarmy boy neon sign, high up on the wall of a barber's shop at the bottom of George's Street. We also shouted at him to keep his hair on, ran past the pantomime emporium and over to City Hall. We looked inside and outside the building. We were back in less than ten minutes and waited across the road outside the Lucky Coady shop near the Pen Corner. Shortly Dad reappeared. 'Now I'd like the four of you tell me the shape of the building, but just on this one occasion, you may all tell me at the same time.'

'All at the same time' – that surprised us, as we were always being told to never speak at the same time. 'Square, roundy,' came the quick replies.

'Yes,' Dad laughed, and ushered us towards the bus stop and onwards to Nelson's Pillar. He explained to us on the bus why both of us were right. 'These smart architects use all sorts of techniques to pull the wool over our eyes and use certain materials and designs to create shapes. The pillars inside are in a circle, so we think we are in a rounded room, and it's actually called the Rotunda or Round Room. However, on the outside, when we look at the building, it is square-shaped.'

'So,' Freckles said, 'we have a round room in a square building, am I right?'

'Yes,' replied Daisy. 'Like yourself. A round head on a square body!'

'Accept nothing at face value,' Dad said. 'Always question. Always double-check. And always notice, but particularly notice what you don't notice! Look at the clouds. Are they really clouds or balls of wool? Where does the rain come from? Look at a raindrop very closely and see it working or playing. What makes the wind? You may feel it against your face, blowing through your hair, yet you cannot catch it. Try and catch it. Why not? So, I must remind you, nothing is as it seems. Like the chap over there making lots of money from his Three Card Trick. Is he fooling them all the time or are they fooling themselves? How come he makes lots of money and they never ever can pick the right card?'

We were somewhat perplexed. Everything we saw seemed to us to be exactly what we saw. Anyhow, we had a great chat over this and asking each other did you see this or that and were you really sure that what you saw was what you were supposed to see according to someone else's ideas. Is the Ballast Office clock time correct? Where does it get its time from? Is the river flowing under O'Connell Bridge the same river flowing under the Ha'penny Bridge? Why was Isaac Newton so concerned about the apple falling on his head? Was it because it tossed his hair? No, because it was rotten! What about Christopher Columbus? He didn't believe he would fall over the edge of the world as everyone else thought. They said he was stark raving mad altogether. And Copernicus and Galileo. Even the holy Pope thought it was a disgrace for someone to be going on and on about the earth flying around the sun, and not the other way. The Pope was completely wrong and he should not have given Galileo the bum's rush. It wasn't his fault he had a good telescope. Telescopes don't tell lies. They do the seeing for you. Or do they? Oh, we really enjoyed all those crazy questions.

Freckles, of course, had his own view on matters. 'It's all rather simple,' he pointed out. 'Take the invisible prince in Mount Jerome. I'll ask you a question to illustrate what Dad is trying to say. Okay,' he went, 'when is someone there and not there?' We tried to figure out the invisible prince angle to the question. However, we shouldn't have bothered. 'When he's not all there!' went the little smirk, who nearly ended having to speedily exit the bus. At this stage I thought to myself that the best thing for me to do when I got home would be to send in some of these 'Riddle me this, riddle me that' puzzles to *Ireland's Own* or the *Our Boys*. I would then receive a nice five-shilling postal order for myself! Then, what wasn't there would soon be there!

The bus seemed to linger for ages on O'Connell Bridge. Dad pointed his pipe towards the river. 'What's she called?'

'The River Liffey, of course,' we replied.

'Quite right, though sometimes called Anna Livia by those with a soft spot for her. I used to swim in there lots of times as a boy and on a number of occasions took part in the famous Liffey Swim. You can still see me in the National Gallery in Jack Yeats's painting, *The Liffey Swim*,' and he guffawed. 'I brought your Mum to see it when we were courting. She is still trying to find me in the picture, though I keep telling her that's me swimming the fastest!' He roared laughing. 'I told her when we started courting that that was when I first saw her. I was a teenager swimming along in the Liffey Race, doing fine until I was distracted by seeing your Mum on a passing tram. She was only a very young child then, but she caught my eye at the time and then I remembered her when we met years later. Sorry, just getting carried away. Tell me, what does the river remind you of? Anyone?'

We all looked down from the bus into the depths of the river. Minnie laughed to herself and then nudged me. 'Queen Victoria doing a wee wee!'

'What? I heard that, you little scallywags!' He tickled the backs of our necks. 'Well, good for you. You are right and nearly right. The *Evening Mail* made one letter typing error when they were reporting on Queen Vic's visit to Dublin a few years before she died.'

'Which letter?' we were dying to know. We had to wait.

'Her yachting party were sailing up the Liffey during her visit and the *Mail* wrote about it,' and here he huddled up to us and whispered, looking over both shoulders, 'now I'm telling you not to repeat or use this word, you promise? Don't let Mum hear you or there will be skin and hair flying!' We promised. 'Minnie gave you the hint – the paper said she "pissed" under the bridge.' He said this with a kind of look of near regret that he was perhaps overstretching himself. Hysterical laughter broke out on the top deck of the bus and was muffled just as quickly.

'Next time we're in town,' said Dad, 'we'll pop into Merchant's Arch there at the Ha'penny Bridge to see a roller-coaster staircase, also called "a cantilevered stair".' Before he could say another word, we had persuaded him to allow us all to get off the bus near McBirney's. We then trooped along by Webb's second-hand bookshop and on to Merchant's Arch. This hidden staircase was in the building beside the arch. It stretched from the ground all the way up three flights to close to the roof. We had lots of fun here running up and down the stairs and sliding on the bannisters. It was quite steep and curving, so we hurtled down one by one and then ran back up to the top again. Dad beckoned to us – 'before the owner catches you,' he warned. Towards the Ha'penny Bridge with us, moving like lightning. 'Great!' said Dad. 'We're here just in time to see Hector Grey selling lots of bargains over there outside the Woollen Mills shop.' Little did we realise that we were going to watch an outdoor pantomime.

We crossed the Ha'penny Bridge, enjoying the clickety-click and the rattle and clatter of our shoes on the light metal rods holding the timber planks together. 'This is the only pedestrian bridge over the Liffey,' said Dad. Once a toll bridge, over the years it was also called the Wellington Bridge and the Metal Bridge. The Ha'penny Bridge name eventually stuck because the halfpenny charged to cross it caught people's imagination and gave the bridge its popular title. Before the pedestrian bridge was built, people used the ferries to cross. Wellington Bridge opened to the public in 1816.

Besides all the people like ourselves crossing the bridge we noticed beggars, musicians, singers and all sorts. Not only that but we had to wade through different kinds of stalls and hucksters at either end of the bridge, and particularly at the open space outside the Dublin Woollen Mills on the north side. There was this small man, Dad called him Hector Grey, shouting and roaring and offering all sorts of bargains at rock-bottom prices. He had brushes, soaps, torches, candles, towels and every kind of household item imaginable. What amazed us was that he was telling the crowd around him that he would sell it to them at a complete loss and would also give them some free items as well! Dad said that was his 'sales talk' and it was Hector who started the tradition of selling at the bridge. He had been selling his wares there over many years. His popularity lay in selling quality items at affordable prices, Dad told us, and he sold them in such a way that you found it very hard to resist his 'patter' and you definitely thought you were getting a bargain, whether you needed the item or not.

There was another man nearby, Paddy Slattery, and he was selling glass and tile cutters. We had never seen glass or tiles being cut and were absolutely enthralled with the simplicity of it. Freckles asked him for 'a go' and Paddy obliged. Now I have to say that I was somewhat envious, what with Freckles having all his nails and tools at home and him with his bony hands. Still, he managed to follow Paddy's instructions and was soon cutting with the onlookers all around him clapping. I thought he was going to bow, knowing how vain he was. Paddy was delighted, of course, knowing full well that Freckles' knack would show people how easy it was. However, I decided I certainly wasn't going to buy one, even if I had the money. Sure, wouldn't I get dagger-boy Freckles there to do the job for me!

As we were mesmerised at all the hustle, bustle, barking and bawling all around us, Dad was browsing through some old books at Joe Clarke's bookstall. I nudged Freckles. 'Hey look over there, you should try that.' He looked over at Blondini the Sword Swallower, who was devouring swords to beat the band. I thought if Freckles tried to do that, maybe the sword might get stuck. Dad suggested that it was a good idea but on another day. While we watched the Cart Wheel Man doing his flips and flops, we heard the crack of a whip and were startled to see the Whip Man whipping a cigarette out of a lady's mouth from twenty feet. Dad told us she was his wife. She shouted to him that if he missed, he would be in big trouble. She reminded me of Daisy. Maybe I could get a whip and practice in the garden secretly and then try the same trick on her. Only this time I would deliberately whip her yap trap shut! I planned to enquire from the man if he had any whips for sale. I was unfortunately distracted when I saw the Magic Soap Man, whose own brand of soap only needed a drop of water to remove the worst stains. That would be very handy for Mum, I said to Dad. 'It would indeed, son,' and he went over to the soapy man and bought a few bars. I was delighted. There was another man trying to sell items to improve our front door. He was known as Grain the Hall Door Man. Dad said our door didn't need improvement since he had only painted it green recently and it had no grain on it. I nodded, not having a clue about what grain had to do with hall doors.

We walked along Bachelor's Walk and around the corner into O'Connell Street. We stood outside the Metropole cinema and gazed up and down the widest street in Europe. Clery's Department Store across the street was buzzing with life and the clock chimed out its musical tones. We had happy memories of being brought to see *Snow White and the Seven Dwarfs* in the Capitol cinema, right next door to the Metropole. The statue of 'Big Jim' Larkin stood directly across the road in the middle of O'Connell Street. As we looked across towards it we saw a group of colourfully dressed people gathering around it. These were huge fans of *Snow White*, Dad said, who went to see it every week, all year around. Another group from the opposite side of O'Connell Street then joined the first group. These were 'Liberty Hall' people, seemingly. 'This is a great Dublin tradition,' Dad told us. The two groups joined forces then, right in the middle of O'Connell Street, and marched around the statue all the while looking up at Jim Larkin's outstretched hands, raised to the sky. They too raised their hands in unison and expressed their thanks with a rousing rendition of their anthem. All over the city centre it rang out: 'Hi ho, hi ho, it's off to work we go; we work all day, we get low pay, hi ho, hi ho, hi ho, hi ho.'

We queued up for Nelson's Pillar and while waiting Dad told us all about the GPO and the 1916 Rising and how the centre of the city was totally destroyed when the *Helga* gunboat sailed up the River Liffey and opened fire.

'It's amazing how old Nelson managed to survive all that,' Minnie pondered.

'Well he didn't survive Napoleon's bullet at the Battle of Trafalgar,' pointed out Dad. 'But yes, I agree, it is a wonder how he survived

1916. This monument with Admiral Nelson on top has been here since 1809.' He said that 'meet me at the Pillar' was a famous and favourite Dublin expression and it, like Clery's clock across the road, was a popular meeting place for people, since everybody knew it and it was right in the centre of the city. He also told us that the man who sculpted the statue of Nelson on top, Thomas Kirk, was buried in Mount Jerome cemetery.

At last we went through the turnstile having paid our 6*d* and started up the 166 steps. We thought we would never reach the top viewing platform. The stairs just went around and around, up and up for eternity – all of 120 feet! It was worth it as there were some terrific views of the city and the Dublin Mountains in the distance. We stood on the platform and had to look through railings covered in wire mesh. Daniel O'Connell looked like a dwarf and we could see down onto the roof of the GPO. Freckles hoped to drop a ha'penny through the mesh but Dad said someone below might not be happy having their head split in two! Sneaky Freckles decided he would do it anyway and he flung a coin outward. It hit the wire mesh and bounced back at him, clapping him on the head. What bawls and what gales of laughter! 'Serves you right,' said Dad. Amen to that, we agreed. I picked up the coin and stuffed it into my pocket. 'Ma Ryan's, here I come!'

After leaving the Pillar, we strolled over towards Grafton Street. As we crossed O'Connell Bridge we tried to figure out which was the taller, Liberty Hall or Nelson's Pillar. While we waited at the Thomas Moore statue, Dad popped in to the Irish Yeast Company, nearby, for a few packets. We passed the exotic Switzer's department store and then Dad brought us into Bewley's. He left us to do some hotel business and we sat near the Harry Clarke stained-glass window enjoying tea and lovely sticky and cherry buns. We chatted about the window with its exotic birds, flowers, sea creatures and butterflies. When he returned, we popped into Woolworths – or 'Woolies' as we called it – bought our little bags of sweets, filled our pockets with every kind of gobstopper and then went to the nearby Grafton Picture House so see some cartoons, the Marx Brothers and The Three Stooges. We came out poking each other and playing tricks. A few years later we had graduated to films such as *The Ten Commandments*, *Mary Poppins*, *The Sound of Music*, *Around the World in 80 Days*, *The Flight of the Doves*, *The Love Bug*, *The Way West*, *Paint Your Wagon* and *Chitty Bang Bang* all holding our attention.

Retracing our steps down Grafton Street, who should Dad meet but only the legendary Noel Purcell, a famous Dublin actor, tall as a house and with a real Santa Claus beard. 'Ah, me aul flower,' he called to Dad and the two had a great chat. 'Why does that strange man call Dad "flower"?' asked Minnie. 'It's Liberties lingo,' replied Freckles, hoping to be taken for a 'real Dub' eventually, despite not having fully lost his 'culchie' accent. 'Will I give yez a bar,' Mr Purcell said to us just before we left. Before we could answer, off he went singing:

> Dublin can be heaven, with coffee at eleven, and a stroll in Stephen's Green.
> There's no need to hurry, no need to worry, you're a king and the lady's a queen.
> Grafton Street's a wonderland and there's magic in the air … In Dublin on a sunny summer morning.

And off he went with us laughing our heads off. We were having a ball and indeed felt like kings and queens ourselves as we headed for the bus stop with a spring in our steps. We sang 'Dublin can be heaven' all the way home.

11

∽⧜∾

THE HAPPY GANG AND LAUGHING GAS

Our Mum was a very happy person, always smiling. Seldom cross, never very cross. And her marriage to Dad was also a very happy one too. They had a wonderful courtship in Dublin during the Emergency, a few years prior to getting married. They met at a dance in the Gresham Hotel Ballroom and it was love at first sight for both of them. They had a few great years going out together, a time filled with fun and activity. Frequently they went on holidays to the English Lake District and climbed mountains in Wales. They also liked the Isle of Man, walking through the Cork and Kerry mountains and Garnish Island. And in those golden years, they laughed with a joy that only love could bring.

Dublin was very fashion conscious in the 1940s and '50s so both liked to dress and look well, despite the widespread rationing in clothing during and after the Emergency. There was a certain refinement and air of manners and civility pervading the city and this was reflected in the penchant for dressing well. Mam liked a loose-fitting midi-length shift dress and matching jacket. Sometimes she wore a black mandarin hat with a spotted veil or a slouch hat in varying colours, a trapeze swing coat with a fancy brooch. One of her favourites was a light blue suit with sequins on top. Shoes were navy blue, suede leather. Her leather handbag and gloves were in a similar blue. Dad liked double-breasted suits and looked very suave and debonair.

By this time, Dad's family had moved from the Liberties to Templeogue. The family numbered thirteen at this stage and space had become a problem, so his father bought two houses side by side and surrounded with an acre of land. The new home was called 'Palmville' and was right in the heart of the village.

Dad was well known in the hotel and catering business, and consequently many doors were opened for him, whether it was in restaurants, ballrooms or cinemas. Conveniently, both he and mum were living in the city centre, and this made it all the easier to enjoy a great social life, going dancing, to the cinema and dining out in some of the best restaurants, including Jammet's and the Stephen's Green Club. Dad had opened what became a hugely popular restaurant in Dublin Airport in the late 1940s, with a view of the airfield. It also held functions and dances and people came out to it in their droves. It was one of *the* places to dine and socialise in Dublin for nigh on twenty years after first opening.

The Theatre Royal (demolished in 1962) on Hawkins Street was a particular favourite for the happy couple. This was owned by the Elliman family. Maurice Elliman had built the Metropole on O'Connell Street and the Theatre de Luxe on Camden Street. The Theatre Royal was, and not just because of its huge capacity, a landmark theatre with its resident orchestra, the Jimmy Campbell Orchestra. Here you could have a film and variety show ('cine-variety') with the one ticket. The programme, which did much to dispel the gloom of the Emergency, also included The Royalettes, a glamorous line-up of twelve high-stepping chorus girls, including two professional dancers, Babs de Monte and Alice Delgarno, who directed the troupe. Other regulars in the theatre's programme included Tommy Dando on the Compton Organ, as well as Jack Cruise, Noel Purcell, Peggy Dell, Cecil Sheridan,

Harry O'Donovan, Danny Cummins, Vernon Hayden, Mickser Reid and the Happy Gang. Jimmy O'Dea also featured regularly. It was also *the* theatre for Hollywood stars when coming to Dublin. Some of these were James Cagney, Danny Kaye, Judy Garland and Nat 'King' Cole. Judy Garland endeared herself to a crowd on Poolbeg Street by singing to them from a window of the theatre. The famous boxer, Jack Doyle and his film-star wife, Movita, also appeared.

The couple's wedding took place in the Pro-Cathedral in the centre of Dublin, with 'Ave Maria' and 'Panis Angelicus' being sung. Mum's young sister, Lily, was the bridesmaid. The wedding ceremony was followed by a reception in Jury's Hotel, where Dad had been a one-time manager. They honeymooned in Northern Ireland near the Giant's Causeway. After having a number of different flats, including Rathmines and Bray, they finally settled in Mountain View.

They continued to have a very happy life together. Dad, being from the heart of the Liberties, enjoyed his pint but once married gave it up. Despite the arrival of two children, Minnie and I, they continued to go to the cinema every Thursday night. Within a few years, Freckles and Daisy came to stay with us Then our fun began! Daisy was left in charge of us and what a time of mischief and adventure we had. No sooner had the adults left the house than we took over, turning off the lights, playing hide and seek, dressing up as ghosts, sliding down the banisters and up and down the linoleum floor in the hall, which consequently was always shiny. We sprinkled talcum powder onto it, which it made it very slippery. Then we had midnight feasts of Rusks and broken biscuits from Sweeney's at the Bridge, the Beehive or the Emmet Dairy, telling each other ghost stories and watching the passing car headlights making moving pictures on the front sitting room walls.

Dad regularly gave Mum cheques with messages on them such as 'please pay the bearer one million pounds of kisses' or 'one million pounds of graces'. Some of their favourite radio programmes included *Friday Night is Music Night*, *Sing Something Simple* with the Adams' Singers on Saturday evenings, *Your One Hundred Best Tunes* on Sunday nights, and *Your Choice and Mine* with Tommy O'Brien. Then there was *Down the Country* with Fred Desmond, which was opened to the sound of the *Elizabethan Serenade*. They loved Puccini and Verdi in particular. When he came home from work in the evenings he would give her a kiss and then ask 'how are the buffs?' Then he would give us bags of Maynard's wine gums. She was always first, however. It was a marriage made in heaven and they spent seventeen years of devoted love together. This fact and the happy memories sustained her for the rest of her life.

Dad suffered from high blood pressure in his later years, often attributed to the rich hotel food in the various establishments he managed. The hotel work was very demanding and had him on call practically twenty-four hours a day, seven days a week. Because of his health, he had to retire early from the business in the early 1960s and became a Commercial Traveller, which gave him more time for home and the family.

It was a few days before Christmas that he had a heart attack at home and ended up in St Mary's Hospital in the Phoenix Park. This was the former St Mobhi's Military Hospital where Mum worked as a nurse during the Emergency. Mum spent that Christmas beside Dad's bedside. We spent Christmas Day at home playing with our toys. I got a toy mouse as a present and this gave me hours of pleasure. The next evening, we were brought to our cousin's house in Donnybrook. Our Uncle drove a white Ford Cortina with XZC 213 on the number plate. We spent the evening in his house and my abiding memory was eating sandwiches while sitting on a bright blue carpeted stairway. I insisted upon sitting there, rather than with the rest of the family at the table in the kitchen. I had never seen or felt such a carpet before. I spent my time just running my fingers through the soft fibres of the thick-pile carpet. That and the pleasing aroma of ham wafting through the house were my memories of that visit.

Dad had another, this time fatal heart attack on 27 December. In a kindly whisper to Mum and holding her hand, his dying words were, 'look after the children'. The watch he was wearing at the time also stopped. He was fifty-six years of age and Mum was in her late forties. She had lost a husband, her best friend and the family breadwinner.

Her heart was broken. She quietly and gently wept.

Later, we spent hours in a big black funeral limousine just down the hill from the hospital as we waited for the hearse and the rest of the funeral cortege. In the darkening Phoenix Park surrounded by swaying and towering chestnut trees, it seemed interminably boring for us children stuck in the car. It was not the custom then for children to say goodbye to a loved one. In a way, they were just brushed aside to be seen later, maybe. The driver of the limousine gave us a bar of chocolate, which helped pass the time. It helped that we played word games with the 'Cadbury' name, even breaking it up to give 'bury' the 'cad'. We laughed despite the serious circumstances.

The funeral took place in the local church with an overflowing attendance. After the main ceremony, we moved to the side chapel for the transfer of the coffin to the hearse. There was much weeping and gnashing of teeth, with me doing both. I was not looking forward to a visit to the dentist the next day. And it was not only for the pain involved.

The Eastern Health Board dentist, on Cornmarket in the Liberties, was famous for his treatment and the use of laughing gas as a painkiller. Once the extractions and fillings were complete, I left the surgery laughing my head off. This was not ideal given the circumstances. When relations and neighbours commiserated with me, offering condolences such as, 'You poor little lad! Sorry for your trouble,' and such like, I responded with 'Thank you very much, ha! ha! ha!' which nobody found funny, including myself. 'At least he didn't die roaring,' I added, just to calm the situation. 'Maybe snoring, more likely, ha! ha! ha!' I could see the situation was deteriorating. 'Unlike them corpses up in the hospice. You can still hear them roaring in Mount Jerome at night! Although Mum did say that they were just the cider drinkers going mad.'

'I'm sure you'll miss your Dad?'

'Yes. He used to bring us home wine gums and jelly snakes and sometimes sticks of rock. Then on Sundays he took us to the park and we played on the merry-go-round and see-saws and afterwards we went to Ann's shop beside Paddy Walsh's for big wafers and broken biscuits. And he told us lots and lots of stories about the old days when people went around smoking pipes, didn't want to be buried standing up, wore funny hats on their heads and played football in their bare feet.' I didn't mention that he would no longer be able to tickle us and ask 'How are my little buffs today?' Or who would take his place and walk bravely across the road with his jacket off, sleeves rolled up and tell that tramp Adler on no account to be scaring his children.

Mum's emotions were her own and not for showing. The only indication of any loss was the black veil and clothing which society stipulated she must wear for at least a year after her loss. As was the custom, the curtains in our house were drawn closed to convey our loss. She sent out black-edged envelopes to thank the mourners for their attendance. She called a meeting of the family and asked us all to do our best to help out in the house until she decided what was to become of us all. Afterwards, we buried a mouse at the end of the garden in Dad's old silver shaving box.

The days and weeks passed and Easter was soon upon us. Not having Dad around meant we were not sure if we would be having Easter Eggs or not. We agreed that we wouldn't even mention it to Mum. The house seemed somewhat gloomy, although Mum was as cheerful with us as ever. We hoped that she would soon be able to discard her black garb as it added to the atmosphere that something had changed. We still loved the swing in the garden and I spent hours on it waiting for the buds to appear on the pear tree. I swung back and forth, back and forth with my feet in the air trying to tip the lower branches of the pear tree, unsuccessfully. The spring shoots were struggling to be seen, causing the branches to be lighter and out of reach.

We missed Dad bringing us to the park and it was even more difficult to push the merry-go-round. There was little bounce and hurtle as when he put his strength into pushing it faster and faster and us holding on for dear life and nearly taking off into space with our hair trying to catch up with us. Instead, we sat on it, side by side, and round and round it trundled, not smoothly or skilfully but twisting and banging and falling in a lopsided fashion. Finally, the cold, spiteful rain forced us to go home. Stephen's Green was little better, with the flower beds struggling to come to life. There was no music on the bandstand and no pinkeens darting about in the pond. People hurried through with a determined seriousness, clasping coats and hats, but not lingering and chatting over the miniature O'Connell Bridge. Even the ducks were ignored, nobody stopping to feed them and smile as they used to do at their quacking when they chased the bread. I had nightmares about being lost in the crowds on the Ha'penny Bridge and being surrounded by turnstiles. Not the small Croke Park type, but the large iron-bar gated turnstiles similar to the ones at the bottom of the steps leading up and into the Phoenix Bridge at Islandbridge.

12

A Crown of Thorns and Tales from the Crypt

It was Good Friday morning a few months after Dad's death and Mum announced that we were going into St Michael and John's Church near Fishamble Street and Wood Quay to hear Our Lady's Choral Society singing the Halleluiah Chorus from Handel's oratorio 'The Messiah'. Mum said that Dad had told her that it was first performed in Dublin in a music hall on Fishamble Street back in 1742. We groaned. We hated the sound of the Halleluiah, thinking it was an absolute fraud with old timers singing it and failing to sound cheerful at all.

It was the custom in Dublin on Good Friday, for most of the shops, businesses and pubs to close, at least between 12 noon and 3 p.m. It was also tradition for Dubliners to visit cemeteries, and off with us then to Mount Jerome to see Dad's grave. Afterwards, we returned by the Orphan Walk and then on to the Hawthorn Walk. Suddenly, Mum stopped near the entrance to the Victorian Chapel and pointed. 'That's the Crown of Thorns Tree,' she said, looking at an ancient, straggling and prickly looking tree. 'Your Dad showed that to me many years ago, when we first moved to Mountain View. He also said that it was one of only two in the country, the other is in the Botanic Gardens.' She walked over to it and put up a finger to touch one of the branches. 'Ouch!' she suddenly shouted, startling us all. 'Sorry, I didn't realise how sharp those thorns were. I'll just put my hanky over this and then we'll be on our way.'

On the way into town we passed St Patrick's, with the mournful tolling of the bells sounding even louder in the quiet city. They must be sitting upside down, I reflected. Each peal seemed a chilling reminder of mortality. Boom, boom, boom. Gloom, gloom, gloom. We alighted from our bus near High Street, high by name and by nature as it looks over the city and the River Liffey towards the Four Courts on the opposite quays. The bus stop was near the beginning of the 40 Steps to Hell, by the side of St Audoen's Church.

Standing in the tiny St Audoen's Park before descending the steps, we were perched on the edge of the old city walls with some of the battlements still intact. The large grey stones that constituted the back of the adjacent Catholic Church, also called St Audoen's, looked quite grim and overbearing when viewed from Cook Street at the bottom of the steps. The long winding steps, dark even on the sunniest of days, were quite difficult to descend because of the width of each step. At the bottom, we passed through a portcullis-type gate and out through the wall of old Dublin. The wall towered above us, impossible to climb and built that way to ensure the Irish would not penetrate the invaders' stronghold. They never gave up, however.

The towering church and the City Wall were side by side, with the back of the church pressed tightly against it, creating the appearance of a continuous wall. There were two large grey-stoned blind windows that seemed to stare right down at us, as if giving directions to the lost. I looked back and the windows seemed to be following us malevolently. They seemed critical, judgemental, asking 'Where do you think you are going?' We weaved and wobbled past the tenements and derelict buildings, vagabonds lurking, our eyes downcast, straight on. To our right, lanes crowded with hovels and dilapidated dwellings, hurtled down to our feet.

We crossed Winetavern Street, gazing at the dark sky through the arch connecting the Synod Hall to the main Christ Church Cathedral. Halfway along the old cobbled lane running at the back of the church, we stopped near a small narrow door. 'This,' said Freckles, having done his research upstairs in Rathmines Library, including looking at Rocque's map with a magnifying glass, 'is one of the entrances to Hell.' Mum looked startled yet she was prepared to listen. 'Come, follow me,' he said, as we entered the cathedral's crypt via steps leading downwards. This was a different entrance to the one we had used when Dad had brought us to see Strongbow and the cat and mouse playing the organ. Unlike the previous visit, there was a palpable atmosphere of dampness and foreboding in the air.

Freckles pointed to a door along the dark passage, which he said was the entrance to where the tavern called 'Hell' was located. It is still called that name by the staff of the cathedral but was used for storage purposes. He whispered to us, 'If one enters through this door, Hell is in front of you!'

'No thanks,' was our response. 'Let's go!'

Freckles told us that because of the name of the tavern in long ago times, the area around the cathedral became known as Hell and developed a very disreputable name with all kinds of dubious taverns, gambling houses and every kind of imaginable strange goings-on. To confuse matters further, there were stories related to why the tavern itself was called Hell. One story related to a crypt-keeper who locked up the tavern for the winter months and inadvertently left behind a customer, who spent the winter there in the freezing cold. On reopening for business, the following spring, the crypt-keeper found the customer still there – but now a skeleton! When the story spread, it might have been the reason locals called the tavern Hell.

He said there used to be a lane called Hell running in front of the cathedral with gates at Fishamble Street and Idler's Corner. We felt it was a good excuse to leave the dark dungeons of the cathedral with their mice and cats playing organ music for the deaf and the drinkers.

To lift our spirits after being to Hell we sang 'Molly Malone', since she was long associated with the fish hawkers of Fishamble Street. Freckles was all chat, meantime, and pointed out the Gates of Hell on the top of the street, nearly opposite the archway of the old Fishamble Street Music Hall. We rushed over to see the Gates of Hell and were somewhat disappointed, since they were just ordinary black, cast-iron, ornamental entrance gates. Freckles, however, told us about the Devil's head, carved from oak, which was over the entrance of the original old gates for hundreds of years. This strange wooden statue of the devil greeted the visitor who dared to venture into the area day or night, he said. When it was taken down, the Devil's head was turned into snuffboxes. Freckles said that some of these snuffboxes had carved on them representations of the Devil escorting a figure to the fires of Hell, and on the inside of the snuffbox lid the following lines were engraved:

'Prime your nose well; I'd have you be civil. This box was
in Hell. And was made of the Devil.'

While Mum popped into a grocery shop near the Harding Boys' Home, Freckles told us all about Darkey Kelly and her house of horrors, which his uncle had told him about. She had what was known as a 'bawdy house' called the Maiden Tower, 'just across the road there on Copper Alley, right in the very heart of Hell. Oh, she was a right one alright,' exclaimed Freckles 'and…' here he beckoned us closer, 'was the Madam of an absolutely shocking house of ill-repute.' He said those kinds of premises were often called 'bawdy houses' in those eighteenth-century times. He didn't explain too much saying he would leave the details to our imaginations. It seemed to us as if he didn't exactly know too much himself. He just said that those kinds of places had drink and gambling and laughing and holding hands and what-not. He said the Maiden Tower was like being on the Ghost Train out in Bray and contained such a labyrinth of rooms, galleries, mirrors and doors that it was almost impossible for anyone to find their way out from the upper stories unless accompanied by a guide acquainted with the intricacies of the building. This was quite deliberate. It was easy to get in but very difficult to leave in a hurry. Many unwary customers were never to be seen again. After the Madam's death, investigators found the bodies of five men hidden in the vaults of the house. Apparently, according to Freckles, she had a secret trap door up in one of the top rooms full of mirrors and curtains always drawn. If she didn't like the look of the man who came in for a chat, she would sit him down in this chair and pull a lever close by. The floor would suddenly tilt downwards and down went the unwary man, hurtling into the dungeons below.

Unfortunately, continued Freckles, greed caught up with her and she was burned at the stake for witchcraft after she accused the Sheriff of Dublin, Simon Luttrell, of being the father of her baby. When Darkey Kelly demanded money from Luttrell, he refused to have anything to do with the child and instead, in order to discredit her, spread rumours among the women of Dublin that she was involved in witchcraft and the murder of her baby – though no actual body was produced. Some said that her having customers from the rich and famous in Dublin was her downfall. It was said that men such as Luttrell 'wanted the wench but not the woman,' whereas she 'wanted the money but not the man.' Daisy was taking notes of all this, going by her twitching eyes and ears.

'What about Molly Malone?' queried Minnie, wanting more scandal. 'Didn't she live around here with the fishmongers, if we are to believe the song?' She was always going around the house singing about the fishmonger's daughter, 'as she wheeled her wheelbarrow, through streets broad and narrow, crying cockles and mussels, alive, alive oh.'

'Well I'm not sure if you really want to know the true story about Molly Malone, Minnie.'

'I do! I do! Please tell us, Freckles.'

'Okay, alright. I'll tell you something which you won't like. From my reading, I discovered that she was not exactly what she seemed to be, if you get my drift.' And he tried to wink at us, failing miserably though and ending up with a face that was an improvement on the original. Minnie, however, did not get his 'drift'.

'I know you are full of lies,' replied an angry Minnie. 'Let's hear you anyway, you aul fibber.'

Going by what that aul fibber told us, that day was a very sad day for Minnie and the rest of us. No longer would we be able to sing that song with the same gusto. Our dreams were taken from us. Molly Malone seemingly was a part-time Moll, as her name suggested and which Freckles hinted at. She bounced her barrow up and down the old cobblestoned streets during the day and then in the evenings met a few men, had them sit on her lap and such like and got paid lots of money for it. That was according to his story anyway. Just then, Mum reappeared and gave us all ice creams. 'I was lucky to find a shop open today,' she said. 'So here goes and enjoy. Luckily I managed to get a few cookers to make an apple tart this evening and a few other items.' We cried 'to Hell with Hell' and away with us down the steep and winding Fishamble Street.

13

THE GREAT LIBERATOR AND BERNIE BOTTLE EYES

Near the quays end of Fishamble Street and around into the former Smock Alley, now called Essex Street West, was the back of St Michael and John's Church. This originally had been the Smock Alley Theatre and was where Oliver Goldsmith's *She Stoops to Conquer* was first performed. Daisy reminded us of this, quite sharply. Before she could continue, Mum said her goodbyes, saying she wouldn't be too long as she was just going to pop in to the church to say a quick prayer and then hoped to hear a little of 'The Messiah'. She asked if any of us would like to go along with her but we had no interest whatsoever. We also knew that Daisy was bringing us to the Viking Adventure Centre near the church, which promised to be far more interesting. We agreed to meet at the same place later.

We really enjoyed the centre as there were lots of interactive things for us to do, including painting and rubbing images of Vikings, Normans and King Brian Boru. There was also a café, so that helped too! Freckles and Daisy kept us either bored or enthralled with various stories as we explored the centre. The problem was that they talked down at us far too much, 'getting above themselves', as Mum used to say about some of our neighbours. Daisy sometimes looked at me as if I was one of the Ten Lepers, just out for the day!

Daisy called us over as she was gazing out a window and pointed up to what she called the 'Freedom Bell' high up in a bell tower on the back roof of the church. It seemed to me that the bell must have boomed out of kilter in her head as she suddenly insisted upon quoting Jim Larkin. 'The great are great because we are on our knees. Let us arise.' That's great, I thought to myself. I was just about to get up and go, when I was virtually hauled back. 'But he forgot about women, perhaps. It is women like Auntie who are on their knees,' she said. 'Look at her every day scrubbing the kitchen floor. You should start doing it Larry,' she said, looking at me. I thought she was a bit smart for her own good to make such a suggestion. I had never used a mop or cloth in my life. She had caught me in a bind, so I had to agree to help Mum with the mopping and I knew where I would start – with Daisy' mop of frizzled red hair, cascading down her back now. She reminded me of that infamous pirate queen from County Mayo, Grace O'Malley, and her audacity for sailing up the River Thames and telling Queen Elizabeth what she thought of her. When they met in Greenwich Palace, Grace refused to bow before Elizabeth, because she too was a queen. The two women spoke in Latin and came to an agreement. Grace's twentieth century successor, my cousin Daisy, still seemed to be speaking in Latin, for all I understood or cared.

Now Daisy had a habit of lecturing and not listening. She had no interest whatsoever in what anybody else had to say. 'A mind of her own,' Mum used to say. She should mind her own business, I sometimes thought. When we were out of sight, she was inclined to discuss us with Mum, as if she was a woman of the world and on equal terms. But I was always within earshot, sometimes hiding in the big hot press that was in the kitchen. From there, sucking acid drops or a liquorice stick, and lying on a wooden shelf with my feet resting up against the warm water cylinder, I could hear them gossiping away.

As the rest of us wandered around looking at the various exhibits, including one showing Brian Boru bashing the head off Harold the Viking and the rest of his comrades at the Battle of Clontarf, Daisy again pointed up at the bell tower. I completely ignored, her looking at a replica of a defensive tower, called Isolde's, which was one of the towers around the old walled city of Dublin, and which was located just a stone's throw from where we were. Pulled away from the exhibition, I was annoyed. This time, I thought, the bell was definitely going to come crashing down or something, or maybe she was having a vision. More of the latter, I'm afraid, as it turned out, with a long-winded rant on men and women and what they should or should not be doing. No doubt she was still smarting from recent jibes from Freckles, who really had lost the run of himself. Who does he think he is anyway? I resented his attitude and got a pair of boxing gloves to try and beat him up. Unfortunately, he swatted me away as if I was a puny teenager.

'That's a lie,' Daisy said, eyes blazing and still looking up at the bell. 'That is known as the "Freedom Bell" because Daniel O'Connell, known as the Great Liberator, which is another lie, rang it when the government gave the people Catholic Emancipation. Two damn lies,' she emphasised. 'It's a mockery of women.' We gazed down at the exhibits, hoping Mum wouldn't be long in the church with its Halleluiah what-not. I just knew Daisy had lost the run of herself immersing in so many of these foreign books that gave her all sorts of ideas. You wouldn't find her reading all about the Four Marys in *The Judy* or *The Bunty*. No, she much preferred to attend classes in the Alliance Française and go to meetings organised by Kadar Asmal about Nelson Mandela and black and white people in South Africa. I also overheard her talking about something called Women's Lib and burning her clothes with other like-minded lunatics. She said that as soon as she finished school she was going off to Paris, get an au pair job and meet Jean Paul Sartre – who wrote a book called *Nausea* all about getting sick – and Simone de Beauvoir, a real Countess Markievicz-type, ready to fill you full of holes. She also said she would be making lots of visits to the Shakespeare shop. I mean, what absolute nonsense I had to put up with. She was turning out just like Bernadette Devlin on the barricades in Northern Ireland. Maybe she should forget Paris, I thought, and go there instead and get arrested for flinging petrol bombs around the place. I hoped Minnie wouldn't turn out like her.

I had to duck a few times such were the shards, slivers, slings and slurs hurtling at us. 'Remember Jonathan Swift who wrote *Gulliver's Travels*? Well that book, and the one about fattening babies so they could be eaten for lunch, was published around the corner from here on Fishamble Street.' I yawned. 'What did he say about happiness? It was nothing but self-deceit. He would know, of course, being an expert himself on self-deceit, with two girlfriends at the same time, both wanting to marry him. And, unbelievably, both of them were called Esther. Oh, he was crafty indeed. He turned one against the other and had jam on both sides of his bread, so he did! An absolute rascal, I'll have you know,' Daisy spat out with her face getting redder and redder until she looked like one big red freckle. 'What did he do so as not to confuse himself with the two names? He called one Stella and the other Vanessa. Wasn't he the crafty man? And guess what, didn't one of them die just when the relationship was getting awkward. She was young and broken-hearted and died, very conveniently for Swift, just outside the graveyard that used to be next to St Andrew's Church, down the road there, off College Green.'

I was getting very suspicious of this Swift fellow. There was no doubt that he was an absolute chancer, particularly in the light of our previous visit with Dad to St Patrick's Cathedral, with its 'Chancer's Hatch'. Why didn't he get rid of it? I reckoned that he spent half his time at the hatch chancing his arm to make sure it was supple, able and willing to write all that satirical stuff and giving all his enemies headaches. Now here he was again with two girlfriends, and one very conveniently dying right outside a graveyard! I did not see myself as Poirot, yet I had my strongest suspicions about this Swift in this particular case. In fact, 'Murder Most Foul' was what crossed my mind. The location was ideal for the perfect murder. Esther lived with her family at Foster Place just around the corner from the notorious Daly's Club, the worst type of gambling club in all of Europe in the eighteenth century and well into the nineteenth. Even

Charles Dickens, on visits to Dublin many years later, had heard of its notoriety. Worse still, some of the Bucks that went to that club had a long family tradition of being members of such clubs, including the equally notorious Hellfire Club.

While Daisy rambled on about nothing in particular to no one in particular, I pondered on more serious matters. It was my understanding, then, that Swift persuaded one of these young Bucks to 'accidentally' push one of the Esther's out the club window and, hey presto, she was gone! He was some yahoo, alright. A number of names sprang to mind including Burn Chapel Whaley, infamous for burning down churches in the eighteenth century. His son was equally mad, accepting wagers from his friends, Copper Faced Jack and the Sham Squire, to jump from the first-floor window of his fine house on St Stephen's Green while seated on his horse. He did, and won the bet, but killed the horse. There was also Tiger Roche, who was seen by some as a hero, but by others as a thief and a murderer. Then there were the Pinking Dindies, those student ruffians from Trinity College, who used to go around 'pinking' passers-by with their swords just for the fun of it. Worse, they went around mugging people with their handkerchiefs! They approached a likely victim and took out a hanky with a large heavy key hidden in its folds, pretending to blow their nose. Instead, they swung it at the victim's head, just for fun! There was also a notorious individual called 'The Dolocher' who used to go around the vicinity of Hell at night dressed as a black pig terrorising and murdering the unwary.

Swift's Esther, known to him as Vanessa, could quite easily have been murdered by any of the disreputable individuals such as those mentioned that swarmed around Dublin. Even the poor, if arrested for the smallest crime, would more than likely end up in Newgate or Kilmainham gaols and from there finishing out their sad lives dancing at the end of a rope from a hornpipe to a pirouette. The only consolation to the deceased was that the locals in Dublin might sing about them, as was the case in the popular ballad, 'The Night Larry was Stretched'.

Vanessa's body would then have been deliberately dumped outside the nearby graveyard. Not for a convenient burial, but for a convenient body snatch! In those days, the infamous body-snatchers were well paid for their trouble, particularly by the likes of the medical school in Trinity College, just across the road from St Andrew's graveyard. There was a big demand for bodies and Swift was happy to oblige them in order to extricate himself from an awkward relationship. A complete chancer, I concluded.

'We have a lot to bear, do you hear me?' Daisy hollered. Yes, we couldn't but. And on she went with her rant. 'Now some men recognise this. Very few, in fact. Most don't because they are blinded by lust or their imagination, or loneliness or boredom or whatever. So, with a little help from buckets of Coco or Estée or whoever, the target is sucked in. Men end up just marrying bottles of perfume. End of his and her life as they suck the life out of each other. Vampires both,' she cackled, as was her norm. And I'm looking at one right here in front of me, I confided to myself, humming *Ten Green Bottles*. 'Ten green bottles marching up the aisle. Ten green bottles laughing all the while. La, la, la-la, la, la, la, la, la.'

Oh, she's turning into a right witch, I knew, even though Halloween was a long way off. I was remembering some of her past misdeeds against my good self. I wished sometimes that she would have hopped right back onto her broom and taken a one-way ticket to the moon. Yes, and she was great for criticising us all and real mean sometimes. Hadn't I asked her nicely to be introduced to a friend of hers I fancied, nice long hair and bell bottoms, and she just sneered, 'She wouldn't even look at you.' Wasn't that nice? If someone had asked me I would have said that the only place where anyone would even look at Daisy herself would be in Madam Tussauds – in the horror section! Oh, she had a touch of Darkey Kelly to her all right!

I ruminated further on my many grievances, seeing her as a right nuisance, talking about love and lust as if she were an expert. And she used to sidle up to Mum, 'a right lick,' I thought contemptuously, putting ideas into her head. Maybe Larry should do more around the house to help out. He could do the dishes after lunch, bring in the coal and fill the scuttle, empty the fire grate in the morning before breakfast, set the fire, bring in the milk, polish the front door brasses, sweep the floor, tidy his room, sweep the stairs, cut the grass, gather the leaves, clean the windows, bring out the bins. Unbelievable! I felt she was trying to turn me into a right class of an old slave and me a very busy boy as it was. I had an army to look after. Sixty skulls to knock together. Being a former Head Altar Boy brought its responsibilities and demands on my time and energy. Rotas for all these altar boys to be organised and planned carefully so that I didn't have to serve on any of these early morning Masses. Also, I had to make sure that I served as many weddings as possible on Saturdays so as to collect all those lovely ten shilling and one-pound notes for myself. I did, of course, give Mum half every time, though.

Then there were the orphans in St Mary's to be looked after. What with all those Valentine Cards I had to read. I had received buckets of them only a couple of months previously. The postman just squashed them through the letterbox. I had to complain at the Post Office and ask to have them delivered in sacks in future. Moreover, didn't I have to see Bernie Bottle Eyes from the orphanage up the lane beside Mulcahy's grocery shop? Wasn't she lovely, though slightly plump. But she had a lovely roundy randy face. Nice white skin with the odd spot. Staring *voulez-vous* eyes behind light grey colour-framed glasses, inviting, just me. And holding her close. My first kiss, though not hers, which was just as well for me. It could be love, I thought. No! It's just a silly phase I'm going through! I will survive!

I sent her a Valentine Card, especially handwritten with lines such as 'Bernie bottle eyes, I tell you no lies. You …' I'm still convinced her card to me was definitely lost in the post.

Where were we? Yes, Daisy talking to nobody about lying lawyers. She burned with some firesome anger. 'The famous United Irishmen! Napper Tandy, Wolfe Tone and the rest of them! What about all those millions of Irishwomen that weren't even included or consulted? It was as if the country was populated only by men! Yet that is exactly how they saw Ireland. That Freedom Bell above our head is, as I said, another big lie. It was supposed to signal the ending of the Penal Laws. But he forgot about the Penal Laws against women! Do you know about the

Penal Laws?' she asked Freckles, who was quick to respond.

'Of course, we do. Sure, didn't old King Billy bring them in, after the Battle of the Boyne in 1689, to make sure the people in Ireland had all their power and influence taken from them? Not allowed to build churches or go to Mass and all the priests run out of the country. I am totally in favour of those Penal Laws, I am! They should have been kept. O'Connell has a lot to answer for, you bet! I agree with you there, absolutely. Some Liberator if you ask me!'

We nodded awake and agreed wholeheartedly with what they both said or whatever it was all about. 'Liars, liars, liars!' she suddenly shouted at us.

'We're not liars,' we shouted back. Fibbers at times, maybe, but not liars.

'What's more,' she continued, 'All those lies in the Constitution were put there deliberately for two reasons – to keep women suppressed in the home and to make sure that all the lying liars would make lots of money fighting amongst themselves over the interpretation of those same lies. Sure, if the Constitution said we will give women in the home a decent wage to look after the family, no matter what, then the politicians would have their work cut out for themselves to balance the budget in a new way, lying prostituting lawyers would no longer be making stacks of money for telling lies, and priests would no longer have the upper hand over women in the confessional. But, no. What do we get instead? Half a loaf, that's what! That's why this Freedom Bell is just a lie. We have no real freedom. Maybe half of us think we have, but the other half with the half a loaf know otherwise.'

'It's time to go now,' I kindly suggested. 'Sit,' she barked, showing her dragon's teeth. '1916 was a failure. The men were just shot once. They all had a great life beforehand, working away, making lots of money, living the good life. Then they shot to glory and martyrdom. Suddenly everyone wanted to be like them, including our young friend, eighteen-year-old Kevin Barry up in Fleet Street. He would have served his country far better if he had finished his medical studies.'

She was becoming shriller. 'Hear this. In houses and homes up and down the country to this day, mothers and daughters like me, helping out all the time, are shot every day.' I suddenly perked up. Daisy was about to be shot, sad to hear, of course, but she had to go some time. No, alas, Daisy was still there with us. 'Mothers are shot and they don't die, that day or the next or the next. They never die. Instead they live a life in Hell, here, far worse than those brave buckos of 1916 shot only once and it's all over. Where were the real heroes of 1916? They were the mothers, daughters and sisters left at home darning the bullet holes, forever. Pearse got it totally wrong when he said that a nation without its language is only half a nation. He should have said that a nation without its women is only half a nation or not a nation at all! That's what he died for. Half a nation!' Just a half-baked Revolution, I laughed to myself.

I threw in my tuppence worth, feeling quite smart. 'Well, half a loaf is better than nothing,' I said. She just glared at me as if I had just given her a slice of mouldy bread. Luckily, we saw Mum in the distance.

14

THE PALACE AND THE PAUPER

Mum joined us and mentioned the nasty person she met in St Michael and John's. Apparently, she had gone in hoping to hear Our Lady's Choral Society giving a rendition of Handel's 'Halleluiah'. I was wondering at the fascination with this piece of music since the rest of us nearly laughed at all the Halleluiahs. Seemingly, George Frederick Handel came to Dublin in 1741 to give the world the first performance of 'The Messiah' (1742), which contains all the Halleluiahs. Jonathan Swift, the Dean of St Patrick's Cathedral, was looking forward to meeting him. However, Swift was laid up in bed so Handel kindly visited him in his Deanery. When Handel knocked on his door and Swift was told who his visitor was, he said: 'Oh, a German, a genius, a prodigy! Admit him!' So, two of the great figures of the early eighteenth century met in Dublin. Mind you, not too many people know that Handel got a paralytic stroke while in Dublin, caused by overeating! The greedy man! It looked to me as if the greedier met the chancer.

In went Mum anyway, to listen to the music of this hungry man. The church was a hive of activity and a babble of voices, but no sound of any music. People seemed to be preparing for something and it was not music. Just then a small thin priest came bounding over to her. 'How can I help you? Are you here for the Via Dolorosa? If so, please hurry along, we can't waste time, can we?'

She didn't like his demeanour or tone. 'I'm here to listen to "The Messiah",' she went, but he quickly reacted.

'Madam, we never have that here on Good Friday. Do you not know your religion? Are you a Catholic? That music is much more appropriate for Easter Sunday, don't you realise? Oh, please spare me this! Can't you see I'm busy preparing for our annual Via Dolorosa?' He seemed to relish those two words by slowly emphasising them and repeating them. 'Yes, our special Via Dolorosa. Do you even know what that means? That means, to lay folk like you, the Way of the Cross. In other words, the story of the Passion.' I understand alright, thought Mum, as his words pierced her. *Your* way, *our* Cross. He persisted. 'Are you here by yourself? We could do with someone to help carry the cross. If so, go over there and Father Byrne will give you an old cloak to wear. Then you may join in the procession. No!' he seemed startled. 'You tell me you have children waiting for you in the Viking Centre? That is absolutely dreadful, Madam. You should be minding them, and not gallivanting around town. Letting them wander around by themselves, I can't believe it. Bad habits, Madam! Bad habits indeed! Don't you know a mother's place is right at home in the bosom of her family? That's where you and they should be right now and also attending to your religious observances. Excuse me, I have more important matters to deal with.' He disappeared into the babble.

Not a great start to my day, Mum thought to herself. The incident brought back memories of her nursing days in Dublin when she was living at Gardiner Place and undertook much 'agency work'. This involved visiting the homes of mothers who were 'expecting'. One of her patients lived off Nicholas Street in some of the old tenements near St Patrick's Cathedral. She and the husband had seven children and decided that was enough. One day after Mass, she arrived home and told her husband that the priest said no one of childbearing age should stop having children. Sometime later she had another. Both she and the baby died during the birth. They were buried together.

Mum also remembered visiting a family around the corner in Ross Street and the stories of a mother who would have been around her own age now. 'From the time I was born, my neighbour Moggy was there. I'd be swinging on the lamp post (or scutting on the back of the coal lorry) and she'd be sitting there at the window, her dog beside her, watching the kids and the people. She had six kids herself and she was left a young widow. She'd wash the dead or anything to earn a shilling to rear them and if she never had a shilling she was always in good form. She'd go around for a few glasses of stout at Corbett's and would come around singing.' Will I end up washing the dead? Mum wondered. Your day will come, my good man, though your words agitate me! Out the door of the church she went, ignoring the Holy Water font.

Mum had planned to find a building near City Hall which housed an old charity Harry had often talked about. She wasn't really sure where she was going or what the future had in store for her and the buffs. Which way should she go? she reflected. What was she to do? How could she cope? She didn't like the predicament and quandary she was in. Where was all the help she needed? Four young teenagers. Four mouths to feed. Four bodies to be clothed and housed!

As she walked up the cobbled Fishamble Street she was reminded of Henry Grattan who was born there. He never gave up his fight for Irish independence, for the country to have its own parliament. He even fought a duel over his principles. As she walked around the corner onto Lower Edward Street, the words of James Clarence Mangan, also born on Fishamble Street, came to mind, 'My Dark Rosaleen, do not sigh, do not weep.' She wiped away the tears that trickled down her cheeks. She thought of Harry again, blew her nose and briskly resumed walking down Lord Edward Street to City Hall, deliberately ignoring the Harding Boys' Home. She hovered outside the Sick and Indigent Roomkeeper's Society. She didn't linger for long, however, and laughed to herself when she saw the name of the location – Palace Street. 'Harry will provide,' she thought, more in hope than belief and hurried back to the Viking Centre via Eustace Street.

Mum suddenly saw a familiar face in the distance, a cousin, one Simon Williams. He had a wind instrument shop beside the Quaker's Meeting House on Eustace Street. She remembered the children used to laughingly call him Slim Sim as he was a stout-looking individual. A character, full of mischief and stories, always huffing and puffing and talking about the kind of work he did, making sure the instruments 'had lots of wind' he used to say. On seeing Annie, he crossed the street. 'I'm just on my way to catch the wind,' he laughed. 'Here, give me your arm, Annie, you look absolutely jaded. Here, take a rest. Look, those hill heels of yours are suicidal on these cobbles. Off with them.' Before Mum could say a word, Slim Sim had her sitting on the steps outside the Quakers, had taken off her shoes and replaced them with another pair.

'What! I can't believe this, Simon. Where did you get these?'

'The Missus. I have just collected them from Clegg's and I knew you had lovely feet like hers, Cinderella.' Mum breathed a sigh of pure relief.

'Do you know, Annie, I was in with the Quakers behind us here only last week, just for a coffee and a chat, and I heard your name being discussed. Not you personally, mind, but your namesake. You won't believe it but they are planning to put a bench in honour of one of your relations in St Stephen's Green.'

This was certainly great news and Annie was somewhat astounded to hear about an unknown famous relation. 'Who? Who?' she wanted to know.

'I think you probably know, though you may have forgotten or not been aware of their work. It's Thomas and Anna Haslam, the suffragettes who fought for women's rights at the turn of the last century. The Quakers knew the full story, and I told them I was related to an Annie Haslam from County Laois who had a mother called Annie Williams who married a Thomas Haslam. They told me to call back later and said they would check it out in the meantime. So back I called and they said that our Annie Haslam, your mother, must have had a connection to Thomas Haslam who also hailed from County

Laois. They said that it was too much of a coincidence having the same name, particularly since most of the Irish Haslam's had settled in Laois. They agreed that you had to be related to these great fighters for women's justice! Next time you are over in the Green, check out your own bench!' and he laughed. 'There's rumours about that the Corpo are planning to erect one there!'

'I always had that feeling,' Annie said thoughtfully, with her shoulders thrown back and life returning to her face. 'I just knew it.' She remembered discussions at home near Clonenagh, when she was a child, about the Quakers of Mountmellick and Portarlington, the latter also known as 'Tanner's Corner'. 'And what a wonderful location for the commemorative bench! I love St Stephen's Green and we bring the children there all the time!' She suddenly grew sad at the word 'we'. She rebounded quickly, however, and smiled. 'Well, what a coincidence, Simon, and I was only thinking as we visited Harry's grave this morning of another heroine who campaigned for equality.'

'Who do you mean?' asked Simon.

'Speranza, of course. She was Oscar Wilde's mother, or as some of the children prefer to call him, Fingal O'Flahertie! His mother was known as Jane Francesca, Lady Wilde, and wrote under the pseudonym of Speranza in that great patriot newspaper, *The Nation*. She was very courageous, and, like the Haslam's, fought for women's suffrage, equality and other rights at a time when women were not even allowed to vote and loads of other things. They weren't really regarded as humans at all, merely slaves of convenience.' Mum was not quite finished. 'I still remember what is carved on her headstone: "Tread lightly, she is near. Under the snow. Speak gently, she can hear, the lilies grow." Now isn't that nice?'

'Yes, very nice indeed,' said Simon.

'I have to meet the buffs over at St Michael's, Simon. Many thanks, you've given me a great lift and you've made my day.' What a transformation. It was as if she had a facelift and hairdo all in one go. Good old Simon, she thought, and hurried along. Wait till the children hear the news! And she realised that they were no longer children.

15

THE VANQUISHED AND THE VIOLINIST

We had a quick snack in the Viking Centre when Mum arrived back. She thought it a complete waste of money eating in such places, but 'needs must,' she said, and smiled at us. We knew we'd be all right and she seemed in good cheer. After much chatter and hearing her adventures, off we marched, reinvigorated. We continued along Essex Street and Temple Bar towards Fleet Street and near our bus stop for home. Freckles kept us amused with stories of Pimping Peg and such matters.

Well, it must be said that 'amused' was not quite the correct word. Freckles has a strange way about him, you see. He had no problem, as a mere teenager, discussing adult matters in front of the rest of us. Worse still, he regarded himself an adult and advised Mum, which I happened to overhear, to discuss 'such matters' with me. Now I knew or at least heard all about 'such matters' from Bernie Bottle Eyes. She was very amenable in 'such matters', including all the introductory offers. Moreover, if we had stayed any longer at the back of the convent wall underneath those stained-glass windows, they would have mistaken us for statues.

Unfortunately for me, Freckles sticking his nose in other people's business resulted in Mum placing certain magazines strategically on the corner of the breakfast room table just before I happened to walk in. Magazines such as *The Messenger*, *Reality* and the *Far East*. I wished I could see Freckles and Daisy packing themselves off to the Far East, that's for sure. I mean, some of these had articles by 'agony aunts' such as Angela MacNamara advising teenagers on this and that. I skimmed through them when no one was about just to make sure I was up to scratch on developments and future options. And they were enhanced further listening to Frankie Byrne on the radio or having a peep through Mum's *Woman's Way* magazine where I discovered Mary Marryat giving lots of interesting advice. She advised, for instance, that a girl wouldn't become pregnant through any kind of kissing. One letter writer wanted to know if her bust would get any bigger.

However, I was just so embarrassed by it all. And now to hear Freckles going on again about Pimping Peg in front of Mum and me there as well. To hear some of the things he came out with. I just spluttered and my hard-earned crisps shot out of my mouth all over the place. 'Are you all right, Larry?' Mum asked. I pretended I was not hearing anything and lingered behind a little, gazing into Rory's Fishing Tackle shop and the Regent's Barber and the old dilapidated buildings around Merchant's Arch. My two ears were, however, keenly listening to everything that was being said. I had an 'inquiring mind' and 'had great potential', a teacher once wrote home on my Christmas Report. Daisy said that read 'a no-hoper'.

As I said, I was absolutely mortified to be in such company when 'such matters' were being discussed. I already had my fill of Darkey Kelly and Molly Malone, another imposter. There were imposters everywhere, it seemed, and Pimping Peg was no exception.

According to Freckles, Pimping Peg was known by this name for 'certain services' she offered the very well-off people in Dublin at the end of the eighteenth century. Fame came at a price, he pointed out, and the bankers, politicians, movers and shakers had to pay this

Pimping Peg person a very high price for the privilege of sitting on the edge of her bed.

'How come she was able to command such high prices?' we wanted to know. 'What was so special about her?'

Seemingly, they all wanted to be with this bottle of perfume, masquerading as a woman. Anyway, Freckles told us a fascinating yet tragic story.

Like my sister and cousin, she was a very independent-minded person. From the age of fifteen (after she became pregnant and was abandoned by her upper-class boyfriend) she continued to mix in upper-class society to ensure her survival. First, she was the 'kept woman' of a succession of wealthy men. Not for her a conventional marriage involving a life of docility and subservience. Echoes of Daisy here, I thought. She met Joseph Leeson, a wealthy English merchant from whom she took her assumed name to enhance her respectability. He was known as 'Game Cock Joe' and later became First Earl of Milltown. Leeson fell for Pimping Peg's charms and put her up in a house in Ranelagh. She was a right one though. While Leeson was away she would sneak her other lover into the house, one Buck Lawless. Leeson finally found out and on discovering her carry-on left her penniless. She later said that she was more 'distressed by the loss of his purse that the loss of his person'. Buck Lawless went on to become her longest boyfriend and they lived together for five years, having five children. However, as ever, tragedy struck: their money eventually ran out, the children died one by one and Lawless absconded for America, leaving Peg heartbroken. Despite that, for social standing purposes, she kept her original 'keeper's' name and so styled herself 'Margaret Leeson'. She never married subsequently but moved through various relationships. She regarded marriage as an unfair contract but accepted the name Leeson to lend her respectability.

Daisy butted in just then, telling us, 'Well isn't that a good one. That's just what I was suggesting back at the Freedom Bell. This Pimping Peg and I have a lot in common.' Well for once I had to agree with Daisy. They had a lot in common. Money-grabbers, users and connivers, with no heart for the poor kind men doing their best for them. All the men wanted were a few kisses. That was not enough, however, for Pimping Peg, or Daisy for that matter.

With the departure of Buck Lawless, Peg returned to a life of prostitution and found that many wealthy men were willing to pay her way. These included a Lord Lieutenant of Ireland, Charles Manners, Fourth Duke of Rutland, known for his convivial nature and ample banquets in Dublin Castle. He insisted on sleeping only with Pimping Peg, swearing he would pay his fortune if only his wife was as good in bed as she was. She had certain standards, however, and refused to have as a client another Lord Lieutenant, John Fane, the Earl of Westmoreland, because of his ill-treatment of his wife. This was becoming an absolute ear opener for me and I could see Daisy' eyes all sparkling and she nearly jumping out of herself with glee.

Pimping Peg wouldn't take any nonsense from the high-and-mighty. When Signor Carnavalli, a celebrated violinist, came to the Smock Alley Theatre to perform Italian operas, he barred certain kinds of people from attending, or as Pimping Peg put it, 'every lady of my description'. She turned up at the theatre nonetheless, took her usual seat, but, on Carnavalli's orders, was unceremoniously thrown out by the doormen. Furious, she got a warrant against them for assault and robbery (for holding the ticket she had paid for) and returned to the theatre with four of the nastiest bailiffs she could find, who then hauled Carnavalli and the doormen off to Newgate prison.

On another occasion, and also in the Smock Alley Theatre, Charles Manners, one of her most important friends, appeared in the regal box at the theatre on the same night that Peg was attending the show. Some characters in the gallery began shouting at her, 'Hey Peg! Who slept with you last night?'

Peg gave them a severe look, threw a quick glance at the Lord Lieutenant and in a scolding tone said, 'Manners, you dogs!'

Daisy screeched with laughter on hearing this. 'Hurrah for Pimping Peg,' she shouted, jumping up and down. 'See! What did I say? We may fly like butterflies but we'll sting like bees.' And you deserve a good box, I thought, meanly.

Daisy, of course, had to get the last word in. 'That's just what I was saying to the rest of them, Auntie, when we were waiting outside the church. Pimping Peg was like the actress in *She Stoops to Conquer*, and maybe Oliver Goldsmith modelled her on Peg. Yes, I think that's exactly what happened. Peg certainly stooped to conquer and she succeeded very well.'

Daisy looked at Minnie. 'When Peg stooped to tie her shoelace, as it were, she, like us all at some stage, couldn't manage it the first or second time, yet she, like us, persisted until she understood the knack of tying the knot, so to speak. To get this knot the way she wanted it, she used that particular talent that nature gave – a broad range of womanly wiles to knot the husband she really wanted.'

'Hang on,' went Minnie. 'Just what do you mean by womanly wiles?' I thought Minnie was getting like Freckles, full of awkward questions.

Freckles, however, took the bait. 'You know, all that blinking of eyes, like there was a fly or something caught in your eyeball, wearing loads of red lipstick, putting stuff like powder rouge on your face to make it look pink instead of ghostly white, smiling like a cat that has just got the cream. All that kind of stuff, but in buckets for the occasion! You know, wearing a mask, like. Eventually you will get what you want.'

'And if you don't, what happens then?' persisted Minnie.

'You do what Pimping Peg did,' added Daisy. 'But this time you get the best to pay the most. Men often prefer to pay for comfort, when they haven't the patience or guile to play the game of life and love. Peg was not one of those wailers who go about whinging "I have to find a man". No way. For her, it was "no man, no cry", but "if he pays, she'll play".'

16

SUNLIGHT SOAP AND THE SWASTIKA STRIKE

We passed the old ruins of Isolde's Tower and stopped near the junction of Essex Gate and Parliament Street, gazing up at the Sunlight Chambers on the corner to our left. Mum paused and looked at the curious eye-catching façade. Underneath the filth and grime, we could still make out the colourful images of men, women and children toiling in the fields and homes. With a terribly sad look of resignation and looking at Daisy and Minnie, she said, 'This is our life.' Two lines of coloured stone in Art Nouveau terracotta/ceramic frieze work, curved around the front of the building, showed the story of hygiene, soap and washing. The beauty and uniqueness of it belied its horrible message. The nice colourful carving was essentially an advertisement in stone for Sunlight Soap, the same as we used at home. The grimy story depicted washing, scrubbing, playing children, filthy men toiling in the fields getting their clothes dirty. Women were shown drawing water from the well, using scrubbing boards and visiting washing rooms, just like the one Dad showed us at the back of the Iveagh Markets. This was the past and the future as depicted in the carvings up high on the wall. It also reminded me of the blocks of Sunlight soap we used at home, with their strong laundry smell.

'Work, work, work. Endless scrubbing of brats, and pots and pans. This is a monument to women's oppression,' remarked comrade Daisy. 'That's all they want us to do, in their nice fancy pictures. Buy lots and lots of soap. But they don't tell us that the soap won't do the job itself! We have to! Well, it's certainly not for me!'

We strolled from Parliament Street and around the corner, over the ragged cobblestones of Essex Street East, and past the Dolphin Hotel. It brought back memories for Mum, as often times Dad and she dined there, in some style, and then rambled up Crane Lane to the Olympia Theatre.

Being Good Friday, the pubs were closed, yet we could detect raucous singing from the back of some ancient closed pub. It might have been the Foggy Dew. I recognised the ballad, 'The Little Old Woman from Wexford'. Faintly the words came through a window, 'There was an old woman who lived in the woods… they took her out, and she got hung… a weela, weela, wileya…' Mum paused and closed her eyes. We felt slight drops of rain, heard the throwing of furniture around in the distant sky, and saw jagged silvery forks dancing in attendance.

Approaching the centre of Temple Bar, flag-waving crowds seemed to seep from all sides as if going somewhere important. Different coloured scarves and hats were in evidence, but predominantly black and white. Mum seemed somewhat alarmed, particularly when we were enveloped in a sea of ruffians. Some of the flag wavers pushed and shoved past us heading towards Merchant's Arch and Mum was struck on the face with one of the flags, with the culprit just laughing and disappearing through the throng. We stood beside her, shocked and trying to help her. This was serious. 'Take me home,' she pleaded.

We continued along the cobblestones, Mum still very distressed as the crowds milled around.

'There were some famous actresses who worked and lived around here, once upon a time,' Daisy said.

Mum agreed in a much stronger voice, glad to have escaped the Tolka mob. She said that Dad and she used to go to the new Theatre Royal over in Hawkins Street many times before and after they got married. But there was an equally famous Theatre Royal once located on the corner of Crow Street many years before the Hawkins Street venue. 'I used to hear your father talking about it and an actress called Peg Woffington, but I never heard the full story.'

'Wasn't she the one who told her boyfriends they could go to Hell?' Daisy suggested, laughing. 'Well, she had some attitude, that's for sure. I heard about her up in the Mountain View Musical Society during a fundraising quiz.'

As we were chatting on the corner, a hippy-looking young lady with jewellery and coloured beads dangling all over her, and with flowing skirt dripping on her sandaled feet, came out of Claddagh Records. 'She looks like she has just come from the Sultan of Turkey's harem,' I whispered to Minnie, remembering Ali Baba stories.

'I heard what you were saying about the old Crow Street Theatre,' she said, 'and Peg Woffington.' 'We were only talking about her recently over in Trinners, when we were studying *Hamlet* and David Garrick and his connection with the Smock Alley Theatre up the street there. The Smock and Crow Street Theatre had huge bad vibes between them and Peg opted to work on the stage in the latter.'

She was 'some tough nut,' confided the student. 'Really way out,' she said in hippy-speak. 'An inspiration for modern girls if you ask me. I'd say she'd be popular with Germaine Greer and Simone what's her name, you know, Sartre's girlfriend. I can't think of her surname. This weed is doing my head in. I must have got some bad grass!' Minnie, Daisy and Mum were intrigued and amused. 'Yes,' continued the self-made cud-chewing hippy, 'she was the famous actress who rose from rags to riches and who told David Garrick that no man was going to direct her – on stage *and* in bed!' She then shrieked into her jumper which had seen better days in Nepal.

Daisy joined the chorus, true to form, and let out an almighty peal of laughter. 'Did you hear that, Auntie, Peg would take no orders from anyone? She sounds like you!'

Dublin Be Damned!

'Get on with you,' Mum replied, trying to deflect. We waved goodbye to our new hippy friend, with me saying 'far out' to her. She replied saying she would love to see me and Jimi on the Isle of Wight, whoever he was, and wherever that was.

Another lady who was not going to be directed was Delia Larkin, Jim's sister, whose union HQ we had just passed, heading for our bus. I had hoped Daisy wouldn't notice the Irish Women Workers' Union sign over the door when passing and distracted the rest of the family by pointing to a plaque on the building opposite. It was Kevin Barry's birthplace at No. 8 Fleet Street.

'Ah, we'll come back to Kevin Barry some other time,' she wickedly responded. 'First, I want to remind you all about the incredible Delia Larkin. What did Jim Larkin famously say?' Daisy asked Freckles, hoping for sheer ignorance.

'I will arise and go now and go to…'

'Getting there,' she conceded.

Before she could utter another word, Mum proudly answered the question. '"The great are great because we are on our knees. Let us arise". I have always liked that,' she admitted, much to our surprise. Yet we liked that she liked that. We smiled and the clouds drifted off towards the Irish Sea.

Daisy, of course, had not quite finished. 'I mentioned at the church about all these liars, yet our friend Delia Larkin also had to deal with them. First of all, her good brother, Jim, had to fight the Vulture of Dartry Hall…' Suddenly we were awake again. We wanted to hear all about vultures. What were they doing flying around Rathgar, down the road from us in Mountain View. I had read about them in the Sahara Desert, waiting for the dying to become rotting corpses in the heat of the day before swooping. Well we were all shocked after hearing her story about William Martin Murphy, a vulture disguised as a person who sucked the blood out of the workers during the 1913 Tram Strike in Dublin. For months and months, he refused to give in to the workers' requests for an extra few bob to feed their families. He sacked them all instead and with all the money, it was rumoured he built a mansion up in Rathgar off Orwell Park. He even built turrets so he would be able to look down on the city on strike, and prepare to dive, like the vulture, so strikers said.

'Did the workers win in the end?' asked Minnie.

'Not really,' said Freckles. 'They had to agree to go back to work, couldn't join a trade union and had to behave themselves and do what they were told.'

'But the bosses got the message loud and clear,' interjected Daisy, always ready to clarify the facts.

'What about Delia?' piped up Minnie, reminding us that she was there.

Daisy took over again. 'Well, with the amazing courage of Delia, the workers of Ireland today, and Uncle Harry, rest in peace, were able to have two weeks' holidays every year, thanks to her going out on strike.'

'What did she do?' Minnie persisted.

'She stopped washing the laundry. That's what she did,' Daisy laughed. 'Wasn't she an absolute genius?'

'But how did people get longer holidays just because she stopped washing dirty laundry?' I asked, beginning to get interested.

'Simple. How would you like to be going around in smelly clothes, although I think you do sometimes?'

Smelly? Me? What a liberty! I think I will go on strike, I thought to myself, picturing pickets and marching up and down outside our house in the cosy cul-de-sac. An all-out strike. No holds barred. Workers of Ireland unite. 'Sorry, comrade, can't pass, an all-out strike here. Exploitation of the masses here, you know. The Vampire of Mountain View has forced this upon us. There she is, called Daisy, peeping out through the curtains and hoping we can't see her! Power to the people!' I thought meanly to myself. 'Come the glorious day, comrade, and you're first to the wall!'

Luckily for me she answered her own question as I pretended to be seriously pondering the gravity on the situation of dirty laundry. 'Quite simple,' she emphasised, and we heard the full story of Delia Larkin, the nearly forgotten sister of a famous brother. 'Where is her statue?' shouted Daisy, getting all angry again. 'Well good old Jim has a statue in O'Connell Street, but the powers that be ran out of blocks and mortar and couldn't do one of Delia. Otherwise they would doubtlessly have built one,' says she venomously.

'There, there, Daisy. Don't get too worked up about statues,' went Mum. 'Take heart that Delia was probably delighted that in 1925 Oonagh Keogh became the first woman in the world to be admitted to a Stock Exchange, and that exchange is just up the road there on the right-hand side of Anglesea Street.' See, Mum had a way with her. Daisy relented.

A cheerful bedraggled wino went staggering past, talking to himself. Suddenly he stopped, right in front of us, and roared at Mum. 'Here you, Missus, you look in bits. Take a swig out of this,' and he shoved his bottle of wine into her face, splashing some over her. Mum, calm and collected as always, remained nonplussed, while Daisy, with a shriek, told him to be off with himself or suffer the consequences. He laughed heartily and staggered on, singing 'Alive Alive Oh, Alive Alive Oh.' Mum was tiring. Home with us then on the bus quietly singing 'Kevin Barry' who '…gave his young life for the cause of liberty…'

17

PILLOW TALK AND PIANO MARY

'We're going to visit Uncle Jack today,' Mum informed us one sunny morning during the school holidays, a few weeks later. Well, not exactly just him. A few more uncles and aunts, including our favourites, the hilarious and outrageously dressed Auntie Aggie and Auntie May who had been with the Royalettes in the Theatre Royal years previously. Mum's old friend and former army chaplain, from her nursing days, Father O'Byrne, was also going to be there. All very secretive as far as we were concerned. Uncle Jack lived just off Gardiner Street and around the corner from World's End Lane in the heart of Monto. World's End Lane was the first name of the street, which was always having its name changed, including to Montgomery Street, and hence the name 'Monto', before eventually becoming Foley Street. Many of the older residents still used its original name.

The notorious Monto area, a mere square mile of streets, was within that part of Dublin bounded by Talbot Street, Amiens Street (near the Five Lamps and Connolly Station), Buckingham Street, Sean McDermott Street (formerly Gloucester Street) and Lower Gardiner

Street. In its heart was the Gloucester Diamond, which got its name from the diamond-shaped intersection at Gloucester Place and Gloucester Street. Colloquially, 'The Diamond' referred not just to Gloucester Place but an entire area surrounding it. So, people still liked to say they were from the Diamond. All these name changes and aliases were very confusing for us. So, you might say you are from the Diamond, but maybe not from Monto, although the Diamond was in Monto!

Foley Street, which ran parallel to Talbot Street, was called after the sculptor, John Henry Foley, who designed the Daniel O'Connell monument on O'Connell Street. This street, and an adjoining street now called Railway Street but originally Mecklenburgh Street, was the very heart of this disreputable district called Monto. Some of the few names that have survived from the heyday of the Monto era included Beaver Street and Mabbot Lane. Bella Street and Bella Avenue off Buckingham Street were called after the Madam of them all, Bella Cohen. Monto was in a great location to attract customers for certain services, being near Aldborough Barracks, Amiens Street train station, the Dublin docks and Sackville (now O'Connell) Street.

So here we were, at World End's Lane, visiting Mum's in-laws and Father O'Byrne, for some unknown reason. Uncle Jack was a widower, having lost his young wife just a few years earlier. His wife had been Mum's younger sister, Lily, her bridesmaid. Naturally enough, he was devastated and his life and thriving medical parts business went completely downhill since. That was the reason why he was living in a flat in Monto, having lived in fine houses over the years elsewhere in Dublin.

Being avid readers of all sorts of mystery and murder stories, we had our suspicions about the visit. Number one of these was a marriage proposal, which she had presumably considered, given each family's circumstances and which seemed to coalesce following Dad's untimely death. We had heard them chatting along such lines in the front seats of his car, a Volkswagen Beetle, with him proposing in a casual joking fashion, but totally serious. We were in the back, not listening but hearing it all. It was difficult to know when Uncle Jack was sober or not sober. He was never obstreperous, always garrulous and laughing. Sometimes when he came to visit us, he would drop his children off at our house and would disappear for hours into the Bottle Tower up the road or the Beggars' Bush down the road. He always seemed very relaxed and walked around with his hands constantly dug into his pockets, jingling change. He was a short, stocky man, and had the appearance of a retired American millionaire – bright jackets and huge, baggy beige trousers as befitting his bulk. Unlike most Irish people, he never wore dark clothes. His had been a very happy, if short-lived marriage. He was left with two young boys around our ages.

He loved motorbikes and regaled us with stories of his younger days, particularly when courting. We found it quite funny to hear that he used to tear up and down the roads and mountains of Ireland, with his girlfriend, our aunt, on the back. As a wind-cheater, he would have masses of newspapers under his coat, protecting him from the chilling winds. We imagined the newspapers fluttering around him as he took a corner or went hurtling down a hill. How would one arrange newspapers around one's body? All very odd, we thought. Yet, we liked him very much and he was good to us as children, particularly after the death of Dad. He was quite charming with lots of jokes and laughter and had nicknames like 'Beelzebub' or 'Rat tat tat' or 'Moppy' for us. He regularly drove all the way in to us, and off to the Bog of Allen, Silver Strand, Donabate, Wicklow, everywhere. Six young teens (including his own two) and two adults squashed into a Volkswagen Beetle – two of us sat on a ledge, just inches above the engine, which was underneath and behind the back seat. That was the Uncle Jack we were going to visit.

We got off the bus at Nelson's Pillar and Uncle Jack's was less than ten minutes away down by Talbot Street. We passed Guiney's Department Store and all the old pubs where smoke and drink competed with cheap perfume, and raucous laughter came from everywhere. Uncle Jack had a two-roomed flat in a big four-storey Georgian house that had seen better days. Faded carpets and linoleum, practically worn away, revealed old floorboards. Greasy fly-covered bulbs with dust-covered shades swayed ominously over the stairs and landings. Wallpaper, once cream-coloured and patterned, was now grimy and blackened, only the top part betraying an original colour. The flat was little better; dark, gloomy and untidy, like a jungle. Clothes strewn about, dishes unwashed, smells from hell, with not a schoolbook or schoolbag in sight. Uncle Jack sat just gazing at the TV, a permanent fixture in the enormous armchair, itself dwarfed by the high ceiling and huge windows. Yet we always knew to expect adventure when we visited.

After tea and sticky buns, Mum suggested that while she, the relations and Father O'Byrne chatted, we should take us for a stroll to the park on the square with our other cousins, Mossy and Maybe. The latter could never make up his mind and hence the name. Always whinging and whining and wiping his nose on his sleeve. He had a thing about Tina Turner and told us he just loved 'Nutbush City Limits'. He was also a great fan of Mary Poppins, even going so far as to try and emulate her amazing feat at the end of the film, where she took off into the skies with the help of an umbrella and everyone singing, 'Let's go fly a kite, up to the highest height...' Luckily, he had a soft landing from a haybarn roof onto a rick of hay. Despite that we liked our cousins. We didn't mind that they had a bad influence on us, just temporary of course, as they were quite wild, and we had great potential.

We all bounced down the stairs anticipating adventure. Mossy shouted 'howya' to a haggard-looking girl climbing the stairs. 'That's Lollie,' he told us. 'Always coming and going at odd hours and bringing new boyfriends up to her room.' Just outside, I remembered my cap and while the others waited, flew back up the stairs. Coming down again I saw this haggard-looking young lady who was on the way up. I stood on a landing for her to pass.

'Do you know what?' she slurred, looking right at me. 'Do you know what? Sex is violent whether for love or money, in love or in war!' This was followed with a long deep sigh.

'I couldn't agree more,' was my reply. 'In fact, it is an absolute disgrace.' Before she could get a word in edgeways, which would have been difficult anyway, given her wobbly state, I said, 'There was I, with these two country girls, in and out, backwards and forwards, up and down, doing my utmost to keep to the rhythm. Going like the clappers and me pores pumping. And guess what?' I continued as she peered closer at me. 'I ended up bruised all over.'

'Why's that?'

'Those girls had two left feet and hadn't a clue about sets,' I said, remembering my recent set-dancing carry-on in the Gaeltacht, my first and definitely last time going there.

Grabbing hold of the bannisters after a number of attempts, she bent down in front of me and slowly, very slowly, prised off her high heels. I gasped. Seeing and believing. My face reddened, thinking she was going to continue undressing right there. She swayed back up and started laughing, a real smoker and drinker's rasping, phlegmy laugh. 'You're a hoot,' she went, laughing, falling backwards and again grabbing the bannisters. She leant back, tilting dangerously so, still laughing and swearing, and then flipped over, legs everywhere and down. I had heard about someone having the last laugh. I moved towards the stairs and met her staggering back up. 'I'm off, just off,' she hiccupped, slightly sobered and slightly battered. A baby's pram in the hall had broken her fall, though I wasn't sure if there was a baby in it or not. I glanced in as I passed through the hall door. Two marbles stared at me from a pancake.

Back outside, Mossy told us all about the War of Independence in Monto, informers, the Cairo Gang and Shanahan's pub, where Michael Collins hid out and used to have secret meetings.

'What were they doing here coming all the way from Egypt?' asked Minnie.

'They were desperate secret agents that had worked previously in Cairo doing the government's dirty work for them before they came to Dublin to do more of the same. But Michael Collins got rid of them all one night while they were sleeping in their beds! In fact,' Mossy continued, 'there is a strong belief in Monto to this day that the War of Independence was won because of Monto. Not only did the Big Fella have lots of his important meetings here – the Black and Tans were afraid of the area – but because of all the pillow talk they managed to get lots of information, guns and uniforms from the enemy!'

'What's all this "pillow talk" business?' Minnie wanted to know.

'It was when the Tommy's were full of drink and chatting to the girls on their beds at night that they passed on secret information. The girls then passed it on to Michael Collins and the boys, many of them paid assassins who were called the Twelve Apostles.' Mossy seemed to be well-informed and he also told us lots of stories about 'informers and spies' who hid out in the area.

Minnie wanted to know why it was called a 'red light' district. Good for Mossy as he knew the answer. He said that long ago all the miners used to carry red lanterns when coming up from the mines, all worn out. All they wanted to do was just have a chat with some nice ladies. The nice ladies always obliged and the miners left their red lanterns outside the girls' houses. Mossy then paused. 'Listen to this. There is an old Dublin street song that children around here used as a skipping rhyme and some of them still sing it as I've heard it a few times since we moved here.'

> Down in Mabbot Lane lives a big fat lady.
>
> If you want to know her name, you have to pay a shilling.
>
> Soldiers two and six, sailors two a penny.
>
> Big fat men, two pounds ten. Little kids a penny.

He told us how he has a feeling it was still going on as before, despite the Corpo making a big 'hush hush' about it. 'Lily of the Lamplight was a famous girl who used to walk the streets here,' he said. We also heard how all these girls all made pots of money just sitting around, drinking, laughing, singing and chatting. He said that people didn't know the half about James Joyce and his writings, where and how he got his ideas. This is getting all confusing, I thought.

Only Daisy seemed to know about James Joyce. 'A famous Irish writer who went to school in Belvedere College not too far from here,' she told us. 'When he was in school he used to go on the mitch and come here to Monto to chat to the brazen hussies.'

Maybe sniggered when he heard them called 'brazen hussies'.

'What's that?' Minnie asked.

'Close your ears,' ordered Daisy. 'And you,' looking at Maybe, 'rinse out your mouth with soap the minute you get home.' Of course, Bossy Boots knew everything. 'They are girls that wear loads of bright red lipstick and plaster paint on their faces and get big fat men to sit on their laps and pay them money. Fat men with cow dung on their boots or reeking of rotten fish,' she emphasised. 'And they went around on high heels, smoking and drinking, walking up and down O'Connell Street and Grafton Street, saying rude things to passers-by.'

'Like what?' persisted Minnie, dying to know.

'Like, psst, psst and…'

'Ah, you're telling us all fibs,' was Minnie's reaction.

Daisy was not amused and stared at Minnie. 'All these fibs are absolutely true,' she insisted. 'And I'll tell you something. I had heard about the priests in the Pro-Cathedral reading James Joyce off from the altar.'

'Why did they read James Joyce from the altar then if they didn't like him?' queried Minnie.

'Who is this Joyce chap?' she persisted.

'Ah, he's the chap that wrote a book like *Around the World in Eighty Days* and never came back,' went the Luke Kelly lookalike. Real smart like.

'No, no, no!' said an irritated Daisy. 'That was Jules Verne. You, Freckles, don't be putting the wrong ideas into their heads. Joyce wrote about one day in the life of a man name Leopold Bloom and all the adventures he had when he was doing his business in Dublin. Hear this as well. Joyce had Leopold Bloom living near Emmet Bridge on Clanbrassil Street. So, ignore all Freckles' nonsense, Minnie. Joyce was read from the altar, which means he was criticised because they didn't like what he wrote about meeting bold girls.'

'Yeah,' chipped in Freckles, determined to make amends. 'He created a real stink with his former teachers in Belvedere College because he wrote about coming here to Monto and chatting up all the Lillies and Lollies. They really hated him for that because he used to sneak out from school and come over here. Then he sneaked back and wrote all about what he had seen and done. Oh, yes, he was in big trouble, he was.'

'And, guess what,' interjected Mossy, us nearly forgetting his story, 'this place is full of Monto babies! Why do you think that the two most popular names here are Tommy, Albie, Vicky and Eddie?' He glanced knowingly at Minnie and I, and we tried to look back knowingly, failing miserably.

What we didn't hear that afternoon: we were shocked to hear about kings, princes and the well-to-do coming to Monto via secret underground passages. Mossy brought us down into the basement of an old abandoned house and showed us these passages. He said they linked Monto via Talbot Street to the Custom House, where the important people used to disembark from their private boats and come to see the Madams in the 'flash' houses who were in charge of the chat girls. He said that thanks to King Edward, it is said that many of the local children have blue blood running through their veins and are really princes and princesses! We asked Freckles to show us his hands. We knew from the look of his bony fingers that he did not have a drop of blue blood. Then we heard all about the concrete-faced Madams and bully boys. We just lapped it all up. Before long we were all singing 'Take her up to Monto, Monto, Monto. Take her up to Monto, langeroo, to you!' We barely knew what it meant but sang it anyway. The Dubliners were always singing it, so why not us too!

Coming around the corner from Gardiner Street we approached the 27 Steps at the Gloucester Diamond. Minnie, Freckles and I wanted to race up and down the steps when Mossy got an idea. 'How about hearing some old stories about Monto from a chap who actually grew up here and knows a lot of the characters that worked and lived here, including Crusher and Dizzy?'

'Lead on, Mossy,' we said, 'but first we want to do the 27 Steps,' and before he could say another word we were racing and chasing up the steps. After a breath-taking fifteen minutes of flying up and down we finally calmed down and away with us up Corporation Street and then down Foley Street. Mossy brought us to the flat of Razor Ryan, who welcomed us in, sat us down by the fire, gave us some Gur cake and regaled us with his reminiscences of the area where he grew up. He was an elderly man, though still muscular and tough-looking from his days as a docker. We could guess why he was called 'Razor', what with all the scars on his gnarled face and half his teeth missing. We are somewhat in awe of him and remained near the door.

Razor told us the name 'Monto' came from Elizabeth Montgomery, a well-to do lady married into the Gardiner family who built many of the fine Georgian squares and streets in the area. 'But with all the name changes over the years, not only were visitors and the customers confused, but so were the residents!' he laughed.

'How did it all begin?' Freckles wanted to know.

'For two reasons,' was the answer. Monto started thriving slowly in the decades after 1800, firstly, because Hell in the vicinity of Christ Church Cathedral was being bulldozed by the Corporation, with all the old lanes and alleyways obliterated. They wanted Dublin to be full of wide streets so that traffic would flow easily. 'That old street, Exchequer Street, though, which was also full of 'shady houses' managed to escape', Razor noted. Secondly, with the *Act of Union* which came into effect on 1st January 1801, 'as we say here, "the rich marched out and the poor marched in." The well-to-do hob-nobs decided that henceforth London was the place to be, since Dublin was no longer to have its own Parliament.' 'Bear in mind,' continued Razor, 'at one time this district was very fashionable with many grand houses. Like all those lovely houses on Merrion Square, Stephen's Green, Parnell or Fitzwilliam Square. Just imagine only one family staying in the whole house, and not being in flats and tenements like now!'

Throughout the nineteenth century and early twentieth century, until the 1920s, the 'powers that be' turned a blind eye to the goings-on, so long as it remained in the Monto area and did not spread like a disease elsewhere. Consequently, the red-light district of Monto not only prospered but was renowned by soldiers, seamen, medical students, politicians, race-goers, cattle dealers and all and sundry.

Drinking and prostitution was tolerated on a twenty-four-hour basis. Anyone could open a brothel and this was compounded by the very important fact that there was no legislation in Ireland outlawing the burgeoning business. They said, 'Ah, well, it's the oldest profession in the world, it's too late to do anything about it now. We'll just put up with it so long as it stays out of sight.'

However, despite that, Razor said that without certain classes of customers Monto would not have existed. One of the main reasons for its survival was the thousands of British soldiers based in Ireland, acting as the garrison, holding the fort for England here, as it were, but also coming and going to wars in Europe, from the Crimean to the First World War. This situation lasted until after the War of Independence and the evacuation of British soldiers back to Britain. 'The soldiers marched out and the Legion of Mary marched in – the party was over! And it was downhill from then onwards.' Razor found this very funny.

Razor knew the names of some of the old Madams like the back of his hand. He rhymed off the principal Madams that included Nora Seymour, Teasey Ward, Liverpool Kate, Mrs Mack, Meg or Maggie Arnott, Lizzie Arnold, Maria Lynam, Mrs Meehan, Bella Cohen (called a 'massive whore-mistress' by Joyce), May Oblong and Becky Cooper. 'Some of the Madams of Monto were larger-than-life characters,' he told us. One owned thirteen brothels and was a formidable woman, both physically and in personality. They also had 'fancy men' or pimps such as Crusher Kelly or Dizzy Johnston (who was regarded as being mad) to protect their business. Perhaps the most feared of all the Madams was May Roberts, a tall and broad woman better known as Madam Oblong. She was noted for her cameo earrings and her vivid facial make-up. One risked one's life if you crossed swords with her – she always had a bacon knife near at hand!

Another infamous Madam was Mrs Mack. Reputed to be an extremely greedy woman, Mrs Mack was so well known that the whole area was sometimes called 'Mackstown', such was her influence and control in Monto. The medical students of Dublin had a bawdy song that began:

Dublin Be Damned!

> O there goes Mrs Mack; she keeps a house of imprudence.
>
> She keeps an old back parlour, for us poxy medical students.

Oliver St John Gogarty was one of those medical students and a friend of James Joyce, both regulars in Monto. He once described this famous Madam as the owner of 'a brick red face on which avarice was written and she had a laugh like a guffaw in hell.' Another Madam, Becky Cooper, was also celebrated:

> Italy's maids are fair to see, and France's maids are willing,
>
> But less expensive 'tis to me: Becky's for a shilling.

Razor was great for these rhymes. 'Not great at all,' he replied. 'We heard them all the time here growing up, so we did.'

For all the condemnation of their occupation, the girls who walked the streets were generally considered to be decent, unfortunate and kind, forced into a life on the streets through circumstance; quite a number ended up in penitentiaries or Magdalen Laundries, like the one on Gloucester Street overlooking Monto. The younger ladies were generally pretty, well-dressed, mostly didn't drink, whereas the more experienced ladies had a battered look to them from being on the streets every day for years. Traces of young beauty might still linger but their eyes would have a wretched and melancholic look. They would have aged long before their time. Often, they would have made themselves deliberately drunk each day as a preparation for their street life. Black eyes, broken arms and sleeping in doorways were a regular feature in Monto. All this was ignored by the authorities. Some prostitutes were even murdered, including Harriet Butler, Honor Bright and a number of others.

Razor recounted how some of the girls who became pregnant were tossed out on the street by the Madams. Despite that, the local women looked after them. Oftentimes as they huddled and sheltered in tenement doorways, locals brought them tea in 'tenement china', the name given for a jam jar of tea. Some of the girls would leave their babies with the local women, promising to return. Most never did and these new-borns were known as 'Monto babies', and it was not unknown for some of them to have Royal features, mannerisms and characteristics in later years. Sometimes the mothers would return at Christmas and give out presents to the children.

'What did I tell ye?' went Mossy. 'Didn't I mention that the place was full of Monto babies now grown up and they all look like kings and queens?'

We liked some of the names used by the popular prostitutes, which Razor said had not been forgotten from the old days of Monto. Fresh Nellie, Connemara Maggie, Minnie Maypother, Fleury Crawford, Irish Nanny, Beautiful Nelly, Manchester May, Lottie L' Estrange (who pushed a soldier into Spencer Dock), Cork Annie, Lady Limerick, Julia Rice, Aunt Betty or Lady Betty, Maggie Ballard, Meena La Bloom, and the Goofy One, were just some of the names he remembered. One of the Monto ladies, Maggie Ballard, was known as the 'Queen of the Spunkers' and she had been over twenty years in the area. 'Spunk' was a slang expression at the time for methylated spirits and many of the ladies drank it because it was cheap and an easy way to stay drunk by just adding water every so often. 'To see them standing around together passing around the meths was like watching a witches Sabbath,' Razor had heard it being said by Frank Duff of the Legion of Mary.

Piano Mary was another well-known prostitute. She acquired this name from a habit of running her fingers up and down the spine of a customer while they were in bed. Kitty D., a local girl, was regarded as a particular beauty with long black hair down her back. Another figure in the area was Lily of the Lamplight, such was her custom to always tout for business under a street lamp.

Razor was warming to his story. 'These days we have many people coming to Monto to see the place where that little aul whoremaster, James Joyce, wrote about.' We were a bit shocked to hear his intemperate language to describe James Joyce. 'I can read your minds. But that's what he was. He came in here, had a good time and then went off and wrote about it and it made him famous. What about the girls he used and abused, I ask you? They made him famous and where did they end up. In the Joy, or a pauper's grave in Glasnevin or in the Magdalen

Laundry. And that's a fact, I'll have yez know.' You could see he was getting hot under the collar at this stage.

As we were listening to all this, I could see that Daisy was becoming redder in the face. Not from blushing, which I nearly was, hearing all about 'such matters'. She was 'hopping mad,' she told us, 'at the cheek of James Joyce to go about passing himself off as a great writer while all along he was nothing but a little whoremaster as Razor said.'

'Hear, hear,' chimed in Minnie.

I thought I better approve whatever she was gassing on about. 'There, there,' I said, and was met with disapproving glances.

After hearing all these shocking and revealing stories about kings, princes, madams, pianos and bone crushers, we were speechless but in total awe. Giving our thanks and saying our goodbyes to Razor, we decided to go back to Uncle Jack's. The cousins, however, saw some friends from the Diamond and headed off for a game of football, while Daisy and the rest of us continued the walk back to the house.

'I know there's something up,' she suddenly said. 'I know what this is all about. Auntie is going to marry Uncle Jack and that is why we are all over here together today and that's why she told us to go for a walk.'

'I think she is going to become a Madam and Uncle Jack will be her Crusher Kelly,' I said.

'No,' said Freckles. 'I'd say she is going to pack you lot into the laundry and then marry Uncle Jack. Hang on a minute,' he suddenly said, 'I see Auntie over there.' She was talking to a tall and severe looking lady and they were both gesticulating.

'Quick,' said Daisy, 'hide here so she won't see us.'

It must have been the longest five minutes in our lives but eventually Mum hurried herself off in the direction of a building across the road from Sean Mac Dermott Street Church. She went through a door beside a shop with Mattress Mick's emblazoned over it. 'That's the Magdalen Laundry, I think,' whispered Daisy. 'That's where all the brazen hussies end up, washing and scrubbing other people's clothes. This is a terrible place. Auntie shouldn't be bringing us here with all these buildings falling down and children going around half-dressed.'

We were really dumbfounded by all this intrigue and strange goings on. 'What on earth is she up to?' wondered Minnie out loud as we trudged back to Uncle Jack's.

'Time for home,' Mum said, no sooner had she returned. 'Goodbye all, will be in touch,' she said, brushing her hair and touching up her red lipstick in the hall mirror. Just like Lily of the Lamplight, I thought.

By the time we were leaving Monto there was no doubt that she was somehow changed. She had taken on a new look. Gone was that look of sadness, dejection and resignation and instead there was a look of determination on her face. Her eyes were bright, her face had colour, shoulders thrown back, head held up high. She looked like she had sprung up from one of Mattress Mick's best sprung mattresses. She had a spring in her step as we walked briskly to our bus stop on O'Connell Street.

'I'm going to become a Madam,' she suddenly said, laughing. All except Daisy, we were shocked and horrified. In the space of a few seconds we went from redskins to palefaces and back again. Daisy just looked at us and nodded.

'What did I say!' whispered Minnie to me. 'I just knew we came to Monto for a reason. And I don't like this.'

Mum looked almost pleased. 'At the weekend, we are going the National Gallery to see my favourite painting,' she informed us.

18

THE 40 FOOT AND SWIMMING AGAINST THE TIDE

That weekend couldn't come quick enough for us. There was just one question foremost in our fevered minds. What was going to happen to us? On that Saturday morning, we went with Mum to the National Gallery on Merrion Square to see Jack B. Yeats's painting *The Liffey Swim*. Mr Yeats lived his last days in Portobello Nursing Home, and Mum knew some of the nurses looking after him. She used to meet them in Findlater's shop in Rathmines before we were born. She liked to hear about his progress, and that he was still sketching even though he was unwell. Before Dad died we were regulars in the gallery and he had known the Director, James White. I always thought that his name was very appropriate for one running a picture gallery. A blank canvass waiting for the brushes and colours. One day when he was chatting to Dad, we overheard him mentioning something about 'taking pictures'.

'Great!' shouted a very young Minnie and off with her. We found her half an hour later, sitting on the floor, with a small stash of priceless paintings around her.

Dublin Be Damned!

For some reason, Mum wanted to revisit this particular painting. She sat in front of it and gazed. The annual race was from Victoria Quay to Butt Bridge, a distance of one and a half miles. It usually took place after work in the evenings. Dad seemed to glide through the Liffey waves almost effortlessly yet she could see from his eyes, chin, shoulder and arm muscles that he was fighting and working his way through the choppy waves and against the incoming tide as he neared O'Connell Bridge and towards the finishing line. She could also see his bright face and sparkling eyes looking towards the tram. There she was, on the lower deck, leaning forward and craning her neck to see. She was beside a woman with a huge, broad hat. She was looking directly at him. Mum let out a deep sigh. You could see her starting to relax on the one hand while gazing at the painting, but on the other her eyes were working overtime. She was finding a deeper relevance and resonance. We decided to leave Mum to her thoughts and rambled off to explore by ourselves.

I was distracted rambling around the gallery and thinking of Dad and another place he loved to swim – the Forty Foot Gentlemen's Bathing Place at Sandycove. This was, as in the case of the Liffey Swim, strictly confined to men. Women swimming in such public places, on view to all, offended modesty, which had to be safeguarded, according to those who knew all about these matters.

On one visit to the Forty Foot, Dad was thrown on to the rocks and sustained a burst appendix, yet he still managed to swim to shore. The Forty Foot was very popular with Dubliners because no matter what time of the day or night you visited, despite the ebbing and flowing of the tide twice a day, you would always be able to have a swim there, unlike most other beaches because of the permanent deep water. It was often quite choppy and it was more of a swimming spot for hardened swimmers than a beach. Any sunbathing was done on a small patch of flattened rocks between the entrance and the sea, or else on the surrounding rocks overlooking the swimming area. Much to the annoyance of the regulars, Mum chose to ignore the 'Men Only' sign and used to go in with Dad and sit on the rocks while he swam. She used to tell the curmudgeons that as a nurse there was nothing she hadn't seen before and laughed. 'Anyway,' she went, 'aren't you lucky to have an SRN on duty!'

The name of the bathing spot is said by some to have derived not from the depth of the water but from the fact that the 42nd Highland Regiment of Foot was based at the nearby Martello Tower during the French Revolutionary Wars. From the end of the eighteenth century onwards, the English government was afraid the French would invade their country through a back door – Ireland – and so they built all these Martello Towers with their cannon guns along the east coast to repel any possible invasion. Dad said the only invasion that ever occurred in the area was that of jellyfish, some of which were known as Portuguese man o' war and gave a terrible sting!

That evening Mum called a meeting in the dining room – the very room in which Dad had his first heart attack and from where he was taken by ambulance to hospital, never to come home again. The curtains were drawn closed tightly. She was still wearing black. I started to wonder with trepidation what could be in store for us. The rest were the same. We were not chatting among ourselves. Over and after Christmas we had overheard various conversations from relations and some of our cousins had told us what the adults were talking about on the matter of our future as a family. The parish priest had called and we overheard the word 'orphanage' mentioned. He said that Mum 'couldn't possibly cope with four children' and 'the cousins should be sent back…'. Voices were raised and he left the house looking very vexed, ignoring the sad-faced children standing in a line in the hallway. And there was an orphanage not too far from us, in St Mary's, where the girls looked somewhat on the wan side, except one or two. I had visions of myself marching around Croke Park with the Artane Boys' Band, dressed in an orange pleated skirt called a 'kilt', playing misery music and banging a drum to the words of 'Sinne Fianna Fáil' and everyone sitting down before we had even finished. And there were suggestions that Mum should go back to her nursing career. We also knew about Uncle Jack and his hopes. Mossy and Maybe had confirmed that to us not only on our recent trip to Monto but also down on the farm in Clonenagh. On one occasion when we were digging coins into St Fintan's Wishing Tree, which was up the road from the farm and between two ancient graveyards on the road to Mountrath, Mossy said that it looked as if we would all be living together. We had mixed feelings on that.

Certainly, there were choices. People would not have been surprised if she had placed us in orphanages. How could she possibly look after four children on her own? If she intended to mind them at home, the State Widow's Pension would be derisory in relation to her needs. Well, when the issue arose as in our case, what Daisy had said to us about priests, politicians and lawyers proved to be correct. They were all 'liars' she had told us. 'Promises, promises and more promises.' Mum could marry Uncle Jack. There could be problems, however, with that option, not least his own. And Mum would be in a worse predicament having to look after six children. She would become a slave and effectively some kind of kept woman like Pimping Peg or Peg Woffington. What a raw deal! Was Mum going to become a Madam like the ones we had heard about in Monto? Would she end up with a brick-red face and have a guffaw from Hell? All these thoughts raced through my mind.

We hadn't reckoned on Mum's decision. She told us that she had come to the conclusion that the only person able and willing to look after us was herself. We breathed a sigh of relief. However, for this to happen she had decided to become a businesswoman and rent out some of the rooms in our house. We were going to stand on our own ground and on our own two feet, she told us. This would require an 'all hands-on deck' approach and she asked us if we were willing to roll up our sleeves. We were absolutely delighted and all gathered around and hugged her. We were just so happy. Mum had no intention of anchoring herself in the past or to anyone or anything. She decided to refuse the offer of marriage, refuse to go to work, refuse to place her two children and the two cousins in orphanages and the Artane Industrial School, and refuse to listen to any more bad advice. She was going into the accommodation business, as a landlady. Our worst fears of her becoming a Madam were allayed. Moreover, this was an exciting new adventure with new people moving into the house into bedsitting rooms, or 'bedsits' as they were known. Mum said we had to move as fast as possible to get the business up and running. 'A matter of weeks,' she said.

Freckles and Daisy, delighted not to be going back to Limerick or anywhere else, got stuck into painting and decorating. Mum organised for the gas company to install gas fires, cookers and meters and for the ESB to sort out the extra wiring needed. A plumber was called to install wash hand basins. The tenants would share the bathroom with us. I was appointed as floor painter and given a tin of dark brown/ black 'stain' to paint the area surrounding the large linoleums. We converted our former large sitting room and dining room into two completely self-contained bedsits. Upstairs, two bedrooms were converted into a two-roomed flat.

Mum called into Christy Bird's at Portobello Bridge and Mattress Mick's in town. Both are legends, the former for second-hand furniture and the latter for divan beds and mattresses. Mattress Mick was a great character, looking like a cross between Gene Wilder in *Young Frankenstein* and Slade's Noddy Holder, wishing a Merry Christmas to everybody. On his skull was a massive crown of frizzled wild hair, topped with a bushman's hat. He was immensely proud of his hair. He had a handkerchief sticking out of his blazer's breast pocket. His eyes darted everywhere behind huge spectacles. His teeth seemed to be battling each other trying to find room to grow. He had 'mattresses' running up and down outside his shop, enticing and cajoling potential customers. 'Get your best sprung mattress here,' the humans hidden inside the mattresses shouted. 'For the sleep of your dreams, try our springs!' His attitude underpinning his business was that 'everyone has to go to bed!' He lay on the mattresses Mum was interested in, just to prove a point. Mum bought loads of beds and furniture and had them delivered by van. While they were doing that, I was down on my knees painting the doors and cleaning the windows, slaving as usual.

I was sent into town on my bike to the offices of the *Evening Press* to place an ad for three nights. The paper promoted itself as the 'best for small ads'. I felt very important doing business at the main counter and seeing all the bustle of activity around me. We had to try and fit as many words as possible into as little space as possible as we paid for every word. Our ad eventually ran:

> Mountain View Villas – Beautiful large double bed/sitting room on ground floor level. Divan beds with spring interior mattresses, large gas fire and easily cleaned breakfast cooker, own meter. Everything supplied except linen. Free electric light, hot water. To be seen any evening between 7 and 9 p.m. or afternoon 3 to 5 p.m.

The *Evening Press* was indeed the best for small ads as rarely did we not have tenants. Saying that, we did have a few cold winters over the years when we had empty rooms. Luckily it was seldom that all the rooms were vacant at the same time. On those occasions, cold winds seemed to be blowing from everywhere, yet Mum kept the ship on an even keel. She stretched every penny and eventually we had more tenants. Most times there were eleven or twelve people staying in the house, including us four children, all sharing one bathroom minus a shower.

With the arrival of tenants, usually five – two in each of the two bedsits, one having a two-roomed flat upstairs – space was always going to be an issue. The house was nine-roomed, and the five of us in the family therefore had three bedrooms between us. A small bedroom on the first floor, next to the bathroom, was to be the boys' room, with a bunkbed. The girls had too had bunks in a small room, and Mum had her own room.

To some extent we enjoyed having tenants in our house, although there were frequent problems. First and foremost was the reaction of many of the neighbours. They strongly objected to Mountain View turning into 'Flatland' or 'bedsit land' like Rathmines. This objection was expressed verbally and non-verbally, as in holding their noses and directing their heads elsewhere when they walked past.

Then there were the tenants that absconded, owing rent and other bills. Furniture and facilities were invariably damaged or made unworkable. Not all the tenants were suitable and in one case we found a cache of bullets under the floorboards after one tenant evacuated fairly quickly! Moreover, some tenants didn't like sharing the house with the landlady and/or her children so we had a high turnover, with many only staying a few months. This would increase our workload, not to mention having to place more expensive ads in the *Evening Press*.

There was often drama. One incident was when a tenant called Hans, a student who had told us he was from Heidelberg. He liked to call himself 'Rock', dressed very sharply, was always combing his hair and liked to check himself into the hall mirror at every opportunity. On one occasion he decided to test his poker face skills on another of our tenants, who also prided himself on his poker face. Well, the two poker faces spent the whole evening looking at each other's poker face and trying to best each other. They both looked like Jackie Gleason in *The Hustler*; hair greased back, waistcoats, cigarettes dangling from the sides of their mouths in a smoke-filled room. Unfortunately for us, Hans played like Paul Newman and had cleaned Jackie Gleason out by breakfast time the next day. There was uproar in the house as the tenant admitted he had no rent money for a month. He later told us the house had changed hands a few times overnight!

We had some kind-hearted tenants. One husband and wife let us into their bedsit to watch *The Riordans* and the *Sunday Matinee* with Walt Disney. Since we didn't have our own TV we would have watched anything. Coming out after *The Riordans*, a soap set on a farm in the heart of rural Ireland, manure included, we like to quote actor Tom Hickey's favourite phrase. Consequently, we kept jibing each other to 'get up the yard, there's a smell of Benjy off ya'. That particular tenant then used to go across the road to the chipper to buy us all burgers, chips and doughnuts.

Another tenant was the tough manager of the Four Roads pub on Sundrive Road and the Blades pub in Terenure. He had married one of the Healy girls of Healy's pub on Mountain View Road, but she died at a young age. He was later the manager of the smallest pub in Dublin – the Dawson Lounge. Back in the 1950s he had a falling out with the Catholic Church, after he boxed a priest to the ground. He was with us for a few years, occupying the top floor flat. As we got older and circumstances improved, we needed more space. We decided we could take back his flat and use for more space. He was given a few months' notice and was not too pleased. It didn't bother us in the least and we used to slide down the bannisters singing, 'O'Brien has no place to go!'

Then there was the case of the black-faced tenant. Now we all knew about black babies; hadn't the nuns asked us many times to give a penny to help the poor black babies in Africa. We also collected red and orange metallic foil tops from the milk bottles and brought them into the nuns, who sent them to the Missions for the same reason. Now we had one of those black babies moving into our house. A very big black baby, who was studying medicine in the Royal College of Surgeons. We felt proud that all our pennies had helped him come to Ireland to study. We were very nervous, however, never having seen a black person before. We had seen pictures on the front page of the *Sunday Press* of Cassius Clay after his victories over Henry Cooper and Sonny Liston. We had heard Louis Armstrong singing but had never seen him. Daisy said she knew all about black people, having seen Sidney Poitier in *Guess Who's Coming to Dinner*. She said she also knew all about Martin Luther King. I said I did too, having heard about him in history banging his menu up on church doors just to annoy the Pope. She just gave me that look of hers. Some of us whined to Mum that she should have told us well in advance of who's coming to our dinner. Minnie and did not sleep well for a few nights as we had heard people talking about the Baluba cannibals in the Congo after the UN stint of the Irish Army there. 138 soldiers were surrounded by 3,000 starving cannibals clamouring for an Irish stew. The cannibals didn't get their stew after the Irish showed them that they were not called the 'Fighting Irish' for nothing. It gave us no comfort, however, and I made sure my knife, fork, spoon and bottle of tomato sauce were stashed away safely under my pillow.

Our black tenant used to spend hours every day just gazing out the front downstairs bedsit window. He used to pull back the lace curtains and look at the people and traffic passing by. This did not go down too well with our neighbours, with many complaining that we were turning the area into a ghetto. Many of them were in shock also, never having seen a black man before, one who stared out at them every time they passed up and down the road. One neighbour blamed us for her nightmares. She complained of dreaming of hordes of little black babies covered in milk bottle tops chasing her around Mountain View Park. Many others walked along the opposite side of the road for fear of being looked at too closely.

His name was Patrick Cedric Job and I, trying to be sociable, said that he must be Irish. He looked at me mournfully, saying he was from the Cameroons, wherever that was, but it sounded musical, like macaroons. It didn't matter as I knew he was from Africa anyway. I introduced myself to him and, trying to cheer him up, told him that 'I hope the sun always shines on your shiny face. I know all about slavery,' I added. 'In fact, some of our relations were slaves, in the West Indies.' I paused and, getting no response, continued: 'Yes indeed! My Dad said that Cromwell shipped over 6,000 Irish children to the West Indies after he defeated the Irish at the Battle of Rathmines. Yes, we're living here for hundreds of years, ever since my great-great-grand-uncle helped King Brian run the Vikings out of Ireland long ago. Unfortunately, we were not so lucky with Olly Crommy and, as I said, some of our relations from Rathmines were sent abroad. That's why I think I have a sweet tooth – from my ancestors working in the sugar plantations. They gathered the sugar all right, but they helped themselves to lots and ate it raw, poured on to butter sambos. So, I blame my slave relations for my manky teeth. That's how the dentist described my teeth – "manky". Anyway, you just relax. You are amongst friendly slaves here in this house!' I also told him that my Dad once said that one of the nicest sounds you could hear is an African speaking with a Dublin accent. I added that by the time he would be going home he'd be 'a real Dub' like Phil Lynott from Thin Lizzy. And I was sure he'd have no difficulty in getting a job as a witchdoctor. For good measure, I whispered, 'And if you are ever stuck for a job, I'm sure he'd find room for a drummer.' I decided I would call him Massah, which I thought sounded more African.

One tenant called Milo, used to leave his wife behind and go to England for a few months' work. It never lasted and he came back and things quickly, after a brief drink-filled honeymoon, returned to abject abnormality. Back home he brought English tabloids such as *The News of the World* and *Titbits* and leave them in the hall. I personally didn't mind but this really annoyed Mum. He accepted an offer of a job with in an hotel and after a week told the chef what to do with himself, in the process practicing his knife-throwing skills. Then he joined CIÉ as a bus conductor but after six weeks he came home. Only years later did we discover the reason. 'Making the rent' it was called. 'Go ahead' or 'you're all right,' a non-paying bus passenger would say, giving you a fraction of the fare with the ticket for nothing dropped on the floor. His wife, Deirdre, and the rest of us were happy that he was working on the buses. All, that is, except the CIÉ accountants, who figured out the scam. 'Strange,' they said. 'How come the bus is on the busiest route, full of passengers, but little return?'

'Ah, they just hopped on and hopped off,' he said.

'Very good,' they replied. 'You too may hop off.'

He used to beat up his wife, black, blue and all the colours of the rainbow. We used to be terrified. Mum used to go in and comfort her and give her iodine from the medicine cupboard. On one occasion when we were all out, he cleared the house of Mum's wedding silver and good china. We saw them in the window of Kilbride's pawnshop months later. Mum was absolutely furious but did not ask him to leave in order to protect his wife. Otherwise they would have been on the street.

Another tenant, this time from Ceylon, called Raj, absolutely loved himself. He spent hours in the bathroom washing, shaving, having a bath every day. Tenants were supposed to ask Mum to have a bath – once a week. Mum then had to heat the hot water tank with a coal fire, every day, even in the summer. The rest of the tenants and ourselves had to wait until he was finished. When he finished, we couldn't believe our eyes. He left everything dirty – filthy soapy water still in the sink, towels strewn on the floor, often with poo on them. The bath had this line of dirt around its rim (I had never heard of a plimsoll line until he moved in). Mum, full of apologies to the other tenants, had to rush in and clean up the mess, and towels replaced. Eventually we managed to get rid of him, but not before Mum had found an immediate replacement as she could not afford to be out of pocket. I liked a young attractive female tenant who seemed to have lots of different boyfriends. Mum sent her packing too. I was disappointed as she was always nice to me, saying I must pop into her room any time for a chat and a smoke, even though I didn't smoke. She was a fan of Mae West, who I had never heard of before, and this tenant advised me frequently, 'You only live once, but if you do it right, once is enough.' On another occasion, holding her cigarette in her hand, she looked right into my eyes and said, 'When I'm good, I'm very good. But when I'm bad, I'm better' and laughed.

The then there was the tenant called D.J., a name which we found strange, yet understandable, since he hailed from the heart of the Bog of Allen and was a farmer's son with no interest in milking the cows or sheep shearing. He always needed to borrow our cooker at mealtimes for his motorbike. He liked to think he was a 'Hell's Angel' and dressed appropriately at times. His spark plugs were full of oil and he needed to use one of the cooker jets to burn it off. 'What about your own cooker?' we asked. 'Oh, I'm cooking on it,' was the cheeky reply. He was in too much of a hurry one day and he grabbed a saucepan of boiling water from Mum, accidentally spilling the contents over her. She was absolutely scalded, with her exposed skin quickly turning an awful burnt red colour. We were completely shocked that such a thing could happen to Mum. My face turned bright red and I could feel my forehead sweating. I didn't know what to do and I didn't like what I saw. We were reminded for weeks afterwards of her sore blisters. I never forgot the red fuchsia in the yard as it brushed against the kitchen windowpanes.

I did know what to do when my new second-hand shoes, sent to me from England by an aunt, disappeared overnight from the hall. Probably borrowed by a sleepy tenant with the same-size feet as myself, I surmised. I had to step back into the ones I had previously worn – the ones with holes and pieces of cardboard to try to stop the endless wet feet I was getting. I really missed those shoes as they had leather soles and heels with a metal strip on the tip of each of the heels. They made a good heavy sound on floors and the steel heightened the effect and gave me an air of some importance as I strolled down the school corridor. So I was very upset.

I ended up walking around with 'holey' shoes, a problem in the rain but even worse when serving on the altar. I had to wear an extra-long soutane when serving Mass and made a particular point of tossing the hem of the garment over the backs of my shoes when kneeling so no one would notice. On one occasion, serving at a wedding, when I stood up to perform my altar boy duties, I forgot to disentangle the soutane from the heels of the shoes, with the result that the top part of my body was suddenly jerked backwards. Worse was to follow with the contortions I had to undergo in order to extricate myself from my captured heels. It was as if for some inexplicable reason I had taken to Dervish dancing or Houdini-style escape capers on the altar in front of the happy couple and guests. The blushing bride turned a brighter red and the non-blushing groom turned a whiter shade of pale. The crowd called out for more, I didn't doubt. At least they would have had a memorable day, no extra charge. I didn't even have the consolation of looking forward to receiving a nice big one-pound note after the Mass, for services rendered, as was the custom, with the best man doing the honours. I would even have settled for a ten -bob note, or even half-a-crown. Doubts would have been sown, however.

Once our tenants had settled in, Mum called another meeting and assigned us all jobs around the house. Daisy and Freckles really rose to the occasion. Daisy brought her management skills to the fore and was assigned to collecting the groceries every week from Lees, Five Star or H. William's supermarket in Rathmines and Mc Cambridge's in Ranelagh. I had huge sympathy for the staff as she checked the price of every item on the receipt. I was to get the daily 'messages' such as the *Indo*, *Evening Press* or a pint of milk, usually from the Beehive Shop or Sweeney's Grocery. I also had to empty the fire grate of the ashes, bring in the coal and set the fire. I also had to dry the Delph.

Taking care of the fireplace was the worst of all jobs, as I had to do it really quickly in the morning before I left for school and I was usually covered in dust from the ashes or the new coal in the process. Putting out the milk bottles every night before going to bed was an important job. Sometimes in the mornings, when bringing the milk in, I would find the tops had been tampered with by early morning birds who liked their cream. As did we, and, like the birds, we helped ourselves to the inch of cream which the Dublin Dairies kindly topped up each bottle with. We replaced it with water, much to Mum's annoyance. We only drank it when we had to from then on.

Bringing the bin out each week was a difficult job; as the bins were made of iron with a handle on each side, the bins themselves were heavier than the contents. I also had to whitewash the walls in the yard on a regular basis, as well as doing gardening. 'Making the tea' in the evenings for Minnie, Daisy and Freckles, was not as easy as it sounded, as some of the diners had exacting standards. In those days, most people had dinner during the day, no lunch, and had a smaller meal in the evening, called 'the tea,' which involved tea and sandwiches or maybe a 'fry' 'High Tea' included cakes and buns and was usually arranged for uncles and aunts. When I made 'the tea' I used to give them scrambled eggs or beans and tomatoes on toast or boiled eggs or a fry with a few slices of fried bread, which was very popular.

We were blessed with Freckles also, as he was particularly talented 'with his hands' and could fix anything. For many years after Dad's death, he was able to repair anything in the house, from small plumbing jobs to replacing slates, fixing gutters or leaks, painting, decorating, and even re-wiring the whole house in his late teens. Mum allowed him to convert an old shed into his workshop, where he built up a collection of tools over the years. He was always in and out of Murdock's Hardware, getting all his requirements including every conceivable type of nail. Minnie was terrific also, as she acted as a regular babysitter for a neighbour's child, thereby making pocket-money for herself. They were forever playing and skipping to 'Banana Splits' out in the yard and garden. In a way, then, we were like the bedsits we advertised in the *Evening Press* – 'completely self-contained, everything supplied'.

Life soon took on a certain chaotic normality. Looking after tenants was like running a business – in fact, was a business! There were teething problems with tenants; they weren't happy with this or that or wanted extra baths, utensils, cutlery or bed linen. Or they were temporarily out of a job. Then there were the house maintenance jobs, bigger jobs that Freckles couldn't manage, such as walls needing re-plastering, replacing ceilings and water tanks. There were also four children in tow. As a result, Mum would have no holiday for twenty years, not even on Christmas Day. It was a constant struggle with no let up for her.

An example of the many dramas that constantly beset us was the case of a bunkbed mattress, which caught fire. I awoke one night, coughing and trying to breathe. I got out of bed and somehow managed to feel my way to the wall light switch and peered out the bedroom door. With the light on I could make out a mattress in a tenant's room smouldering, Hans snoring and sweating whiskey with the remains of a half-smoked cigarette lying near his face. I shouted 'Fire! Fire!' and woke the whole house. Freckles and I grabbed the mattress from under the dazed tenant and tossed it out the bedroom window into the yard below.

We did much reading in the one bathroom, with toilet paper shortages necessitating such a tradition. We had no fridge, no washing machine, no hoover, no phone, no TV or record player, only a radio, which was enough. We had the radio on all the time. When money was scarce we had no toothpaste but made do with soot or salt instead. We stuck the toothbrush up the chimney and scraped around for some soot. Sometimes we got more than we needed and it came down, landing in a heap at our feet with a thump and sending a shower of black dust up into our faces. At least we provided our own chimney-sweeping service.

Rarely did the chimney itself catch fire but when it did the vibrations coming from the chimney tunnel gave us terrible frights. The whole house quaked and shook and thundered. We would immediately quench the fire in the grate and eventually the fire in the chimney burnt itself out. On one occasion, however, we had to call the Fire Brigade. Rarely we got in the chimney sweep. He was Paddy Walsh's brother and lived up one of the lanes behind Deveney's off-licence. We fled when we were very young at the sound of the put-put-put of his motorcycle outside the house. What with his long brushes and black face lost in soot, he was as horrifying looking to us as the coalmen carrying in the sacks of Polish coal once every five years, when we could afford it. Usually we relied on sacks of turf delivered every fortnight, courtesy of the government on account of Mum being a widow. Neighbours would notice this and come to their own conclusions – not very nice considering the number of noses that seemed to be pointed upwards more and more. Turf was an inferior source of heat to the big sacks of Polish coal delivered to the surrounding houses. Despite that, we had heat and the sun still shone forever for us.

Mum always seemed to be on her knees. Bear in mind we had no hoover, so she had to make do with a sweeping brush and a dustpan. She also had a mop for the kitchen floor. She was forever scrubbing and cleaning the kitchen, polishing the lino in the long front hall with a tin of Mansion polish and a rag, peeling potatoes and cooking, non-stop. It was go go go, just like the dancers in the nightclub of the same name in Lower Abbey Street. At least twice every day she carried a big red basin full of washing for the clothes lines. We had two of those – one in the yard outside the kitchen, the other at the end of the garden. She had to endlessly wash huge sheets and then lift them, soaking, from the sink and wring them out. Work, work, work. Cleaning and making meals for six mouths. Not to mention teenage and other school problems faced by the four girls and the boys themselves. Most days she went out for some groceries to Rathmines, Camden Street or to Gowran's in Mountain View. She walked the miles there and back carrying heavy bags. 'Mind the pennies and the pounds will look after themselves,' she used to say. Or, as we were told in school, 'every mickle makes a muckle'. Yet she always found time to bake an apple tart, a fruit cake or rock buns. 'A labour of love,' she would tell us in later years. 'Sure, didn't I love you all!' She seldom bought new clothes, yet whenever she went out she had her best coat on over whatever was well worn. Moreover, she always wore a bright smile on her face. Whenever the doorbell rang, or a tenant knocked on the breakfast room door, behind which we effectively spent most of our time, before answering she would straighten herself, throw her shoulders back, smile and then answer the call.

We doubted if any of the nearest neighbours would have cared if she just dropped dead or went away. In fact, they probably would have preferred that if the truth were told. Her circumstances niggled at them. Sister Declan of the Sisters of Charity in the nearby hospice was one of the few exceptions when it came to helping us. She was a tiny nun with a kindly spirit. She ran a food kitchen for homeless men in a shed near the nun's chapel. She suggested Mum send one of us up to collect four or five sliced pans once a week. I was delegated and had to collect them in a brown suitcase, like I was going on holiday. Winter was fine, as nobody noticed me hurrying along and up the dark hospice avenue to the shed. Most times I joined the stream of men tramping up the hill for a simple hot meal. There, I had to sit with all the down-and-outs who were generally reeking of alcohol, meths or urine. Sometimes they drunkenly offered me 'a drop of the craythur' which I had to decline, saying I was 'off the drink for Lent', even in winter! Then it came to my turn to go into the storeroom and pack my suitcase.

With the longer and lighter evenings, I must have attracted a certain attention, flying along with my brown battered suitcase, nearly as big as myself. One evening I was stopped by Rats, Eho and a couple of their corner boy pals at the entrance gates. 'Just where do you think you are going with that suitcase?' They were always asking us for 'any odds' and we would have to empty our pockets and hand over valuables such as elastic bands, marbles and slings. These were sadly missed, having had a multiplicity of uses, including targeting birds and meting out pain on some unsuspecting lad in the classroom. Having seen these ruffians lurking at the gates a few times I was expecting to be jostled. 'I'm dying,' I sighed.

'Dying?'

'Yes.'

'Then why are you always going up and down real sneaky like?'

'I'm waiting for a bed. They told me to keep coming back and I might get one eventually. Then I can go in and do my dying. In the meantime, they are trying to find a coffin for my size. I told them I didn't mind a second-hand coffin or being buried standing up. Hopefully, they will include a bag of bull's eyes and acid drops.' With that I limped off, weighed down with the ways of the world and my heavy load of sliced pans. Not another word was said. See, we had our own ways of dealing with bullies. Name-calling often worked, for instance distorting their family's surname to create an even worse sounding name. This could be done with any name. Take Zender, for instance. Change it to 'bender' or 'render' or 'mender' or 'up ender' and just add a few choice words. It usually works wonders in annoying the beneficiary of your revenge. Using other bullies is equally helpful, particularly if the other bullies are madder than the original bullies. There was one in particular, known as Bernard the Heron, who we used to sub-contract work to on a regular basis. That, of course, depended on when he was available from Grangegorman. But he was highly successful at cracking skulls. Lastly, of course, being a really fast runner was an absolute imperative, if all other options failed.

Another nun behaved completely the opposite to Sister Declan. Even her habit was different, dreary brown in contrast to stark black with a touch of white. This one was from a convent a half-mile from our house. She came knocking on the door one day and Mum answered. The nun was carrying a meal on a tray and Mum was delighted, but not for long. 'Do you mind if I bring this in to Father? He's laid up in bed with a cold,' said the nun. 'His housekeeper is away for a few days and I don't want to have to get him out of bed. I can only get into his house by his back door – I therefore need to use your lane if you would oblige.' The priest's house was two doors from ours and the four houses on the terrace shared a right-of-way passage at the back. Mum let her through our house and on her way, but the cold experience left her shocked.

The neighbours on the other side of our house were no better. The house right next door to ours had two retired Irish Sweepstakes ladies. Their house was always being painted and decorated, with the table and furniture polished every day. The grass in the back garden was cut with a hand mower to such precision that each blade of grass stood at the same height as its neighbour. The flower beds and borders were maintained with equal care and concern. Every so often our ball accidentally went over the hedge and into their garden. They strongly resented handing it back, often complaining to Mum, so we took the initiative and popped through the hedge to fetch it back ourselves. The garden was so immaculately kept we felt we were in paradise. They always knew when we visited the garden as the grass would show our footprints. These two ladies spent a lot of their time playing bingo and chatting over their garden wall to three other retired ladies in the house next to theirs. One of the lady's hairstyles used to cause me to wonder. Her name was Maggie and she wore her hair up in a 'bun'. I could never fathom the reason for this description and it intrigued me for years. The two ladies gradually fell into poor health with the passing years. Luckily, help arrived quickly – the nuns from down the road in the convent. Every day they would call in bringing trays of food and helping in various ways. When they died, the nuns turned the house into an extension of the orphanage across the road.

Some of the aunts and uncles and Dad's friends were helpful from time to time. Uncle Syl from Grosvenor Avenue in Rathgar used to collect the sacks of turf from a fuel depot on New Street in his blue Volkswagen Estate for us. Next door to the depot was the famous cabaret lounge, Gulliver's Inn. Overall, however, Mum was left to her own devices. Some neighbours seemed indifferent to us or watched to see how Mum would cope. It didn't particularly bother us but on occasion when we noticed noses going too high, we found it necessary to fling rotten tomatoes, accidentally, while hiding behind hedges. Or if none were immediately at hand, and we were in our back garden, some bee-infested rotten but juicy apples or pears somehow found their way hurtling towards some unsuspecting busybody.

It was a definite and ongoing struggle trying to make ends meet; however, we had an incredible woman at the helm, a veritable anchor for us. She was single-minded in her determination, had fire in her belly, with courage, resilience and business acumen learnt with life's experiences. She was also an SRN with years of medical experience, dealing with people often in dire circumstances. She didn't drink or smoke, was terrific at planning and budgeting, and despite difficult circumstances she was single-handedly able to rear four very happy children. If you were sick, which rarely happened, she'd whisk out her silver-cased thermometer and stick it under your tongue. Then she'd check your forehead and if the situation looked bad it would be 'straight to bed' and hot drinks. No sooner would you be relaxing in bed than in she'd pop again to check the patient. 'You'll be grand, you'll soon be back to yourself,' as if I had been away somewhere.

She was extraordinarily patient. One day she asked me what I was doing leaning on the sweeping brush. 'Just doing what the Corporation men do after working hard,' I said. 'Taking a well-earned rest.'

'Well, have you started yet?' she wanted to know.

'No, but I'm having my rest first, to save me the trouble afterwards.' You see, a very patient lady indeed. What with having to report down to my school and explain to the Principal, Brother Flour we called him, why her non-smoking son was caught smoking in the toilets. She had to field all sorts of queries. Why was Minnie cheeky in class? Why was Daisy thinking she knew better than her teachers? (She always did, even going to the Principal saying she would take over the class from a certain teacher.) Mum had a thousand things to do. Four mouths to feed and a business to run. All told, at least ten people in the house at any one time.

She was a self-made woman of the world, not afraid to have her own views, conservative and liberal, forged in the smithy of her own soul. 'I'm a homemaker, not a housewife' she used to say. Let's not forget that she had been an Army Sister during the Second World War based in St Bricin's Military Hospital. She had seen life in all its shades. After the Emergency, she had worked for a few years before she got married in Shaen Sanatorium in County Laois, nursing TB patients, many of them young and beautiful. The location for the sanatorium was deliberate – miles from humanity for fear of contagion, in the very heart of the Bog of Allen, maybe in the hope that the bog air would grant the patients some respite or in the faint chance that the bog might share some of its secrets for preserving the dead and preserve the living.

She had huge respect for Dr Noel Browne, the young doctor and Irish Government Minister who helped to eradicate the scourge of TB from Ireland. She shared his confidence and courage. She nursed – and that word is too mild a description – those ravaged with that blight. She also witnessed many patients in workhouses, or in their hovels, being told to 'turn over and die' by those looking after the poor. This was a widespread practice. The carers were harried and consequently hurried things along with very cold comfort. She undertook 'agency work' and could be sent anywhere at short notice and saw many terrible deeds also at short notice.

She herself wasn't given much comfort when she lost three babies in the first few years of married life. The doctor just told her to 'forget it' and 'get on with it' and go home. Her firstborn was called after herself, Little Annie, and ended up in an unmarked mass grave with the rest in Glasnevin cemetery. The plot was only recognised decades later as the 'Angel's Plot'. Yet, above all, her very essence, her spirit, was shown by one salient act. When she was strongly advised by her parish priest to banish us to an orphanage or to the Artane Industrial School, when Dad died, she refused.

She was tough, but in a nice way, burnished like soft steel. I never saw her angry – annoyed maybe, and she might say to one of us, 'You'll be the death of me' or 'You'll rue the day', yet she never, ever raised her voice. She loved her husband and her children unconditionally, yet could be gently strict, as we sometimes saw at home. She had strictness tinged with humour and mischief. It was a joy to behold her chuckling to herself. At Christmas she used a bottle of stout in making the pudding and cake. Overnight we sampled the stout. The next night we went to sample some more, only to find the bottle stuck to the shelf. We pulled and up it came – all over us! She laughed and laughed.

She expressed any anger or frustration in her own singular way. Daisy and a boyfriend were lingering for what seemed like ages one night outside the front door of the house. Mum was worried, as well as being tired from waiting up. Up the stairs with her to the small bedroom over the hall, the window of which overlooked the hall door entrance below. She leaned out and dumped a large basin of water on the happy couple. 'That'll put a halt to their gallop,' she said. 'That'll dampen their ardour.' No nonsense, the message was conveyed loud and clear. I didn't escape either, although luckily, being a middle child, I was invariably lost in the scrum. On one occasion, at the age of fifteen, I was happily ensconced in the snug of the Stag's Head after a game of snooker. There I was, chatting to the lads and making plans to ask for the next round to be 'put on the slate', as I had heard many of the regulars saying. Suddenly, I felt this awful stinging pain. Some force had grabbed me by the ear. 'Out with you,' she uttered under her breath. 'You'll rue the day you came into this pub,' and hauled me home. Oh, she was absolutely right. Never could I go into that pub again. Luckily my last remaining friends understood, or at least pretended to.

Even with Hans, who had no intention of moving until his student days were over and who generally made a right nuisance of himself, she often reminded us (quoting what someone said about a famous medieval philosopher): 'This dumb ox will someday rule the world with this bellowing.' And he did, becoming lead singer in a rock band. Yes, she was philosophical. 'I'll go my way, pay my way, and smoke my pipe alone,' she used to say. She liked these country sayings. I sometimes felt like a bog-man using such expressions as 'when the cows come home', 'you're like a hen on a hot griddle' or 'I'll be there in two shakes of a lamb's tail'. I didn't know anything about cows or lambs and I didn't want to know, except for making money from shovelling up the cow dung along the main road. She always smiled. At the world, with the world, for the world, and never against the world. Always, she would say, 'put your best foot forward,' or 'walk tall and look the world straight in the eye'. Her smiles went many miles and into our hearts and heads.

During the week she was an avid fan of *The Kennedys of Castleross*, a fifteen-minute soap that ran on Radio Éireann for many happy years. She also liked Leo Maguire, who presented the Walton's Music sponsored programme. This was a very popular programme promoting the famous Walton's music shop at the corner of Parnell

Street and North Frederick Street in Dublin. He used to finish with the line, 'If you sing a song, sing an Irish song'. On Friday evenings she sat herself in front of the fire in our breakfast room and listened to *Friday Night is Music Night* and some of her favourites included the Verdi's 'Hebrew Slaves Chorus', 'Flight of the Bumblebee', 'Blue Danube', 'The Dance of the Sugar Plum Fairy' and 'Bolero'. She liked being called the 'Merry Widow' after one of her favourite operettas. She never tired of the voices of Maria Lanza and John McCormack and she was often heard humming 'Ah! Sweet mystery of life I have found you...'. The 'Indian Love Call' from the musical *Rose Marie* and sung by Jeanette MacDonald and Nelson Eddy, had her in raptures. When Minnie became involved in the Mountain View Musical Society, she became a great fan and loved the amateur scene with productions including *The Student Prince*, *The Gypsy Baron*, *Carousel*, *The Lily of Killarney* and, a particular favourite, *South Pacific*. To her consternation, we enjoyed going around the house singing 'The Drinking Song' from *The Student Prince*, with our emphasis on 'Drink, drink, drink ...'

19

THE RELUCTANT GUNMAN AND THE GESTAPO

My spell of three months in Stoney Ward in the Royal City of Dublin Hospital, or 'Baggot Street Hospital' as everyone called it, was one of the many crosses Mum had to bear. Once again, I had diced with death, but on this occasion I had greatly inconvenienced Mum as, while I was relaxing in the hospital bed covered in blood and bruises and a smashed-up leg, Mum had to do the traipsing around to visit me on a regular basis. This accident involved my being whacked by a Mercedes car on the Merrion Road.

It followed on not too long after another life-threatening situation – the strange incident of the pig in the haybarn. Or should I say, 'mystery'? I certainly didn't see the sow or know that it was there when I hurtled myself off the pile of hay and bounced off the pig, much to the surprise and consternation of us both. The hurt pig chased the even more hurt boy – around the farmyard we ran, the fat pig intent on revenge and me in terror. I rushed around the haybarn and then across the farmyard and into our aunt's County Laois farmhouse, where we were staying. It was supposed to be a holiday but turned into a week's stint of slave labour. All I seemed to be doing was milking cows, sowing potatoes, churning the milk, bringing in the hay, gathering apples and cleaning the loft — endless hard work. Milking the cows was the worst as I had to sit on a three-legged stool and try fruitlessly to get the milk flowing. Meanwhile, the cow was getting impatient and kept whacking my face with its tail. Swish, swish, swish, it went, and I was once again baptised, this time with Laois's best cow dung.

As anyone being chased by a huge and angry pig would do, I grabbed uncle's double-barrelled shotgun, intent on inflicting damage to the said fatted pig, which was equally intent on doing the same to me. Unfortunately, the shotgun was somewhat on the heavy side for me, and, consequently, I had great difficulty rushing anywhere. I didn't remember John Wayne having that problem in *True Grit*. I called upon the slave driver, that is, my sour-faced aunt who was always criticising me for refusing to eat her 'country butter' and her turnips, parsnips and all her other rotten old vegetables, to show me how it worked. I breathlessly told her what I intended to do. Unfortunately for me, being the old biddy that she was, she absolutely refused in her best 'don't you dare' country accent. It made one want to reply, 'Aroo from Coirk? I am arrah! Do ye ate potatoes? I do de ah! How d'ye ate them? Skin an' all. Do dey choke ye? Not at all!' She was no help at all and, thankfully, she packed the 'Jackeen' back to Dublin the next day, saying I was no use at all.

So, ending up nearly dead was becoming part and parcel of my life. Saying that, luckily, I wasn't conscious when the priest came in to Baggot Street Hospital to give me the Last Rites. Or when Redser and Four Eyes were told to say their goodbyes, permanently, to me. Sometimes it's best to be somewhat aloof in these circumstances.

The near tragic circumstances had begun when Redser, Four Eyes and myself were making courtesy calls on the various embassies in Ballsbridge. We hoped to meet the ambassadors to discuss their countries, the political situation, the economy, life in general. This was for some school project and we thought the best thing to do would be to bypass the library and go straight to the ambassadors to get the full story straight from the horse's mouth. And they would give us brochures and all sorts of goodies into the bargain. That's the last I remember of what happened; all I recall was waking up in the hospital with torch lights shining into my eyes and some voice with a Pinocchio nose shouting into my face.

I had read of these people in the *Hotspur*. The Gestapo they were called. 'Just checking to make sure you are still with us,' came a voice. What? They didn't need flashing lights to see me. I was there in the bed right in front of them. They may have had their lights on but there was certainly no one in their upstairs as far as I was concerned. However, to be on the safe side, I replied. 'Heil Hitler, how's it going?' Then I tried to give my best Hitler Youth Movement (Mount Jerome Branch) salute. To no avail and I quickly realised they had immobilised me. I knew then that Gary Barry, the apprentice petrol bomber altar boy who had been despatched up to the Northern Ireland barricades by Canon Brady, should instead have applied his talents to the Swastika Laundry. I understood everything. The Gestapo had infiltrated Mountain View and the country using the laundry as a cover – sacks of Nazis masquerading as sacks of laundry.

Staying in hospital for a few months was an unusual experience for a teenage lad. Firstly, I had to have at least two operations to try to fix a shattered tibia in my right leg. This involved inserting a gold plate with gold nails to hold the shattered pieces of bone in place. When I was in pain I could never understand why they insisted on giving me an injection in the bum where I had absolutely no pain whatsoever – up until then! Then I was given a pair of crutches and told to walk up and down the corridors. To make matters worse I was given a bed pan, which I had no idea what to do with, having never seen one before. The man in the next bed eventually told me and I tried to do a one-arm balancing act. That and the glass jar to do a wee in really embarrassed me no end.

Cecil Hannah was the man in the bed beside me. He was from South Africa and was very nice, as were the rest of the men in my ward. As I was a teenager, the hospital authorities didn't know where to put me so I ended up on the men's ward rather than the children's. Cecil painted me a picture of the Concorde and the rest of the ward patients signed it. After a few weeks, he was able to leave hospital but came back fairly quickly. Within a few days, he died in the bed beside mine. I awoke one morning to find the nurses pulling the curtains around his bed. I guessed it probably would be my turn next and so I started making arrangements with the morgue attendant. Over a bottle of Stowshus and a Fanta we distributed all my worldly goods and chattels, including my share in the bunkbed, sunglasses and an all-season brown polo neck jumper.

There was much comings and goings in the ward, a hive of activity with trolleys bringing patients to the Pulmonary Unit or the morgue. You never knew which one you might be going to. I often thought that some of the patients that came back looked worse than when they went away earlier. 'Maybe they were meant for the morgue and came back on the wrong trolley,' I thought. Or else they changed their minds when they got to the morgue. Every so often an orderly came in to give someone a shave. I couldn't fathom this as I hadn't realised they supplied hotel-like services in hospitals. I liked the food too, never having had a plate of bangers and mash before. I had read about it in the comics but had never seen it close up. The nurses were very kind to me, with one even going as far as kissing me. I wanted more of the same and the next time she came into the ward I made such a suggestion to her. I ended up with a smack for my troubles – I had asked her twin sister! That was another thing some nurses were good at, particularly when you may have become inadvertently aroused unbeknownst to yourself. They would just flick or smack the growing offender, which would quickly subside until the next time.

I had a Plaster of Paris cast on my leg for months. It was often the custom for people to sign their names or draw on it. The physiotherapist was a friend of Ronnie Drew of The Dubliners and he was a regular visitor in the hospital. She organised for him to come along and autograph my leg for me. Very kind indeed and I asked him to sing his favourite song for me. 'No,' he said. 'What will ye have yourself,' he went in his deep, rich, gravelly voice full of the sound and the music of his beloved city. 'How about "Monto"?' and away with him with all the patients gathering around and joining in. 'Who's going for a jar?' says he, no sooner had he finished. The ward emptied and off with them to Mooney's pub on the corner of Baggot Street, pyjamas, dressing gowns, wheelchairs and all. I was stuck in the ward in my wheelchair with Fanta for comfort and my plastered leg sticking out in front of me. I smiled at one of the twins, taking a chance that she could be the right one. All I got was a promise.

Every so often I had to walk up and down the corridors getting used to the crutches. In the process, I transformed from a puny teenager into a Tarzan-like figure having developed great shoulder and arm muscles. On one occasion as I was wandering the corridors a number of Gardaí hurtled past me. Seemingly one of the patients in a nearby ward had 'escaped' in his pyjamas. He had been under close guard and managed to climb out the window, on to a drainpipe, down to the street below and vanish. This was at the height of the Troubles in Northern Ireland and the escapee had been under armed guard yet still managed to elude the law. This was also the era of the 'Heavy Gang', tough members of the Gardai, who Dad had once said, were regulars in The Chinaman pub, at the back of Dublin Castle.

The days and weeks flew by and I continued to hobble about, eventually being discharged after three months. I spent the next few months limping about with the aid of the crutches. I also attended physiotherapy in Baggot Street, which included learning how to walk again. Physiotherapy was another experience as I had to undergo ultraviolet light treatment, which involved having to wear huge vintage motorbike-type goggles in the process. When I finished with my physio, the only thing that saddened me was that I hadn't any present to give to the physiotherapist to express my thanks. I was very lucky though, as I had my Mum to go home to. Back in school I was greeted with a new name – Hopalong Cassidy!

20

ROSES AND SNOWBALLS,
PAGING AND CONDUCTING

Life was starting to return to one of routine and normality. Every day we were glued to the 1.30 p.m. news on Radio Éireann, listening to the sombre tones of Charles Mitchell or Maurice O'Doherty report on the battles for civil rights in Northern Ireland. It felt as if we were there at the barricades. We could hear the shouting and roaring of people storming the barricades, the sounds of breaking glass, army trucks and the police sending out warning shots from their rubber bullets and tear gas. The bottle and stone-throwing seemed non-stop. Bonfires blazing all night long. We could hear it being broadcast live. We couldn't believe it, not just the actual violence itself, but the fact that we could hear it right in our own home. There was the young Bernadette Devlin, not much older than ourselves, her long hair flowing down her back – so brave, so diminutive, at the head of the marchers, encouraging them on. Then there was the burning of the British Embassy on Merrion Road following the Bogside Massacre on Bloody Sunday.

It was also the decade of other kinds of assassinations, particularly those of President J.F. Kennedy, his brother Bobby and Martin Luther King. *The Late Late Show* on Telefís Éireann was much talked about, although we didn't have a TV in those years. People seemed to be talking about a former 'Singer' boy called Gaybo and him getting mixed up with a bishop's nightie. Even the Pope got a mention with Paul VI and 'the Pill', going by the front covers of the *Catholic Standard, Sunday Independent* and *Sunday Press*. Moreover, in an unprecedented move, the farmers of Ireland marched on the Dáil and the Department of Agriculture, demanding better money for their products. There was also much talk about the Foot and Mouth Disease and the pioneering Dr Christian Barnard in South Africa, transplanting hearts. Then there was the left-footed artist, Christy Browne. All the lads tried to emulate him and Redser said that some were 'complete naturals' and 'why bother using their hands in future'. They also tried to emulate football greats such as George Best and Pelé.

People were still talking about the blowing up of Nelson's Pillar on O'Connell Street in 1966 and a few seemed delighted to have a piece of old pillar as a souvenir. Even pal Conkers said he had a brick. We knew that without him telling us. We also listened on the radio to the Apollo space mission to the moon and were riveted when Neil Armstrong issued those words about a big step for man and mankind when he stepped on to the Moon's surface. All this was against a backdrop of pirate radio stations such as Radio Caroline operating from the stormy North Sea off the coast of The Netherlands. Radio Luxembourg then came on the air with lots of our favourite pop music. Every song we heard we loved including *Hey Jude, Dedicated Follower of Fashion, Itchycoo Park*, songs about shooting arrows, the green, green grass of home, lazing on a sunny afternoon, and going to San Francisco with flowers in one's hair. What with Dana singing about snowdrops and daffodils, the threat of a nuclear fallout following the stand-off between Khrushchev and Kennedy, which people years later were still talking about, and us all having to live in a yellow submarine, we were living in a crazy world. Every household in the country received a large booklet outlining in great detail what to do in the event of a nuclear holocaust – hide under the table and suchlike. We were also warned to retain this booklet close at hand and so we kept it for years tied with a string on the back of our kitchen door. In the meantime, Louis Armstrong sang about 'what a wonderful world'. Maybe it was. For us it was a non-stop rollercoaster of action and music. In complete contrast to the pop menu we were fed, there was also that bearded man with the strong and gravelly Dublin voice singing about 'Seven Drunken Nights', taking her up to Monto, whiskey in the jar and how Jim Finnegan broke his skull when he fell off the ladder. Joe Dolan singing about being in love with a girl who lived in a house with a whitewashed gable, Johnny McEvoy with his 'Goodbye Muirsheen Durkan', Danny Doyle with 'Step it Out Mary', and the Barleycorn singing about Long Kesh and 'armoured cars and tanks and guns, the men behind the wire' – all these fuelled our minds in varying degrees. This included us marching around the garden with hurleys over our shoulders.

In this hurdy-gurdy world, we managed to get part-time jobs. This involved delivering cards and envelopes to local houses every week. I also went around doors selling 'the pools' and 'be a brick, buy a brick' raffle tickets for the school. Copying the boy scouts and girl guides, I undertook bob-a-job activities which included gardening, cleaning windows, washing cars, painting, delivering groceries, collecting messages from shops and doing the newspaper round. You name it, I did it, even polishing people's shoes for them!

One fairly lucrative job was collecting dung from the main Mountain View Road after the cattle, sheep and pigs had been walked from the local farms to the slaughterhouse at Mountain View Bridge. There were at least four farms in Mountain View right up until the 1980s. There was one attached to the enclosed order of Carmelite nuns at The Cloisters on Mount Tallant Avenue. Another was behind Mount Argus Church. The Hospice had one bordering the cemetery, and St Mary's Convent also had a farm. These were quite small farms – ranging from a few acres to twenty, yet they managed to provide much food for the owners. Their cattle were regularly sent to the abattoir or, as we called it, the slaughterhouse at Mountain View Bridge. As children, we loved to come to our hall door and watch the cattle being driven along the road. Sometimes we helped the drovers and out we'd go roaring and shouting at the beasts, real herding as we imagined it to be. Our long sticks went flying all over the place, with us going 'whup, whup, whup' and causing many a stampede. Minnie was somewhat startled at all the farting going on from the cows. 'That cow just farted in front of me!' screeched Minnie. 'What a pong!'

We found it much harder driving the sheep as they were inclined to go all over the road and into people's front gardens. Some even followed us back into the house. Freckles grabbed one and frantically tried to pull its wool off to make a bawneen sweater for himself. He got barely enough to make a sock. Well, it was a start, we agreed.

Immediately the cattle or sheep had gone their merry way, out I'd rush out with my barrow and shovel and load up the freshly deposited steaming dung. The removal job involved using a wooden-handled steel-tipped shovel which scraped along the road surface, creating lots of noise and sparks. Then in one quick move, I scooped up the heavy load and tossed it, thumping and squelching, into the barrow. Lace curtains quivered nearby, eyes peered, shocked and horrified. Lips and jaws worked overtime and feverishly. This place is turning into a happy haven for senior squinters, I thought to myself. Still, the job had to be done and I managed to scoop up every thud, thump, splash and splat. Then I would wheel my loads up to the priest's garden behind the Presbytery, which was in the grounds of the church. This garden was an old orchard, crammed full of all sorts of fruit trees and with paths between the various rows. There was also a potting shed, so the location was ideal for my business. Once I had unloaded the dung into a big heap in the sunniest part of the garden, I would add straw, paper and old dried-up leaves and mix it up. Then I would leave it drying out for up to six months. The sheep manure usually took longer. If it rained I would throw black plastic sheets over the heaps. I would check regularly to see if the dung was drying out and losing its stench. Then it would be ready for customers.

I went around all the roads in the area ringing a small hand-bell I had borrowed from the church's sacristy, and now re-christened the 'dung bell'. There was a great demand for good manure from householders who used it as a garden fertiliser. Most houses had big long gardens at the back and smaller ones to the front. Some of the houses I visited in nearby Rathgar had even bigger gardens, with some stretching to half an acre. I borrowed the priest's bigger wheelbarrow and called to houses selling 'best well-matured dung'. For a few years I used to go around the various roads in Mountain View and surrounding suburbs shouting, 'Best dung for best results' and 'No pong dung'. Having heard ads on Radio Éireann for some fertiliser called '10.10.20.', I often roared out, '10.10.20. right on your doorstep, while stocks last!'

I made a point of looking after my regular customers, popping in for chats on progress and the general wellbeing of their gardens. I was able to assure them, for instance, that since roses were high maintenance, the dung would cut their workload immeasurably. It seemed to work, as I had no complaints and so I made lots of money, which the lads called 'dung dough'. Customers used to compliment me on their roses and rhubarb. I also became somewhat partial to Mum's rhubarb crumble, as our garden also benefited. The roses at the end of our garden also thrived and were regarded as some of the best in the neighbourhood.

The young non-gardening types lurking around sniggering had no appreciation for the power of dung. They wouldn't have known the difference between a blade of grass and a Wilkinson's Sword blade used for shaving. That's the reason why these ruffians sometimes called me 'Hu Flung Dung'. Not that I minded, as I had a growing interest in Chinese roses. Yet I felt that one needed to prune these developments just like one cared for roses. In the process, I also conceded, I could improve the diet of certain of these lads as well. So, one nice summer's day, after a prosperous few hours of hard work and having a few pats of dung left over in my barrow, I leant against some front garden railings and relaxed. I bathed in the warmth of the sun, listened to the twitter of the birds in the hedges, the smell of freshly cut grass. Suddenly, under the perfectly blue sky, I heard this cacophony. 'Who flung dung? Who flung dung? Yoo, hoo, hoo, hoo. Who flung dung?' There they were, lurking about as usual — the local dung catchers. Just my luck! However, on this nice sunny day, I had all the time in the world. So, at my leisure, unobtrusively, I bent over my supply of second best dung and adjusted my gloves. Then, with a few neat grabs, tosses, turns and twists, I made what I needed. Suddenly, I did a swivel on the balls of my feet that Christy Ring, Mick Mackey, Jimmy Doyle, the Rackard brothers, Jack Lynch or any decent hurler worth his sliotar would have appreciated. I shouted 'catch' and in quick succession flung a few very well aimed, and complimentary, dung balls at the fleeing bunch. They surely deserved relegation these dunk catchers, not even standing their ground! Whop! Splat! Splat! Splat! What sweet music as missiles and targets embraced. The birds in the air cheered. Swarms of ants and flies chased after them. 'It's an acquired taste,' I laughed to myself, 'they'll get used to it. Next time I'll garnish with some Weeya Sauce!'

One interesting side-line emerged from this venture and involved me being called a 'Picaroon'. I wasn't sure if that was an insult or a compliment. I had seen coal lorry's delivering sacks of nice Polish coal to some of our neighbours and noticed that with all the tugging and lifting by the coalmen, quite a few lumps of coal spilled from the lorry onto the road. As I noticed this, I happened to have my Roche's Stores altar boy bag in my hand, containing my surplus and soutane. When the coalmen disappeared into the houses with their sacks thrown over their shoulders, I collected a bagful of coal lumps scattered on the road. We were delighted at home as the heat from coal was stronger than from the turf we had to use. It also gave me an idea. I enquired from a coalman down in Gordon's Coal Merchants at Mountain View Bridge as to where they got their coal from. On being told 'down the docks', I borrowed a messenger boy's bike from Paddy Walsh Cycles, threw a few old coal sacks I had borrowed from Gordon's into the large wicker basket and pedalled furiously along the canal and down to the docks. It took me twice as long to come back as the front basket was weighed down with two full bags of coal I had picked up beside the ship that was unloading coal. It was then that one of the neighbours called me 'nothing but a Picaroon!' Well, my view was that the Picaroon had plenty of warm fires for weeks to come!

Shortly after that, I transferred to the egg business, availing of payment-in-kind on the local farms, in return for helping out. Then I called at the local houses with 'freshly laid eggs'. This became a very profitable enterprise and I became known as 'the egg lad'. And then there was the home-made jam-making business. This involved cycling on summer evenings up to the fruit fields near Lamb Doyle's beyond Rathfarnham. There I would collect buckets of raspberries, gooseberries and blackberries. Using a borrowed messenger boy's bike from the kindly Paddy Walsh, I would bring the fruit to Bosonnet & Sons jam factory on St Clare's Avenue. There my friends Little Chip, Jammy Jemmy and Old Time Irish would do the necessary and most weeks I would have nearly fifty pots of jam, which I called 'Clare's Homemade Jam'. These soon found happy homes in Mountain View. Then I collected the empty jam jars, returned them and was given free jam in return. And the whole cycle started again!

I seemed to gravitate more and more towards the catering business and when I was fourteen I got a job as a lounge boy in the nearby Blades Pub. My request for a job resulted in being interviewed by the owner, Larry O'Carroll, a rather stern-looking man with heavy black eyebrows overlooking even darker eyes. His dad was called 'Mr O' and always came downstairs to the bar from his flat above at the end of a night to have a quiet whiskey and mingle with the slow-departing customers. Looking around the bar, I wondered how all these drunks managed to get in. Did they too have to have an interview and provide references? I wondered. Maybe all that was required was the ability to shout and roar and sing a good bawdy song. Not to worry, all I had to do was to take orders for pints for him and Snowball or Babycham for her and sometimes a Bloody Mary for the hair of the dog.

I liked the names of some of these drinks but refused to take an order for a Snowball when I was just starting, thinking the customer was pulling a fast one. I told him straight, 'If you want a Snowball you had better ask for it yourself. Next you'll be asking me for a glass hammer!' Then someone else asked me for a Redbreast. Not knowing that this was a whiskey, I told him he'd find one in his back garden. It was an unusual job in that instead of the evening tapering off drearily or boringly, as in most part-time jobs, the vast majority of customers at the end of the night were in great spirits, giving us loads of tips and laughing their heads off. Not only that but I made more money in tips than the job itself actually paid. I was being paid twice. I had never, ever heard of a job where you were paid twice.

Just after closing time, Nobbby, a fellow lounge boy, and I got the opportunity to vent our spleen on all and sundry. 'All together now!' we'd roar. 'When you're ready!' 'Let's move quietly towards the exits.' 'Have yez no homes to go to.' 'This is a drinking house not a lodging house.' 'Pleeese move quietly towards the exit.' 'Take your drink with you but leave the glass behind!' 'If yez don't leave now we'll set the bleeding dogs on yez.' 'Hey, you over there! Yes you, baldy!' Nobody noticed our ranting and all eventually left for home. For us it was one of the perks.

I usually had a few part-time jobs going on at any one time and did much juggling to ensure that stayed the case. Mum received at least half of everything I earned. During the summer months, I worked in the hotel business, starting at the age of fourteen as a page boy in Wynn's Hotel on Lower Abbey Street. This job included opening and closing doors for guests, carrying suitcases in and out of the hotel, bringing guests up to their rooms, polishing the brasses and cleaning some internal windows. I was also sent on messages to the nearby China Showrooms or the Happy Ring House to collect some purchased item. Oftentimes I was sent around to the Abbey Theatre, the Gate or the Gaiety, to book seats for guests. I liked collecting laundry from the New York Dry Cleaners across on Middle Abbey Street. There I would linger outside over a pavement grill as warm air gusted up from below.

I worked alternatively the eight to four or the twelve to eight shifts. Sometimes I had to work on Sundays, although this was inclined to be a quiet and dreary day. The boredom was compounded by having to listen to the even drearier music of the Salvation Army as they marched and trumpeted up and down the streets near their headquarters down the road from the hotel. I had never heard any music so less enticing.

Being a page boy was as equally lucrative as the bar business, and

Dublin Be Damned!

I made as much in tips as in wages. The American guests were great tippers, particularly when they were hopping into their taxis going to the airport. They would empty their bulging pockets of Irish change and put the whole lot into my small hands. I always kept my eyes open for these kinds of guests and hurried over to be of assistance. On one occasion two of us were in such a hurry to be of assistance that I was forced to jostle the other page boy nearly out of this world. Another perk in this job was the food, of which I much approved. Meals were provided free to the staff and we had our own canteen in the basement, which was under street level. The reinforced glass squares embedded into the street above and along by the front of the hotel were part of the ceiling of the canteen. These were not just any kind of meals. Only the very best, the same as guests themselves had. I used to go to the kitchen, hand in my plate and the chef would pile it high for me. Never in my life had I dined so royally.

Further opportunities to dine regally were provided at the wedding receptions held every weekend in two of the hotel's ballrooms. I used to have to help set up the tables and displays and during receptions I made sure the carpets were kept clean and tidy, I'd bring empty drinks glasses to the bar and generally make myself handy. As the evening progressed there would be much banter, singing and dancing, and, of course, drinking. On many occasions I was mistaken by guests as another guest, and, not wishing to offend, I did not contradict. I chatted away, being thought of as a nephew of that baldy man over there or of the bride herself. Well, tongues were wagging to beat the band itself as it pumped up the volume. 'Sit yourself down there and get stuck into that nice Chicken Kiev like a good lad,' a short dumpy lady went. 'Tell me now, who do ye think that *amadán* he married really fancies? Can you tell me that? Well, I'll tell ye for sure.' Off they'd go with me tucking into a nice meal and everybody around me talking to me or at me or to God knows who. I just nodded and agreed with everything. They wanted to pour drink into me but I had to regrettably decline, saying I was driving my mother home and she lived down in Kerry. I agreed, however, to a quick twist around the floor and away with us dancing the 'Huckle Buck' to the sound of Brendan Boyer and the Royal Showband. Brendan Shine's 'Do You Want Your Aul Lobby Washed Down?' was also popular with revellers. Sometimes, someone grabbed me to do the 'Hokey Pokey' or 'Shake, Rattle and Roll'. As my Dad used to say, 'When you're in the hotel business, you have to do everything!'

I used to travel into work on the 54A bus and sit upstairs in the front looking out at the shops and streets as we rattled along. There was also the bonus of piped music, which had only recently been added to the bus service. On one occasion, I remember being upstairs on a lovely warm summer's day enjoying the view and listening to the happy 'piped' music and the sounds of Mungo Jerry. He was singing a real catchy number, with lines such as, 'in the summertime, when the weather is fine, you got women, you got women on your mind.' I hadn't, but the song changed all that. On reaching the Quays, I descended the stairs thinking of one thing only and it wasn't work. This was only the beginning of the problem as I immediately fell in love with the hotel receptionists. Most of them 'lived-in' and were always gliding up and down the stairs in their miniskirts or hot pants. This, inconveniently, coincided with my kneeling down trying to polish the ornate brass rods holding the carpets in place on the stairs. These receptionists were better looking than models, as this was a time when such jobs were as much sought after by young ladies as jobs in the bank or as air hostesses with Aer Lingus. When hoovering the bar later, I said to the suave, handsome chap in the mirror, 'My name is Bond, Larry Bond!'

I spent three very enjoyable summers working in Wynn's. At the start of my second summer I was offered a job as kitchen porter, which I foolishly accepted, thinking I could manage an adult's job. The work nearly killed me as I spent all my time slaving in the kitchen cleaning huge pots, pans and cauldrons the size of which I had never seen before. I even found it difficult to lift some of them. Scrub, scrub, scrub, I went, with the perspiration filling up the sink. To boot, the chef would regularly throw a pot back into the sink for re-cleaning. I came home in the evenings and just lay on my bunkbed, shattered. I told the Manager the job was too hard for me and he kindly gave me one more suited to my talents – as a House Porter. This involved swirling around the hotel hoovering the bedrooms, ballrooms, bars and restaurants and everywhere else. This was a demanding job, all the same, full of responsibilities, as the guests' rooms had to be spick and span. The chambermaids were always trying to get me to clean under the beds, although at times I wasn't sure if it was me or the hoover they wanted under the beds. Two rooms in particular caught my attention, or my nose, rather. The Assistant Manager had his bedroom on the top floor and I was required to hoover it every other day. There were two difficulties here. Firstly, he had so many socks and clothing scattered everywhere that it was nearly impossible to get into the room let alone hoover the carpet. Secondly, the pong was just unbelievable! So bad, in fact, that I sent the hoover in by itself with me just guiding it from outside the door.

The second room was much easier to hoover but was only to be cleaned when unoccupied. This was the Powder Room, a name I had never heard of and didn't know what the other staff were talking about when it came up in conversation. 'Would you clean the Powder Room today?' asked the Housekeeper. 'Most certainly,' I replied, not having a clue as to what she was on about. So, I had to go downstairs to the Head Porter, a very genial man called Terry, but one to keep well in with, and ask him what and where was this strangely named room I had agreed to hoover. Just as well as a guest had asked me only recently where to find the Powder Room. I was distracted by the fact that I had noticed a large timber inscribed wall plaque over the fireplace in the hotel's lounge whenever I was hoovering there. It celebrated the hotels' role as a meeting place for the 1916 leaders prior to the Rising. Consequently, I thought the Powder Room might have something to do with that event. Maybe she was looking for the Gunpowder Room? 'Never heard of it,' says I. 'You could try the Ladies over there,' and I pointed to a glass door with a fancy looking lady carved on it.

A similar conundrum arose when asked for the 'Rest Room'. I never knew the hotel had such a room and I presumed the guest was looking for the restaurant or the bedrooms and I usually referred him to the Reception Desk to book in. Sometimes I referred the gent to the nearby bar and advised him to take the weight off his feet and order himself a nice creamy pint of Stowshus. One annoyed guest said he didn't want any more drink – he wanted to get rid of it! I was quick off the mark this time. 'Ah! It's the jacks you want! Over there and down the stairs to your right.'

The same stairs also led to the basement and where Old Ted, the boilerman, worked. He was seldom seen but had been in the hotel longer than anyone else. Sometimes I had to go down for cleaning supplies and he would start chatting about the old days. The basement was very hot, with a huge furnace rumbling away somewhere in the background. He could recall, as a child, seeing Queen Victoria sail up the River Liffey during a visit to Dublin. 'She looked like the roly-poly Michelin Man, sitting there in all her finery!' he laughed. One day he said to me, out of the blue, 'Did ye know that all the banning and burning started right across the street in that holy shop?' He continued, 'and people queued for hours, around the corner to O'Connell Street just to get their hands on that booklet, *What not to do on a Date.*' When I heard this, I started listening. According to Old Ted, 'Dem over there in that holy shop hated yer man Jem Joyce and banned everything in the country because he went up to Monto and brought disgrace upon them.' Apparently, according to Old Ted, back in the 1920s 'secret meetings' were held in the 'holy shop', also known as Veritas House, to launch a campaign to persuade the government to ban all the 'evil and indecent literature' in the country.

After the meetings, delegates flocked over to the bar in Wynn's Hotel, as most of them were staying there before returning home to Ovens, Blue Ball, Spider Hill, Muff, Doody's Bottoms, Toe Head in Skibbereen, Lover's Leap in Mallow or wherever. Lay observers hailed from faraway places including Effin, Slutsend, Hackballs Cross, Fannystown, Lower Balix and Lousybush. Old Ted was the barman and so he heard all the gossip. Pioneer Pins were surreptitiously consigned to pockets, and 'they just drank and drank,' he said. 'All the time calling for more Stowshus for Sure and Stowshus Extra Strength and singing, Ól é, Ól é Ól é Ól é, Ól é, Ól é.' He also remembered the man with the rich and powerful voice, which seemed as if it had rumbled all the way from the very deep south of the Bog of Allen. He always chipped in with 'Praise the Law. I say to you, brothers! Praise the Law! Amen, Amen!' Everyone else in the bar joined in. 'Praise the Law. Praise the Law. Amen. Amen!' 'They went absolutely mad,' said Old Ted. 'Some of them even trying to do cartwheels up and down the corridors on the way to their rooms. There they were outside their rooms, practicing their secret handshakes and trying on their cloaks with the pointy hoods. And later, singing in their rooms at night as they enjoyed a drop of the craythur. I could hear them as I went around the hotel checking doors and lights. There they were…' and he, in his battered old cap and croaky voice, gave a rendition: 'Al-el-uia, Al-el-uia, we're coming at ye! Al-el-uia. ¡Al-el-uia, ¡Al-el-uia, coming to get ye! Al-el-uia. ¡Al-el-uia, ¡Al-el-uia, say, burn the book, yeh! Al-el-uia. ¡Al-el-uia, ¡Al-el-uia, we'll ban the book, yeh! Al-el-uia. ¡Al-el-uia, ¡Al-el-uia, ¡Ye better watch out, ye! Al-el-uia…' He paused, breathless and looking like a long-retired Gospel singer. 'I'll never forget that singing. They were unbelievable times,' said Old Ted. 'It even got worse during the Eucharistic Congress a few years later in 1932, with savages from all over the world descending upon us.' He nodded his head. 'I can tell ye something! Those Volunteers must be swivelling in their graves at all the goings on here.'

There were two reasons why I decided to apply for a summer job as a bus conductor. From my early years, I had an inclination to throw snowballs at bus conductors, not because I disliked them. No, most of them were very nice in fact. However, the problem was that they were absolutely asking to be snowballed. In the cold winter months as the buses trundled up the Mountain View Road, there they would be, standing alone and forlorn on the back platform of the old-style buses. The driver was warm and snuggly in his cab at the front of the bus and well sheltered from the elements. What were we to do with our snowballs when the bus passed us by at the junction with Leinster Road where we were hiding behind a garden wall? Snowballs were made for targets and targets were made for snowballs. Consequently, any bus conductor was a ready-made target for our evil intentions. Just as the bus passed us, an avalanche of snow hurled itself at the platform and clobbered our good friend the conductor. Of course, if there were any passengers standing on the platform and holding the long silver pole waiting to disembark as the bus stop, well, that was even better, and they benefited from our snowballs. The fun got even better when the conductor banged the bell for the bus to stop. He hadn't a chance as he jumped off the platform and tried to chase us. We had planned for this eventuality and he received even more snow the second time, which stymied his progress and speeded our escape.

The CIÉ buses were the last of the old-fashioned type, and the bus conductor's role was being phased out, the plan being to have one-man-operated buses driving a more modern fleet, with the passengers embarking at the front. The few remaining bus conductors still working on the old-fashioned buses heralded the end of an era in transport in the city.

The popular comedy film *On the Buses*, however, made the biggest influence on my decision to apply for a summer job on the buses. It depicted the driver and conductor having a parallel life while working on the buses, including taking wrong turns and running into and out of the houses of desperate housewives at each terminus. I was accepted by CIÉ for a summer job and after a week's training, received my new uniform, my ticket dispensing machine, and a money satchel. I was ready for duty and was assigned to the Ringsend Bus Depot. I was the youngest bus conductor in the country, at sixteen, the personnel department misreading my age on the application form as eighteen and me not wishing to contradict. I used to stand in a little alcove on the platform with the bell over my head. Every so often I banged it once for the bus to stop or twice for the driver to move on. Some people enjoyed chasing after the bus, grabbing hold of the silver pole and jumping or hoisting themselves precariously on to the bus. It gave them a sense of bravado. Rightly so, because you could end up running at fifty miles an hour and holding the silver bar at the same time. Many of Ireland's Olympians were reputed to have gained their speed that way. Jumping off the bus before it stopped was another Olympian feat. One jumped off backwards in such a way that you then had to run after the bus for a few seconds to slow yourself down.

Absolutely crazy really, yet most people in Dublin did it and loved it.

I enjoyed life on the buses which mirrored the film to a lesser extent as there were lots of characters among the staff and the passengers. I was called 'Slits' by the lads on the buses, maybe because I had an interest in the fashion of the day with the emphasis on slits in young ladies' skirts. However, it could well have been my eyes, since at the time I liked Film Noir magazines such as the *Black Mask* I used to get in the Banba Bookshop in Rathmines. Peter Lorre and his fellow hoodlums used to interest me. Maybe I had evolved to look like him. Trying to earn lots of money in a short space of time was not difficult and some days I worked two and a half shifts. The short experience was one of the best educations one could hope for, as one dealt with drivers and passengers from every walk of life and who had travelled and experienced the world. Not only that but it helped me to discover parts of Dublin I wouldn't normally visit, including beyond Tallaght and beyond Blessington. I also discovered Riddal's Row, Chapel Lane and Samson's Lane near Liberty Hall, when they were building the new Ilac Centre. These were close to the Labour Exchange (aka 'The Scratcher'). Sometimes the drivers and conductors might pop into the Confession Box pub near the CIÉ canteen, and beside the Pro-Cathedral, 'for a quick one', before heading for home.

Before I returned to school that particular summer I worked for a week or two as a petrol pump attendant in Bolger's Motors on Thomas Street, across from the entrance to Guinness's Brewery. This again was the end of an era with 'self-service' becoming the mantra in shops and petrol stations. The lads in the brewery were regular customers to the garage and often gave me a few large bottles of stout for my troubles. At this stage, I had not gone down that particular route yet, despite being a connoisseur of the finest Altar Wines, only dabbling in shandy – a mixture of Smithwicks and lemonade. I presumed they gave me the stout to drink rather than for ornamental purposes and since I worked a long and somewhat boring day I decided to sample the black stuff. Oh, it's definitely an acquired taste but I managed to finish a large bottle of it between serving customers. The trouble began when I went out from my little hut to serve a customer and dreamily poured the remainder of the stout into his petrol tank. Luckily for me, in those days, customers remained in the car and the incident was not witnessed by the owner. I quickly switched from pouring stout to pouring petrol, waved him goodbye and hoped Guinness would be good for his car and give it strength to get him home, or to a garage at least.

What wasn't good for me, however, was the incident of the knife-wielding desperado of a gunman who robbed the petrol station while I was on duty. He looked like he had just stepped off the set of *The Good, the Bad and the Ugly* – a ringer for Eli Wallach. He rushed into my kiosk while I was enjoying my lunch and incoherently demanded the takings. But I knew what he meant! On this particular day, it didn't amount to much as the money had been deposited in a secret stash underground. Not wishing to join the pantheon of 1916 heroes, I suggested he help himself to what remained in the till. As he appeared to be more nervous than I, I offered him a bottle of stout and this he seemed to appreciate. 'They say it's good for you,' I laughed, trying to be sociable. He apologised for holding me up and said he hoped I didn't mind if he locked me in the kiosk while he made his getaway. 'No need for that,' I said, not wishing to trouble myself trying to escape. 'You just run along there now like a good chap and we'll say no more.' Off he went. I finished my squashed sambos and then rang the Gardaí. Only then did I realise how all shook up I was.

21

WHERE LOVE STORIES BEGAN

Not long afterwards I had a stint of working with a former Garda – the legendary 'Lugs' Branigan, who I had met years previously with my Dad down in the Liberties. I got a part-time job as a bouncer at the Zhivago nightclub. This was one of the most famous clubs in Dublin with the catch-call, 'Where Love Stories Begin'. However, if the truth were told it should have been, 'Where Love Stories End'!

On my first night I was introduced to 'Lugs' Branigan. 'Hello 'Lugs',' I went, being all familiar and tough.

'Mr Branigan to you,' he retorted in his best bashed-in face look. 'Sorry 'Lugs'. Yes 'Lugs'.' That's why he was a legend – he just had attitude and he expected the appropriate attitude from you too.

'Didn't see you at the Stadium,' he remonstrated, all those years later. I was there all right, but not for long. During one of my early training sessions, in the fifth round, didn't I receive a knock-out blow that lifted me right out of the ring. I didn't tell anyone it was the blasted punch bag that had landed the killer blow, thus ending a promising boxing career. My only consolation was that the punch bag was bigger than me. My next time in that stadium, I boxed, but for a different reason. The heading in the *Sunday Press* summed it up: 'Box and Roll Causes Mayhem at Chuck Berry Concert.' I didn't cause it but there was a whole lot of boxing going on.

I don't know how I managed to get the job in the Zhivago since I was more bounced against than bouncing from previous visits to other venues. My cousin, Daisy, used to go there a lot and I suspected she had put in a word for me. The club was the first to have special disco lighting in Ireland. This involved all sorts of fancy coloured lights beaming, flashing, twirling and twisting this way and that way, supposedly in sequence, but really in such a fashion that nobody really knew if they were drunk or sober. There was strip lighting in concentric circles on one of the dance floors. The décor was also 'different'. To me it looked like I had just walked into a Turkish harem, there were so many onion domes around the place. The club called itself 'Europe's Number 1 Nite Club' and I quickly pointed out to the manager the spelling mistake. There were a number of rules, including 'no denims or runners'. I saw plenty of the latter coming and going to the 'gents', either inside or outside the club.

The club itself was spread over three floors, with different kinds of music on each floor including reggae, rock, disco, and live bands such as Linda Martin and Chips, or the Go-Go Girls, known as Go Go's Galore. These young ladies wore long cardigans to below their knees. Once the music warmed up, they undid the cardigans, button by button and then let them drop to the floor. They weren't wearing too much underneath and sometimes also wore leather chainmail mini-dresses. 'Hot pants' were popular, not only with these girls but also with many of the customers. One of the floors specialised in 'slow sets', which I imagined was for slow learners. Here, there were couches in red velour where the tired could relax after a slow dance. There were regular DJs including DJ Lee. A popular record often played was James Brown's 'Sex Machine'.

As a result, everybody wanted to go to Zhivago's and be seen there. They had high hopes for the latter as it was virtually impossible to see anyone with the flashing lights and semi-darkness. So, everybody ended up talking to anyone. It didn't really matter since they all had come from the pubs and were talking through their hats before even coming into the place. You could be talking to a blonde one minute and the next moment she would be highlighted with a big purple beam which turned her into a waxwork model from Madame Tussaud's horror section. She would disappear as the lights went off, which was just as well as you too would want to disappear. The girls had similar experiences and I often heard some of them chatting and saying to each other, 'Did ye see yer man I was dancing with there? He looks like a gravedigger, digging his own grave!'

To help me along in my new part-time career I grew a moustache, Mexican-style, to send the message out to any would-be troublemakers. I think it worked, as I soon became known as El Diablo. Sometimes, though, I was called Little Lugs. I also wore Teddy Boy shoes, which had extra-volume and thicker soles and heels that gave me an extra few inches, in case they were needed. These Elvis-type blue suede shoes were known variously as Hush Puppies and 'brothel creepers'. I also took up Kenpo Karate, hoping to become Bruce O'Lee, but nearly ended up in a stir-fry having been more chopped against than chopping.

Monday was a very busy night as many from the Showband and the Irish Country and Western world had a day off from touring the country and used to pop in for a few hours, and then fall out. 'Lugs' referred to them as 'the huckle buck' and 'jiving crowd'. I thought he should have added 'the slurry crowd'. They were very full of themselves, not to mention full of drink and full of Old Spice. One chap introducing himself to me at the door as 'Big' Tom. He was that all right and looked like he had just stepped off his tractor to boot! There he was, humming to himself, something someone said was called 'Four Roads to Glenamaddy'. He must have taken a wrong turning, I reckoned. I overheard some of the girls in the ticket office talking about a singer who called himself 'Butch' Moore and who had a preference for walking the streets in the rain. One streak of bacon who looked like he had just returned from famine-ravished Biafra called himself either 'sticky' or 'Dickie' Rock, which I thought apt given his pink-and-white-striped outfit. I had vaguely heard about him and fans begging him to 'spi' on me Dickie'. I whispered to him that 'my Mammy said you should press your hands on your ears every day and eventually they will flatten down'. He just looked at me, not bothering to say thanks for the good advice. As he passed in, I called over to 'Lugs' in the office, 'Hey, Mr Branigan, your cousin has just walked in!'

Other bands introduced themselves as the 'Mighty' Avons or the 'Royal' Showband. One guy with an English accent told me he was 'Long John' Baldry! He was accompanied by a 'Cat' Stevens. Another chap called himself Engelbert Humperdinck. I thought he had some nerve trying to confuse us all and I told him what's what. 'Hey sham, are you for real? We'll stick to Humpty Dumpty! In you go! Neeext!' One group said they were 'the Hoedowners', as if I didn't know they were clod-hoppers and country bumpkins. All I had to do was look at their ill-fitting country clobber and their 'arrah, go on outa dat, with ye'. I expected them to break out into old time fiddle tunes anytime. You'd think they had just stepped off the set for the *Riordan's* having finished churning the butter with Benjy. Another bunch even had the audacity to say they were the Hillbillies! I thought they had some nerve, trying to lower the tone of the place. At least they were honest and upfront about it, I decided, and waved them in.

I was somewhat more circumspect when a bunch of lads – 'we're drifters' – appeared at the entrance, singing their hearts out. I recall it was some number with the words, 'make me an island' and 'I live in the house with the white-washed gable' or such like. Now, I had nothing against travellers or drifters per se, but I thought they should really be looking for the Salvation Army Hostel. I looked over at 'Lugs', and he gave me the nod to let them in. I gave them a good look over, however, to make such they weren't carrying pickaxes, hatchets, slash hooks or blades hidden in potatoes under their caps. No sooner were they in when a painter in white overalls came rushing up to the door. 'Just parking the caravan,' he laughed. 'I'm Joe and I'm with the Drifters, just gone in.' I knew my suspicions had been well-founded. And here he was, with big black bushy eyebrows, coming to the Zhivago dressed in tight-fitting painter's overalls, which looked more like a suit. He must have had aspirations as he also wore a white shirt. I could see that he was not a dab hand at painting as there was not a speck of paint anywhere on the overalls. Or maybe he just specialised in white-washing farmhouse gables.

'You've a handy number there, pal,' I winked at him, pointing at the overalls. 'Don't strain yourself too much inside!' I knew that when he would be leaving later, his white outfit would be multi-coloured with spilt Harvey Wallbangers, Tequila Sunrises, Pimm's No.1, Captain Morgan's Jamaica Rum, Screwdrivers and every other type of cocktail they sold upstairs. 'At least he would look more like a painter, then,' I surmised. I used to envy those barmen who just threw all kinds of coloured drinks into a container, shook them vigorously, and then dumped the contents into a glass. 'That'll be £20 when you're ready, please!'

No sooner was this Joe chap in the door and sitting at the bar with the rest of the drifters, when a clamour of female shrieks went up. Didn't he get up from his stool and start singing 'you're such a good-looking woman' and gyrating in front of a mob of howling disco dancers. He threw off the jacket of his overalls and tossed it into the crowd. A near riot ensued and I called 'Lugs' to stand by for trouble. I couldn't believe my eyes then. Didn't the women start throwing their knickers at this singing painter, who kept on singing as if there was no tomorrow. Well, although it was not advertised as such, it was party time in the Zhivago that night, and we didn't leave the premises until nearly five in the morning. Before leaving I had to go around collecting all the rubbish and I must have collected enough women's underwear to completely re-stock Marguerite's drapery shop in Mountain View.

I had to refuse entry to young lads who said they were from the Cotton Mill. 'Sorry. You're all underage. This is strictly over twenty-one's only. Step to one side now please. Sorry! You can't come in. No boys or girls allowed in.' Likewise, when a young girl appeared at the door. 'Hello, I'm Dana,' she said, introducing herself to me as if I knew who she was. She looked like a schoolgirl, with long black hair, a very white face, and quite petite. Nearly a dwarf, I thought.

'Name doesn't ring a bell,' I said. 'What's the surname?'

'Brown,' she replied. 'Hmmm. Dana Brown. No, don't know the name, sorry. Are you over twenty-one?'

'No,' she admitted, somewhat shyly. I was distracted by her accent. All kinds of everything ran through my mind including that barricade buster, Bernadette Devlin, up in Northern Ireland. She even looked like her, what with her long hair and size. I decided I had better be extremely careful with this one and not to be taken in with her sweet face. I could imagine her as a right rabble-rouser.

'Are you with Margo and the Country Mushrooms?' I asked, having vaguely heard of some such band.

'No band,' she replied, with her sad little face. I knew I was right. If she was not fighting at the barricades she was probably in the school's children's choir, indoctrinating them to become Mata Hari's. What is she doing coming to a place like the Zhivago? I wondered, suspiciously.

'Run along, now, with you,' I suggested and standing well behind the door. 'Come back when you have done your Inter Cert or when you are older, whichever comes first,' I added, trying to be polite. I was certainly in a very tough business, and it was my job to ensure the smooth running of Ireland's top disco and nightclub, particularly in my role as the Junior Assistant to the Deputy Head of Security Personnel.

Another crowd called themselves the Freshmen, which was a complete lie since they all reeked of various noxious substances ranging from dung to joss sticks. I couldn't understand why they didn't use normal band names such as the Troggs, the Kinks or the Hollies, but most certainly not the name used by that bunch of monks from Skellig Michael, who called themselves Hermann's Hermits. Or, for that matter, the American band calling themselves the Monkees, after a choir of singing monkeys someone must have seen in the zoo.

None of these Monday night music lads fooled me as I knew exactly where they were from. You could easily tell as they were running in and out of the place to 'have a leak' up the nearby lane instead of using the Gents. They obviously much preferred to use 'outside latrines' such as the fields and ditches they had down in the country. I knew only too well the situation down in the country. Why, hadn't I visited my uncle's farm in Laois only recently. I couldn't find the toilet and ended up running out to the haggard behind the farmhouse, just like these other short-taken lads. They may have been out of the bog for the night, I concluded, but you couldn't take the bog out of them. After one night when Skid Row entertained them, I suggested to one or two as they were staggering out that they should learn from Brush Shields and pack in all that hoedown and hillbilly music of theirs. They thought I was being funny and fell out of the place roaring their heads off.

And then I saw his face. 'Hi there! I'm John Lennon,' he said to me in an English accent, as if I was supposed to know the name of every Joe Soap that came into the place. I said to myself, who let this hippy out? I was on the door by myself that night as 'Lugs' was busy in the office. He reminded me of either Charles Hawtrey or Charles Manson, but I wasn't quite sure which. He also looked like he had just been pulled from the wringer what with his bearded face, long hair cascading everywhere around his head, those circular-framed glasses and dressed in hippy-style pyjamas which hadn't seen an iron since the Iron Age. Oh, he looked a real suspicious type of character alright. So, I said to him, 'Step to one side, please.' I then told him to raise his arms outwards while I frisked him down for dangerous weapons. Just then I saw his pal, next in the queue. He looked reasonably respectable with long hair and a beard covering a young face, bordering on the babyish, in fact. To abide by the rules of entry I asked him if he was over twenty-one.

'No, I'm Paul!' replied the real smart aleck and he just walked right in as if he owned the place. If I weren't dealing with this other hippy I would there and then have grabbed that Paul chap by the scruff of the neck and the seat of his smarty pyjama pants and hurled him head-first out the door.

'Mind games,' said the hippy. 'This is what this is.'

'No, sorry. I don't do crosswords,' I replied, wondering what on earth he was doing coming to the Zhivago to play his crosswords. Everyone is going crazy here tonight, I thought. The moment I got home, I decided, I would definitely be taking my spoon of cod liver oil. 'Hold on! What's this?' I pulled out a bottle from his sock.

'Oh, sorry guv. That's just a drop of Stowshus for back in the hotel,' he explained.

I peered closer. Yes, it was indeed and I could see the familiar image on the label of a fiddle right next to Louie the lopsided leprechaun. Below that was the name of the brewer, Tabhair Aire Stowshus. 'Okay, fair enough,' I said, and put it back.

'Ta, mate,' he nodded.

The poor chap, I thought, having some sympathy for him. He obviously regarded the Iveagh Hostel as his hotel. 'You seem okay. Carry on, but no messing, do you hear? I'll be watching you! And tell that pal of yours I'll be keeping a sharp eye on him too.' And off with him muttering something about all of us needing love, giving peace a chance, power to the people, number 9 dream, whatever happened to Jammet's and needing somebody's help. Probably figuring out Crosaire's cryptic crossword, I reckoned.

I never had too much trouble with the clientele, even with the infamous 'Hurricane' Higgins, who arrived carrying his snooker cue, which I insisted he leave in the cloakroom. The only exception was a few Kerry football fans up to see Dublin thrash their team in Croke Park. I didn't like the look of them with their wellies and behaving as drunk as skunks. Worse still, I had already spent the evening cleaning and polishing the bouncy timber dance floor all ready for the real dancers, or those that regarded themselves as being Dublin's version of Pan's People. I had no intention of scraping farmyard manure off the floor at the end of the night. I told them that this was a disco and we didn't do foxtrotting or bog-trotting or whatever they called it. I suggested they take themselves off up to Parnell Square where all the other sheep-shaggers went. 'Off with yez, now. Whist! Whist outa dat! Whup! Whup! Whup!' I hollered.

However, this kindly advice did not go down too well. You'd think they were about to grab hold of the elusive Puck Goat down in the Kerry Mountains beyond Killorglin the way they hurled themselves on me *en masse*. 'The power of drink,' I said to myself and eventually managed to wriggle myself out of the scrummage. Luckily for me, 'Lugs' had shown me a few nifty 'duck and dive' tricks. They ended up knocking the stuffing out of each other before 'Lugs' came along and sent them spinning backwards and forwards out the door. 'Well done, lad,' he said to me. 'You have great potential! And don't forget to keep using them bony elbows. They do a power of good!' He nearly laughed his head off at this stage.

One of the perks of working at the Zhivago was the opportunity to pop in for free to Barbarella's nightclub around the corner on Fitzwilliam Lane. This I used to do on my breaks and since the bouncers in that establishment had heard of El Diablo they always gave me the nod to pop in for a short while. I had only one reason and it wasn't for a cup of tea! This club was unique in having bikini-clad water nymphs lolling and splashing around in some kind of small bath tub or foot spa, pretending to be a swimming pool, and close to the dance floor. This was supposed to be a huge enticement for clients to come in and spend lots of money. In fact, all they did was come in and sit around with their eyes popping out of their heads, completely and utterly distracted and having no interest in dancing or drinking. That's why I wouldn't go near Crocs nightclub, up the street, where the owner had a pet alligator in a fish tank just inside the door – I had no interest whatsoever in seeing my eyes popping out of my head!

My stint in the Zhivago eventually ended, as it was time to go back to school. All in good time I felt, as I had no intention of ending up being more danced upon than dancing. Not that I was a great dancer anyway. I discovered this in Sloopy's nightclub on Fleet Street, on a night out with the lads just before I went back to school. Trying to do a John Travolta imitation to 'Staying Alive', I came to the realisation that the splits literally meant that – you split your trousers and quickly had to split for home. A pity, as I had intended to tell my intended how deep was my love. We also tried other clubs but were told to 'come back in a few years'.

So, Nobby, I and the rest of the lads had to stick with St Mary's in Terenure, where we had to endure a band we called 'The Yewsless'. There was a popular DJ, however, and he always seemed to be playing

Carly Simon's 'You're So Vain' on our entering. That was when Sally first saw me. We also frequented the Aquarius youth club beside the entrance to Mount Jerome. In the words of Sister Sledge this was where we became completely 'lost in music'. Moreover, its lighting system was mesmerising for us as we had never seen anything like the startling luminous effect it gave to one's clothes, especially if we wore anything white. The strobe lighting and the swirling ball in the ceiling bouncing light all over us had us living on a different planet. That is, until some skinhead's girlfriend dancing behind me pointed out that 'ye have all dandruff on your shoulders, so ye have'. I recognised trouble when I heard it. She hailed from Hell's Kitchen, which was part of the notorious area of Mountpleasant Buildings in Rathmines. 'Mots' like her had a habit of carrying a hatchet and/or a Stanley knife in their handbags. So, unless you wished for an embroidered face, courtesy of Doc Marten, you quickly 'locked hard' and away with you. 'Bovver Boys', as they were called, were part of that Bay City Rollers, Sweet, Mud and 'wanna be in my gang, my gang, my gang' brigade. You wouldn't want to look at them even sideways, or you'd end up cross-eyed, for sure.

We were more 'heavy rock' fans, and often frequented Pat Egan's Sound Cellar at the bottom of Grafton Street, or Bluebird Records on the Quays. It was in those darkened emporiums reeking with the aroma of joss sticks that we first heard Free's 'Alright Now' and Steppenwolf's 'Born to be Wild'. That's where we were to be found on Saturday afternoons, after a stint hanging around the Dandelion Market on Stephen's Green. Alternatively, we spent our time lazing on a sunny afternoon near the Fusilier's Arch, watching the girls go by – dedicated followers of fashion.

We liked when the DJ in the Aquarius played Hawkwind's 'Silver Machine'. We had never heard anything like it before - the sound of drums intermingling with rotating helicopter blades and building up to a crescendo. I also liked Jethro Tull's *Thick as a Brick* LP, with its eight-page newspaper cover and articles about 'Lust of the Small Nun', but they never played them. 'Try the Osibisa Club,' the DJ kindly suggested. That was where Wilf and Wolfie, with flowers in their spaghetti junction hair and Afghan coats, even in summer, used to go. They talked about joss sticks and 'way out' all the time. They could never recall where they had been except that it was always 'far out man'. They liked Deep Purple, Purple Haze and Purple Hearts. Not to mention all their chatter about Woodstock and Monterey, Zen, Shay Guevara, Crumb's 'Stoned agin!' poster, and some Indian fakir called Maharishi Mahesh Yogi Bear. They also liked these foreign names such as Marrakesh, Kathmandu and Xanadu, but there was no mention of Timbuktu. They chattered about 'trips' and 'tripping'. Very careless, I thought, as our Mum was always telling us to tie our shoelaces before we left the house. To cap it all they went on *ad nauseam* about the Moon. All sorts of Moons in fact – Keith Moon, who they called 'Moon the Loon', the Man in the Moon just landed from a UFO and some oriental chap called Sun Myung Moon and his band The Moonies. You would feel cold winds blowing if you mentioned the Mamas and the Papas, the Mothers of Invention, the Bachelors or the Beach Boys. Talk about bad vibrations! The Horslips were acceptable, even though we all turned into céilí-dancing air guitarists on hearing 'Dearg Doom'.

Hair was the big issue in those days for us – we wanted lots of it and streaming down our backs. I was blessed with long bushy and wavy hair but I got a jolt one day when the bus I was going home on stalled at the corner of George's Street. I happened to glance at a bright sign halfway up a side wall. This large neon sign leered at me, or so it seemed. It was of a young man's head with the words, 'Why Go Bald' over it. The red and yellow sign flashed on an off showing a Larry lookalike one second, with lots of hair, the next moment looking like a smarmy baldy boy. I had a nightmare about it. Would I end up like Yul Brynner in *The King and I*? Or worse still, like the lollipop-sucking Telly Savalas in *Kojak* and going around saying, 'Who loves ya baby?'

I could just imagine it. Yes sir, please step this way. Yes, it's looking very bad indeed, terminal in fact. Bring your head right over here and we'll have a look. Your cow's lick, did you say? May I beg to differ, sir? It looks more like you were licked by a herd of cows! Please put your head there, sir, and we will organise an immediate fitting. How does that feel? A bit tight? Lopsided? Try this one. Now that's better, isn't it, sir? Here is a small container of Stick Fast glue that will hold the crown topper in place all day long. No, sir. You won't be needing a comb. Wind? No, it won't blow in the wind. Do you like this shade? That's just perfect! Even your Mammy wouldn't recognise you! Oh, £5,000 plus VAT and a weekly maintenance charge to be discussed at your leisure. Yes, that suits you just perfectly! Shall I wrap it for you, sir? Fire escape? Completely unnecessary, sir. We have a complete range of all-weather sunglasses right over here. No charge for the pouch! Thank you, sir! A pleasure doing business!'

I would be in a quandary. What if my Mum didn't recognise me? I would have to introduce myself to everyone, including my family, with hair that made me look like Mr Spock. Perfectly straight, with not a single hair out of place. Shiny black, with a fringe covering my glinting eyes and my ears inevitably turning pointy. All my cow's licks' gone. 'Beam the young man up to the front bedsit, Freddy. That will be one month's rent in advance. Everything supplied except linen.'

It was like a daydream, however, going to the Kenilworth cinema, which everyone called 'The Kenno' (later The Classic). This was located nearly opposite Century House. It was owned by the affable Alby Kelly and he had *The Rocky Horror Picture Show* running there for years. While enjoying the film, everyone threw rice and confetti in the air, reflecting the anarchy of the film. And it was here that the petrol-bombing altar boy showed us how to make smoke bombs using discarded film rolls. He also showed us where and how to buy contraband 'bangers' at Halloween from the Moore Street hawkers. We agreed that he was definitely a bad influence.

22

FROM THE FLEA HOUSE TO FLOUR

When circumstances such as a shortage of funds prevented us from going into town to see films in the Carlton, Cinerama, the Adelphi, the Astor, the Corinthian, the Ambassador or the Savoy, there was one local cinema we frequented every so often, and only if we really had to, which was the Stella in Rathmines. This huge barn of a cinema, which had a balcony, was named after the wife of a publican who at one time also owned the nearby Slattery's pub. This was an old pub, probably one hundred years, and full of atmosphere, low counters and sloping floors to keep the inebriated steady. The original hall at the side of the pub also acted as a long snug, having a bench stretching along the hallway wall. This faced a hatch halfway down the hall and which connected to the back wall of the main bar counter inside the pub. The barman was therefore able to serve customers in front of him and, through this hatch, those behind him.

Coinciding with a gradual decline in its fortunes, the Stella became notorious in its latter years as 'the Flea House'. This had inherited the accolade after the closure on a nearby cinema, the Princess, one of Dublin's first cinemas. It was in the Stella that you got more than a flea in your ear from the usher or usherette. It was filthy and disgusting! The seats were so worn that the original soft covering had vanished and you sat on a shiny, greasy surface, slipping and sliding off onto an even more slippery and sticky floor. Damp and humid, even the huge sagging curtains perspired. In fact, such was its reputation for flea infestation that it was said that if you went in a cripple, 'you came running out'. Despite this people continued to visit, including ourselves, more often out of desperation, boredom or laziness.

However, the local priests in Rathmines Church were not happy with the story of the cripple running out of the cinema. This church is the one with the huge green dome that can be seen from the Hellfire Club in the Dublin Mountains. This dome was originally made in Scotland and destined for Russia in 1917. However, because of the various revolutions which culminated in the overthrow of the Tsar and the Romanov monarchy, it ended up in Rathmines. The Tsar and Tsarina had been deeply influenced by the nefarious Rasputin the Mad Monk. His influence continued as far afield as Dublin and from the lofty pulpit, wedged halfway up the wall near the main altar, the priests warned their flock not to be putting about stories of cured cripples running out of the Stella.

Freckles, always the sceptic, explained to us the real reason for the priest's warning. Mind you, he was a total heretic himself, favouring Martin Luther over Martin Luther King. He had no time for King, being wary of his dreaming about distant mountains. He said that if King had tried to climb up to the Hellfire Club, any such dreams would soon disappear. Anyway, he was likewise not a fan of the Zhivago's music and much preferred Fats Waller, Fats Domino or Muddy Waters and their jazz and blues music. Freckles once asked me if they played the Mormon Tabernacle Choir or the Blind Boys of Alabama in the Zhivago. 'Yes,' I replied. 'And not forgetting Big Tom and the Mainliners!' That's the kind of person he was and had strange views on everything. He said if Martin Luther King went around singing the blues like Fats and Muddy he would have had a bigger impact. He was in two minds about Louis Armstrong, asking what was singing with his 'what a wonderful world' and 'you have all the time in the world'. 'It isn't and you don't,' he said. 'There are a lot of strange things going on in the world and I intend to find out.'

As I said, Freckles was a total unbeliever about everything. Except, that is, Mao Tse Tung. He always carried a copy of Mao's *Little Red Book*, written in Chinese, with him everywhere, and often took it out and placed it on a table in front of him for all to see. It didn't matter to him that he couldn't read Chinese! When you met him you immediately knew he had that heretical look to him. Maybe it was the Luke Kelly-looking hairstyle with no rhyme nor reason to it. Shooting this way and that, bushy, Afro-style but with a loud ginger hue. It also reminded me of Noel Redding from the Jimi Hendrix Experience. Freckles was also trying to grow a moustache, presumably so that people would mistake him for the great scientist, Einstein.

Anyway, Freckles had the inside story on the Stella's cripples and the church. The real situation was that they didn't want people flocking to the Stella for a cure. This would do untold damage to the Lourdes 'racket' he pointed out. 'Who's "they" and what "racket"?' we wanted to know. 'Charging and flying people to Lourdes just to be dunked into freezing cold water. That's the racket. It's a huge business, with lots of people making buckets of money from the plight of people who would get a real cure in the Stella. Just from the fleas,' he added. 'That's why Bruce Lee is known as "the fist of fury" – he uses fly ointment.'

'So,' Freckles Luther-Paisley continued, 'with so many people travelling around the world today, some coming to Ireland, and opening up all these takeaways in Dublin, surely it is not surprising that these amazing fleas should find their way into places like the Stella.' We had to agree and decided the next time we got sick we would go to the cinema and come running out, cured, just like the cripple.

Some people said he had a brazen neck, others said a brazen head and Slattery's pub should have changed its name to just that after one of his visits. Coming out of the Stella on one occasion, Freckles said he was popping into Slattery's to use the Gents. We waited outside. In he went, not to the Gents but to the snug. He sat down and relaxed. There was no one else there except a retired-looking gentleman, having his pint and puffing away contentedly on his pipe. After a short-time the man got up, left his pipe wedged in the ashtray and headed off to the Gents. What did Freckles do? Over he moved, grabbed your man's pipe from the ashtray and started smoking it, 'just for practice,' he later told us. Then, up he stood and tapped vigorously on the bar hatch with the pipe. In a deep smoker's voice, he proclaimed, 'same again when you're ready, Jem.' A pint was shoved through the hatch and Freckles picked it up and drank it back in one go. Then, after having a last quick leisurely puff on the pipe, off with him. 'Let's go,' he said, and off home with us as fast as our legs could carry us.

Even the school principal, known as Flour because of his shock of white hair which looked unusual on someone relatively young, was taken in by Freckles. Some in the school regarded Freckles as a bit of a 'brainbox', probably because he misled them by always rubbing his chin and giving the impression that he was ruminating on something important. Consequently, he would be seen going around the school with Flour, who called him Frederick, helping him in various ways and chatting away like he was the vice principal. He was even allowed to miss classes. The worst thing was that when Flour passed me in the school corridor, there was no such recognition that Freckles was my cousin. I was just treated like the rest of the pupils – an impertinence.

Flour was a tough principal and we were all in great fear of him, except Freckles. All Flour had to do was do nothing. His white-headed presence in the building was enough to maintain control. The rare occasion he was not there, emotions just erupted and the pupils went absolutely berserk, running around, fighting, throwing chalk and dusters – releasing an enormous amount of pent-up feelings. We knew he carried the leather, never visible, yet there. He wore padded shoes ensuring that we never heard him until we saw him, thus turning us all into bags of nerves, jumpy, always looking over our shoulders. We ended up with swivelling skulls like in *Night of the Living Dead*, *Dr Terror's House of Horrors* or *The Return of the Zombies*, all of which we had seen in the Carlton cinema in town. He spoke few words. All he had to say was 'my office' and you knew you were in trouble. His eyes took in everything, knew every boy by name, their family and circumstances. Very bad from our point of view because whenever we met him we knew we were open books, all revealed.

The name of other teachers will give some flavour of their mettle – the Brick, the Killer, Harry Hedgehog and the Dustman. With Harry Hedgehog, we were completely distracted with his massive head of spiky grey hair. Better still, when giving us regular tests on the blackboard, he would write the answers on the opposite end of the blackboard and tell us not to look. Once he turned his back on the class, all hell broke loose with chalk fights ensuring the classroom looked more like a civil war zone with barrages and batteries of the best chalk fired at random at every available target. We had the Brick for Biology and learnt nothing. He was built like a brick and looked like Heathcliff in *Wuthering Heights* with long black hair, black eyebrows, blackened face from endless shaving, black locks, and black eyes that seemed to snarl at us. He might as well have been teaching us Chinese for all the difference it made. We hadn't a clue whatsoever about what he was trying to teach. We must have driven him mad as whenever he asked us questions, we always gave the wrong answer. He might ask, 'How do you dissect a worm?' We'd reply, 'with a hammer and tongs'.

The Killer sat in a corner of the classroom disseminating his meagre thoughts on English literature and grammar. He was young and extremely well groomed and wore a suit that looked like it had just been purchased from Louis Copeland. Yet he seemed to speak and look at you with a sneer and was liable to turn on you very quickly, inflicting lasting damage. The Dustman was very popular with some. We had him for Maths. He also taught Woodwork and Metalwork. Along with his distinctive well-worn attire, having recently returned from working on the English building sites where he had learnt his trades, he used to call us all 'comrades'. He had his own way of communicating to us, starting with 'Well, comrades, I'm going to tell you a story.' He would then spend most of the class telling us all about his time visiting Russia, the political situation in the country, and finishing with 'Now comrades, where were we?' He would invariably speak in a different language, as in 'The thus actual sum of the thus actual square on the thus actual opposite two sides, is thus actually equal to the thus actual sum…,' etc.

When our French teacher, Brother Ardle, went off to become a priest, we were delighted, not because he was becoming a priest but because he was gone. He was tough on us, not immune from using the leather and subtracting marks rather than giving marks. After one exam I ended up with a mark of -40 per cent! We looked forward to our new teacher, having heard good rumours. Despite that, they might as well have brought a pig into the parlour and offered him a cup of tea for all the interest we had in learning French. We just could not grasp the pronunciation, not to mention the grammar. We felt we had to assume a different personality, completely at odds with one's own, when trying to speak French. We found it difficult enough to speak English as it was. We would have much preferred to learn German, since you pronounce the words just as you see them on the page.

His replacement was good alright, but despite our best intentions we just could not learn or concentrate. She was French, which helped. She was young, gorgeous and very appropriately attired in the Bridget Bardot, Ursula Andress, Raquel Welch or Catherine Deneuve style we had become familiar with. Her name was Madame Brasser, with a silent 'r' which we didn't bother with, but which finished us off altogether as regards learning French.

The school was a new one, built as an extension to Synge Street by the Christian Brothers in the early 1970s. I never settled into the school, or 'Singer' as we called it, and for the five years there I just wanted to be out of it. With a principal like Flour and other terrifying teachers, you were living in a complete reign of terror, waiting for the guillotine every day. Robert Emmet's skull might have gone missing, but Robespierre's was alive and well in our school. Despite the advent of 'Free Education' in the 1960's, the education system for me was the same old 'Murder Machine'- lacking head, heart and soul.

I liked certain subjects but never could get a handle on science, such was my fear of the teacher, Brother Mee. He was huge, reeked of chalk dust and had small eyes in a fat copper-coloured face. He was tough and looked like a wrestler. Well, he wrestled the life out of me. If he asked a question, say, 'What is a Bunsen burner?' I'd more likely reply, 'A bag of Tayto,' or 'Yes, I agree,' or 'How's your mother keeping?' My problem started when I missed a few days from school, having my hand stitched in the Meath Hospital. When I returned to the science class, I had obviously missed out on a few topics and could never catch up as I was never updated. I had nightmares about Spirogyra and Chlamydomonas, whatever they were. I couldn't fathom why they called a cell a cell. I always imagined cells to be places in jail, like in Kilmainham where the men of 1916 were locked up. How could I possibly be thinking of the components of a human cell when I was thinking of James Connolly being taken from his cell on a stretcher out to the Stonebreakers' Yard to be shot, while sitting in a chair. Every time I heard of atoms I thought of the atom bomb that blew the living daylights out of the poor people living in Hiroshima and Nagasaki. I felt it was a total disgrace pretending to be teaching us about something while totally confusing us at precisely the same time. The worst aspect was that science occupied two periods, a double class three times weekly. At the end of five years the Department of Education awarded me an N.G. in science in my Leaving Certificate. I supposed at the time that at least it was better than no grade. Freckles got an A.

Maybe it was the method of teaching, or the lack of method. For the most part, I felt I was not being taught anything in any subject, just told. There was no effort to see if I actually *understood*. A case in point being grammar. I rarely missed classes. If I was sick, I went to school, no matter how bad I was. I still remember with embarrassment having very bad coughs on a few occasions which just wouldn't go away for days. There I was sitting in the classroom, coughing all the time like a mad dog and trying to restrain the cough at the same time. In this particular instance, I missed one day's school. The teacher was discussing grammar and adjectives, nouns, verbs, etc. and I wasn't told the next day what I had missed. Consequently, I never learnt the difference between a preposition and a proposition, between a noun and a nun, between a verb and a vibe.

On the other hand, Brother Donald dispensed with all the geography textbooks and taught us his way. Part of his strategy involved placing less emphasis on words and more on charts, diagrams and maps – the picture telling the story. We related to his alternative teaching methodology and we all got A's in geography in the Leaving Certificate. Depending on the teacher, our minds either expanded or shrank. With Brother Donald our minds expanded. More importantly, we enjoyed the subject and appreciated what he was doing for us.

I wasn't the only pupil with such a horror of certain teachers. One terrified pupil was so distraught that he climbed up on the roof of the school, threatening to jump. It took hours to coax him down. Most of us had huge sympathy for him. He was a decent, kind, calm, big bear of a chap and always friendly towards us. Many times, the bunch of us, with him, would straggle home together along the Grand Canal. The only reason why he eventually came down from the roof was thanks to us. On hearing the commotion, everyone rushed outside, pushing teachers out of the way. We all looked up at this tiny fat figure. We waved up to him and he waved back, despite his obvious distress and shouting that he was not coming down. This went on for quite a while until a solution was found. Some of the bright lads at the back started shouting up at him, 'Jump! Jump! Jump!' This was kindly meant, of course, boys always have great feelings of empathy towards each other. There was also the expectation of catching him with a sheet, as in the comics, or else wanting to keenly observe the ratio between object and target, weight and velocity of the object, the possible trajectories and direction, the impact of the object hitting the target, proportion of object dispersed, and cumulative result and analysis. Moreover, the fact that he had Billy Bunter's girth was also an important factor. Would he bounce? Would he do a Batman and fly? We were very interested in observing all these aspects. Don't forget also that this was the era of Apollo, with monkey's flying into space and men landing on the Moon and so we had great expectations. Some David Bowie fan whispered: 'Major Tom to Ground Control – "he's made the grade"', followed by, 'he's floating in a most peculiar kind of way', 'Has he taken his protein pills?', 'You can become a hero for just one day.' School was taking on a new meaning for us. Things were looking up!

Not only were my Secondary School days some of the most challenging in my life but, to rub the horror in, we had to fundraise constantly to expand the school buildings so that the next generation would have more of the same terror. However, when I say 'the most challenging days of my life,' I mean the school part of every day. I had many other lives outside school that more than compensated for the misery experienced in school. This fundraising codology was called, 'Be a Brick, buy a Brick', and it never ended. We always needed money for one more brick, so we had to call on every house in Dublin for years, trying to extricate money from people. We carried around white square cards with small boxes or bricks imprinted on them. When people contributed money, their names would be written on those boxes. Each card had about fifty boxes. No sooner was one card filled in, then you were given another. We all ended up having tiny illegible handwriting. I was just another brick in the wall.

Sports training was no different. Casual and contemptuous. We were sent up to Sundrive Park every week to practice football. It was a former quarry, recently filled in, covered up and renamed Eammon Ceannt Park. One of my challenges was that the family couldn't afford football gear for me. I had no togs or boots. Instead, and luckily for me, in First Year I still wore shorts rather than 'longers' to school, the family again not being able to afford new trousers for me. I got much slagging from the rest of the lads, being the only one still wearing shorts. However, when it came to playing football, I didn't need to tog out since I was already wearing shorts. I then put plastic bags over my shoes and ran on to the pitch, or, most times, slithered onto the pitch. The situation was compounded even further as I didn't know the rules of soccer. I had never been taught and despite asking the teacher, I was told I would learn as I played. For me, however, that was the quandary, as I didn't know how to play! I didn't know the difference between soccer, Gaelic or rugby. When the ball came my way, I didn't know what to do with it except to try to kick it, which was made more difficult with my baggy feet. Most times I missed the ball and when I did make contact I would kick it the wrong way and at times even scored goals – 'own goals' as it turned out! Sometimes I picked the ball up and threw it to someone, thus giving the opposing side a handy penalty. You can just imagine how popular I became. By Second Year I was wearing 'longers' and I rolled the legs up and rolled the socks down and carried on, uselessly. I gradually managed to abstain myself from training after that. I would lie down on the grass and roll down the hill away from the pitch and out of sight. Then I was gone!

It was not the end of my sporting career, however. We had an All-Ireland Altar Boys' Football League, and which was a much more relaxed affair with little emphasis on rules or clothing. We even tolerated mixed matches. This was a tradition going back to the early days when we used to invite the local Girl Guides and orphans from St Mary's into the altar boys' changing room for chats and to play board games. We had got to know them at the Sales of Work run by Sister Pedro. We loved the Wheel of Fortune and it was a great meeting point with the orphans. We also used to meet them at various processions and ceremonies and in Rosary Hall for parties. The father of one Girl Guide always seemed to eye me with pathological hatred, muttering something about my 'intentions'. I knew he had me written off as Jack the Ripper even before I'd ever spoken to his daughter, who had a lovely natural all-over tan.

We reluctantly accepted a challenge from the girls in the orphanage who had a basketball team. We felt it would be a one-sided game to our advantage. We obliged and went along anyway, half-heartedly. What we hadn't anticipated was that some of the team were apprentice Sumo wrestlers and chopstick practitioners. We were literally run into the ground. Just when I was about to pop the ball into the net, I felt this whack at the back of my head and I reeled off, dazed, towards the side lines. On another occasion, I ran in the direction of some girl holding the ball. She ran even faster towards me and barrel-chested me nearly into the next world. That was not all. Another girl, with long, flowing, really blonde wavy hair, crystal-clear blue eyes, perfect skin and exuding an awesome innocence, tackled me when I was holding the ball. Tackled is putting it mildly. She kneed me in a place where it hurts the most. Then I bowed towards her, Japanese style, not out of politeness, but in pain. The Samurai, wishing to finish what she had commenced, kneed me again, this time in the chin, just as I was bowing. I reeled back and was shoved out of the way, as if I was a door that required closing, or in this case, slamming. We lost the game with not even one score to our credit. We agreed to a follow-up match. 'Oh yes,' we said with much enthusiasm. With equal enthusiasm, we failed to show.

23

Dancing with the Grateful Dead

We visited Mount Jerome in an unofficial capacity every so often. Some of the more influential elements in our cohort used to encourage us to play football or rather, kick ball, as we were rambling around. We just kicked or tapped the ball around, real casual, and if I managed to head the ball, well, that was a bonus. Even if we had no football or, as was often the case, it ended up being kicked into the nearby River Poddle which ran alongside the Low Walk, we improvised, using old flowerpots or grave decorations found lying around discarded.

During inclement weather we were forced to find shelter, and where else but in the quaint cosiness of a vault. If someone carried a deck of cards, even better. The particular vaults we took shelter in were near the Victorian Chapel, just off the Hawthorn Walk. We ambled down a sloping passageway between the Harvie and the Dycer tombs, opposite General Cockburn's and overlooked by the Cusack mausoleum. The Harvie tomb was the one with the forlorn dog on top. When you looked through the door grill into Dycer's tomb, a skull with a huge grin would greet you, as if anticipating your arrival. This sloping path led down to another one below ground level, which turned left or right at the junction and which was lined with the doors of vaults on each side. Certain names caught our attention, including that of Marcus Moses, Style Kincaid and the Dowager Countess de Lusi. The Countess had her name on one vault and the Count on another, so we promised to investigate. We were not picky, however, and took shelter in whichever of the numerous vaults were unlocked, near at hand and spacious. Once inside, we rearranged a few coffins to suit our purposes and played a few hands of Pontoon, Poker or Skulls and Roses.

Some of the doors to the vaults had become rusted and broken over the centuries, with a few others having been deliberately broken into, particularly the ones dating from the middle of the nineteenth century. With some patience and practice, we managed to push, climb or squeeze into these vaults, the initial difficulty compounded by the fact that they hadn't been opened for years. Many of the vaults were quite spacious and had upwards of twenty coffins lying on shelves. Some of the coffins had rotted away with the incumbents following suit, leaving just their mummified bones for all to see. The more expensive coffins were lead-lined and had survived robbery, time and the elements. We did not mind our quiet company, being of a tolerant disposition, particularly after imbibing copious amounts of Irish cider made with the finest apples from the orchards of County Armagh. Ample seating was provided courtesy of coffin lids and vacant shelves. One or two had benches provided and there was even a small altar in one.

How some of the skulls had managed to separate themselves from the rest of their bodies we could not guess, but they were found by us anyway, often some distance away from their rightful owners. While having a certain sympathy of course for the beheaded, Morty had the bright idea that they would make suitable footballs if covered tightly with strong socks. He said using skulls in this way was a favourite Irish pastime, even older than the GAA and dating back to the Battle of Carrickfergus of 1597. The Great O'Neill's friends in Ulster, the MacDonnell's, had won another great victory against Sir John Chichester, leader of the English forces. After the battle, Chichester's head was chopped off and used as a football by the MacDonnell clan.

One bright spark, Young Banjaxed, even made a little hole for the skull to breathe, another made two eye holes for the skull to see where it was going. Very thoughtful indeed was the consensus, as one could never be fully sure as to what goes on in someone else's head. Maybe we did it out of a certain respect, also. You have to have standards, Mum used to say. Dad used to say 'backbone', which supposedly meant the same thing although I have my doubts. Lots of these skeletons had backbone, if little else.

Markie was losing the run of himself, however. He suggested ear holes in the sock. 'Are we turning into a knitting club or are we to be a shower of right bowsies or what?' interjected Redser, in an effort to quell the fervour. Redser was good like that. On another occasion, he told Dummy to nip outside and check on the door to see whose family was buried inside.

Dummy came back. 'Looks like some chap called Stuart P.H. Windtuds, farts,' he reported.

'What d'ye mean, "farts"?' shouted Redser.

'That's what it says,' was the riposte.

'Here, outa my way, I'm going to see for myself.' Out he went and back in. '*Bart.*, esq., ye amadán! Some of the lettering has rusted away.' Precise, methodical, calculating, you could see his future laid out for him. Not for him to end up as a grape-picker in Spain. He would own the vineyard. The polar opposite to Four Eyes, who was quite easy-going. He often preferred to play chess over in a corner of the vault by himself. He placed his chessboard on the lid of a coffin. He had a stool on one side of the coffin for himself and two stools on the other side. He sat two skeletons on these, looking down at the board. He said they were there to motivate him.

'Who are they supposed to be?' John Jo wanted to know.

'Oh, just two old friends – Bobby Fischer and Boris Spassky.' Young Banjaxed often joined him. He said he found watching chess very stimulating and helped him sleep. He would sit there for hours, nodding away.

'What's a Bart?' Morty asked. He was dressed all in black 'on this occasion,' according to himself. What 'occasion' we never discovered, as he always seemed to find an occasion to wear black.

'Some of those lawdy-daws that go around jumping over ditches, chasing foxes and hares and riding horses,' pointed out Four Eyes.

'Ah, those sheep-shagger types. They shouldn't be allowed in here, if you ask me,' sneered Dummy, looking unhappily at his hand of two skulls and three roses. He tossed his useless hand on the coffin. Then off with him and his Brasso, shining the name-plates and handles on the coffins, even the door knobs and keyholes – Dummy couldn't resist the opportunity to polish them. Up and down and around he went with his little blue-and-white striped metal bottle of Brasso, forever stuck in his pocket with a little rag, now blackened from extensive use. His other pocket held a hanky and a head of lettuce, from which he regularly grabbed a leaf and chewed away contentedly. Once or twice I saw him grab a large lettuce leaf, thinking it was the hanky, and use it to blow his nose. He then put it back into his pocket.

Conkers was even worse. He was serving his apprenticeship as a painter-cum-decorator and was inclined to bring the tools of his trade into the vaults – usually his paintbrush and a tin of paint or a bucket of whitewash. The problem with Conkers was that he really wanted to be a baker, since he loved buns and cakes and all things with icing. His parents, however, set his compass for him but unfortunately it kept swinging back. Sometimes, when the rest of us were sitting around a coffin playing Skulls and Roses by candlelight, Conkers would be off into the adjacent vaults painting and decorating. He had one in particular which he applied his numerous talents to – the Saxe-Coburg vault. 'This one needs a lot of work,' he told us. 'It needs a bit of life, if you ask me.'

Every so often we stuck our heads in to see how much progress he had made. He seemed to be doing fine with the walls brightened up with whitewash and touched up with rainbow arcs and lines – lots of bright colours were his 'preferred style', he admitted. He dotted the walls with sketched images of royalty – crowns, tiaras, jewellery, horses and trumpets. He even painted a dog which he named Caesar. He also had strange signs painted in black scattered on the walls. One he called the 'all-seeing eye', another was the Star of David with a skull at its centre, while others seemed to be mathematical instruments such as compasses, protractors and squares. The eye seemed to follow us around the vault. Below it he had painted two shaking hands – 'just to welcome you, lads,' he explained. On each side of the hands he had drawn groups of skeletons in football gear, like little matchstick men, making up two teams. 'Just like us,' Conkers pointed out. He also painted a few skeletons dressed as jokers or knaves and playing fiddles. Other images were of skeletons in various poses. A set of three he called Curly, Larry and Moe. Curly and Moe had frowns on their faces and faced towards the viewer. Larry, in the middle, turning away from the viewer, had a smirk on his face.

He carved one skull into the shape of a cup. Then he painted it various colours – purples, yellows, greens and blues. He liked what he saw and began making more cups and soon we had a whole collection of cups in various styles and colours. He added on ear-shaped handles for convenience. 'I used spare fingers and toes,' he said. When finished, with enough skull cups for us all, and 'china skull cups' for visitors, he started on a teapot and then a jug. We thought we would have to pop down to Christy Bird's for an old-fashioned farmhouse dresser for all the Delph he made. 'Let's see if he can make plates!' sneered John Jo. And he did, by using the crown of the skull. He just lopped it off, pared and shaped it. The rest of the skull he turned into pyramid-shaped paperweights, nicely painted and with a little smooth indent at each side for easy gripping. There was talk of selling some of these to the stall-holders in the Dandelion Market and the 'arts and crafts people' would like them 'big time' for their quaint 'ivory' style. He also made hundreds of dice from the leftovers. These didn't need painting as he was quite happy, he said, 'with the natural hue'. They just required a bit of shaping and black dots for numbers. He thought these might also prove popular with some of the Dandelion Market customers, particularly those that liked unusual-shaped dice.

In the end, however, out of respect for the remains of the remains, we decided to forgo the Dandelion Market idea and used the pieces to decorate the vaults instead.

That's what Conkers liked to do while the rest of us played cards – brighten up the skulls by painting as many as possible, even when the skulls were attached to the bodies. In that case, he used a dustpan and brush and cleaned the skull from head to toe. If there were cracks or pieces missing, he would fix it quickly, using Polyfilla. Then he painted the whole skeleton and placed it strategically in the vault, either sitting down next to its coffin, often in a reflective pose, or having a couple standing together looking like they were shaking hands or having a chat. He was very artistic indeed. He believed in life after death and felt the 'skellies shouldn't just be left lying around'. Instead he felt they had a good future if put to work. Having polished them really well, he used a few skulls as flowerpots and gave one or two a pipe to smoke on. Some skeletons he used as standard lamps and put shades on their skulls. He then added a few scented night lights flickering away in small indents to the skulls. Some skeletons were placed strategically in corners with their hands holding lighted candles. One shelf had only the one skull but surrounded by artificial red roses he had got from The Punnet flower shop across from the entrance to Mount Jerome. He dressed a few of the skeletons in painter's overalls, 'to keep me company when you lads are playing cards next door.' One he adorned with sunglasses, explaining that the bearer might like to enjoy the sun at some future date. After a hard night's work, he liked to sit on a coffin, take out his flask of tea, pour some into a skull cup and enjoy it with a huge chunk of Christmas cake – even though it was the middle of summer. Sometimes he became so engrossed in his handiwork that he stayed overnight in one of the increasing number of empty coffins. He brought along a sleeping bag for that purpose and just popped it nice and snug into the coffin. He used to set his clock for 7 a.m. and place it in the hands of one of the skeletons. 'I believe in making them work,' he explained. 'No point in having them just lying around doing nothing, is there?'

Applying his baking skills, and using Papier maché, he sculpted a few life-like effigies he imagined were in two coffins – 'maybe kings or queens,' he said. He then placed them lying down on the coffins. He had his favourite skeleton – which he called Vicky – and was often seen or heard dancing around the vault with her with 'Puttin' on the Ritz' blaring in the background. He grew quite fond of Vicky, because she always smiled at him. To us it looked more like a grimace. 'Do you have tickles?' I once heard him whispering to Vicky. He attached a light wooden pole along her spine and branching off towards her feet. 'Giving her some backbone,' he guffawed. This way he felt he would be able to dance with her 'much easier' and he had a little handle halfway up the pole to manoeuvre her legs while dancing. Then he bought her roller skates, 'as a birthday present,' he told us, explaining that he had known her for six months.

We persuaded a few of the girlfriends, or 'mots' as the lads liked to call them, to join us once or twice. We brought along a few tapes including the Grateful Dead, Blood Sweat and Tears, and Stone the Crows to liven things up.

There was much talk about Les, one of the Harvey brothers from the Crows. In the course of the band's live performance in Swansea, he showed what a real livewire of a guitarist he was. The audience had never seen anything like the sparks and sounds shooting from him and his guitar. He even appeared to be on fire. Everyone just went 'wow, man' and stood up to cheer and applaud. There was more to come when, in what looked like an encore, he and his guitar shot right up into the air and then landed back on the stage with an enormous bang. The audience stood up, shouting 'far out man' and suchlike. The only problem was that while playing the guitar he electrocuted himself when he touched an unearthed microphone and hence all the special effects. He was 'far out' all right – into the next world!

As the Grateful Dead groaned on I became unusually down-spirited. I felt somewhat twitchy and began to think darkly that some of the skeletons were looking at me. Just in time, DJ Markie put on the Rolling Stones 'Paint It Black', followed by Black Sabbath's 'Paranoid'. I felt much better and started to enjoy the party more.

Unfortunately for us, some of the girlfriends were completely distracted, not by our amorous attentions, the music or the drink, but by the attention from our long-gone companions, who still managed to grin at them. We turned up the volume on the Grateful Dead to cheer them up, although they did not appear to be real Deadheads, like most of the lads. Out of the side of my eye I could see my girlfriend, Sally, talking with Nobby in the corner and pointing around. She then moved over and sat snuggly beside me. 'Are ye game,' she whispered, and told me what she had in mind. I was a bit taken aback, but since we were all having a bit of craic I said why not, but 'first blow out most of the candles,' I insisted. 'You know what some of these head-the-balls are like!' She headed over to Conkers and told him what she had in mind and the two of them started moving around the various skeletons, sitting them in a semi-circle facing the rest of us. Conkers then quenched most of the night lights and some candles and we were plunged into near darkness, with huge shadows on the walls behind us.

It was my first and only time ever seeing anything like it. Markie pressed on the tape for Alex Harvey's 'The Faith Healer' and as the volume gradually built up, Sally crept out from behind the sitting skeletons. I should have said she swayed or sashayed out, like one of those belly dancers, though slower, and in complete rhythm to the music. Slowly, very slowly, as the music progressed, and as her body danced, she started undressing, starting with her top. Right there with grinning skulls looking at her. We too couldn't believe our eyes. We were sitting, hunched down, with Sally gently gyrating in the middle of us all. Dancing in the shadows, she seduced us all in one go. She looked towards me and I could barely make out that she was dancing in a way that reminded me of Pan's People and Serge Gainsbourg's 'Je t'aime'. On and on she continued, turning, twisting and swaying this way and that until the music climaxed and she was left with her runners and not much else. We joined in the singing: 'And I place my hands on you, nah nah nah nah nana, nah, nah nah nah. And I place my hands on you...' It took all of seven minutes and twenty-one seconds. I could see Nobby's hands twitching, as if wanting to put *his* hands on her. A few got up and transformed themselves into air guitarists. With the flickering candles, even the skeletons' shadows swayed.

When the music stopped there was complete silence. We then broke into a huge applause for Sally as she quickly darted behind a skeleton and got dressed. Conkers re-lit the rest of the candles and we all drank to the late Harvey brother, saying his music lived on in Alex. 'And Sally too,' was the consensus.

'Fair play, Sally,' I said, when she returned. The way she looked at me with those eyes, I will never forget. Always on green, never on red. 'It's so hot in here,' I said, 'you could fry an egg on it.' She just grabbed me, a bottle of Charnel, and we headed outside. We went up on the vault's roof, relaxed and enjoyed the night's balmy heat and the stars twinkling in a clear sky. Below us we could hear Led Zeppelin's 'Whole Lotta Love' as we climbed the stairway to heaven. Years later, when working in the desert, pumping more perspiration than petroleum, I thought of those days. I reached into my rucksack with its freezer bag and grabbed a can. I took a long drink and savoured it. 'Aaah! That's Bass!'

We used to play cards a lot, particularly Skulls and Roses. We sat around on some of the coffins and placed the biggest in the centre of the vault and used it as the table. Conkers placed a few of his carved skulls at each corner and lit the candles. Then he would bring out the flagon of cider and give us all our skull cups full to the brim. 'For Skulls and Roses,' we'd say and start playing. Once Four Eyes brought along a strange concoction which he said he had made one night after work in the Chariot Inn. It was a strange brew called 'Ullage' and he poured some into our skull cups. We tasted it – 'not too bad' we agreed.

'How did you make it?' someone asked.

'I poured all the slops from the dregs in the glass and mixed them all up,' went Four Eyes, blinking down at us. He nearly ended up a permanent feature in the vault that night. Luckily for Four Eyes, Morty had a calming, paternal influence on us. After half an hour or so, we had acquired a taste for this new concoction called Ullage. I brought along a bottle of wine one night and there was much oohing and aahing. I just said it was a leftover from a wedding in Wynn's Hotel. Which it was, but I didn't elaborate on the facts. I called my bottle of wine 'Charnel' and it went down very well with the lads. It was good to see them sniffing and swirling it around in the skull cup before imbibing. Redser thought that the skull added something to the flavour and it 'reminded' him of Jameson and Powers using old wooden casks to enhance the taste of their whiskeys. We all agreed that he might have a point and refilled our cups to make sure. We also agreed that the only time he saw Jameson or Powers was on the side of a bus.

One of the local know-alls got his comeuppance once when he sneaked up on us playing cards as he was taking a shortcut home through the graveyard one night from a dance. We were all sitting around this coffin playing cards by candlelight. Through the gloom we heard a voice slur, 'What are yez doing here at this time of the night?' What on earth did he think we were doing? He had this little skinny face with sneaky eyes look to him. 'This is what we are doing,' replied Markie. 'Here, on the head, quick, catch,' and he grabbed a loose skull from the nearby coffin and tossed it. Two brainless skulls collided as the legless met the footless. He jumped at the hurled heap, as if imagining himself as George Best or Frank O'Neill of Shamrock Rovers and headed the skull sideways. The skull didn't bounce off his head, but he bounced off it and fell backwards into an old, bone-filled coffin, someone's dearly departed remains. From dust to dust. His roars and shrieks could be heard all over Dublin that night as he bounded out of the coffin and tore from the vault. 'Here, where's my skull?' shouted Markie after him. Nobody believed him the next day when he told his story. 'Ah, too much drink!' they whispered and laughed. 'He must be having the horrors!'

The Skulls and Roses card game was like Poker and was also a bluffing game. It was a real poker and eyes game that was even more daring and enjoyable when played with flickering candlelight, four decorated skulls on the coffin lid, and surrounded with shelves of coffins, some prised half open. The game itself involved having a five-card hand with four roses and one skull and turning cards up to show either a skull or a rose. If a player took the chance and then showed up only a line of roses, he won. But if a skull popped up, he lost. If we were dealt out of the game, some of the hardier amongst us often wrapped a spare skull in a sock and tossed or kicked it around in the vault or the passage outside.

One night, playing poker, Dummy thought he would play a trick on us after he was dealt out. He came back in after ten minutes and started peering over our shoulders at our various hands. 'That's a Dead Man's Hand,' he said to Redser.

'No, it's not. I've not got aces and eights,' was his quick reply.

'Well here you are, then,' went the laughing Dummy as he tossed a skeleton's hand on the lid. We just played on.

Usually there was just the one winner each time – Nobby. He rarely lost and we were convinced he was born juggling aces and spades or skulls and roses, such was his canniness. We were regulars over in his house, not just because of his ten sisters, but because he had a tiny record player and a few albums, mainly Taste, Hot Chocolate, Cream, Bread, Marmalade and Bad Company. He also liked Uriah Heep, the Mahavishnu Orchestra, Yes, Mountain, Focus and the Bonzo Dog Doo-Dah Band. He, like Redser, had a sharp eye for making money, having learnt lots of tricks observing the tic tac bookmakers at the Greyhound Track (known as 'the Dogger') which bordered his back garden. Redser sold second-hand cars, even though he was under age and couldn't drive. He delegated to others and was an expert on the many uses of sawdust. It was said he had a copy of Machiavelli's *The Prince* by his bedside.

Take for instance the time I was telling them I had just come back with Mum from Christy Bird's at Portobello Bridge. We had been there looking for a second-hand bedside locker for one of the bedsits. Previous tenants had left lots of cigarette burns on the existing locker and Mum needed to replace it fairly quickly. Mr Bird was rummaging around his shop, saying he had seen a nice one recently somewhere. 'Come on down to the basement and we might find it there,' he went. While we were rummaging around didn't I see a few old skeletons lying in a corner, just dumped in a heap.

'What are these for, Mr Bird?' I asked, somewhat perplexed, imagining he was an axe murderer.

'Oh, they're just second-hand skeletons for the medical students in Trinity and the College of Surgeons. Every second day they come in looking for one. Then, at the end of the year some are brought back to me and I re-sell them. Unfortunately, because of all the manhandling they get from the students, they quickly become useless and I have to dump them, like our friends over there. I am trying to source a new supply for next year's medical students who will be in again annoying me for more!'

Now, I just happened to mention in passing this story one night in the Marcus Moses vault and off went Redser and Nobby into a huddle and started whispering. They beckoned me over and said it was time for us to refill our coffers. 'What's up, lads?' asked Morty.

'Oh, just thinking of a business proposition for Mr Bird,' replied Redser. Within a few weeks we had arranged to supply Mr Bird with new skeletons, old but fresh from their coffins.

As was to be expected, a few of the skeletons weren't up to standard or would cause more trouble than necessary. One of the vaults we visited was that of Maxwell Redmond. Probably a failed General or politician, I surmised. It had a large rusted bell attached to the exterior wall and near the door. Nobby, for once being serious, suggested we ring the bell first before going in. Unfortunately, it was so rusted the chain wouldn't budge, so we got no reply. Hoping not to surprise anyone, in we went anyway and followed the bell chain, which led to a particularly large coffin. We were somewhat reluctant to prise it open, but Redser insisted that 'business is business and whoever was in there would understand'. Eventually we managed to open it and were quite surprised to find the incumbent in good condition – well mummified and well-dressed in late nineteenth-century attire, including grey jacket and trousers, black waistcoat, white shirt worn with a cravat and new black shoes, as if planning to go somewhere. He even had a walking stick and black top hat at his side. We were somewhat startled to see a terrible fiendish grimace on his face. The dusty remains of the stem of a long-withered flower lingered in his buttonhole. In his waistcoat pocket, we could see an old-fashioned timepiece attacked to a little gold chain. On the shelf near his coffin were a few dust-laden bottles which appeared to be Roe's Pure Pot Still Whiskey and Millar's Black Label Whiskey.

Nobby nudged me – 'Hey, Larry! Look at the lid,' he whispered. In the semi-darkness of the vault it was quite difficult to see what he was pointing at but there appeared to be marks that looked like scratches on the inside lid.

'Oh, that was probably when they were screwing down the lid,' Redser suggested. We didn't see any screw holes, however, as the coffin had been closed tightly rather than permanently sealed. It had hinges on one side, a spring lock on the other. There was also a handle on the inside of the lid so that the person lying down would be able to swing the lid up and climb out. The deceased person also held some kind of metal ball in his hand, which was attached to the chain via a hole in the side of the coffin. A link in the chain seemed to be stuck or wedged in the hole on the inside of the coffin, suggesting that if someone had tried to ring the bell from the coffin their efforts would have been thwarted. The other hand appeared to be pointing or reaching up. One of his knees was bent upwards as if he had been trying to use it as some kind of lever. Deciding to leave this person in peace, we quickly closed the lid and slammed the vault door behind us.

After discussing many different names for our new company, 'for tax purposes,' laughed Redser, we pinned it down to two – 'Spare Ribs' or 'Skulleduppery', to be decided later. The rest of the lads wanted to know where all these fresh skeletons were coming from and we told them that we had been busy going from vault to vault evicting any decent-looking skeleton from his or her coffin. Conkers did the rest – cleaned, polished, filled in any missing pieces with Polyfilla and placed them nice and neatly into a range of colourful 'skelly bags' he had specially made for them from large sheets of plastic. We were delighted with the bags as they would make it easier for the students to look after the skeletons, which would therefore last longer, as well as adding a little extra to the price we would get for them. 'Those medical students are all loaded,' pointed out Redser.

Christy Bird was delighted with the standard and condition of the skeletons, thinking they looked 'brand new'. We were very timely, as UCD medical students had called in looking for skeletons. He enquired as to where they came from. 'Oh, a contact in Hong Kong,' said Nobby, 'but luckily the skeletons don't look very foreign,' said he, looking at their eye sockets and height. We planned to supply Mr Bird on a 'never, never' basis, meaning we would always own the skeletons, get paid commission from Mr Bird for the supply and he would recoup his costs by passing on the charges plus extras to the students. And, as before, the students would return them at the end of the year. We would then refurbish them to the standard required. 'And with that we will have a regular cash-flow situation,' concluded Redser, the new company's director of financial affairs. However, after much discussion, we decided in the end to cut out the middleman, bypass Mr Bird and go directly to the medical colleges and the students themselves.

John Jo wanted to know what happened when we ran out of skeletons.

'Not to worry in the least,' chipped in Four Eyes, who hoped to be taken on as a partner. 'What I'm suggesting to the lads is that someone keeps an eye on funerals and take note where the deceased ends up. Then, all we have to do is go along, dig up the coffin, help ourselves to the body, replace it with a couple of sandbags, and away with us! Nobody will ever find out that their loved one has turned into a sandbag.'

'Hold on, hold on,' interjected Morty, the voice of sense to the senseless. 'We don't need bodies, only skeletons.'

Four Eyes had his answer. 'Exactly! And this is where Keef's the Knackers comes in. Dummy here will do the business because he goes to school in Donore Avenue. All he has to do is bring down the bodies in Conker's skelly bags, one at a time in the front basket of his messenger boy's bike and dump them in Keef's big rendering pot with the sheep and cows. Then, before the men come along to make the fertiliser from the bones, Dummy moves in and takes out his skeletons, nice and clean and job well done!'

The rest of us just listened, that's all we could do. Redser and Nobby nodded and consulted. After a few seconds Nobby went, 'Don't worry, Four Eyes. As soon as we run out of supplies we'll put you in charge of stocktaking and ordering in more. In the meantime, keep an eye on the comings and goings of funerals. Okay?' Four Eyes blinked, hoping he had a future which to us was looking increasing doubtful. 'And we'll have to do something with the rings, watches and jewellery the bodies might have,' he continued and we collectively sighed. 'For instance, what will happen to gold fillings?'

'Ah, don't worry your little noggin with that,' replied Redser, winking at me. We can then either get rid of the gold and jewellery in Kilbride's pawn shop or – yes, maybe it would be safer, as you never know who might recognise a relative's ring on somebody else – we should do as Larry's old dear did and donate the jewellery to John's Lane church.'

Meanwhile, Dummy wanted some clarification. 'What happens if the body doesn't fit into my basket?'

Redser was despairing at this stage. 'Oh, just bring it around to Farren's Butchers and ask him to chop it up into nice little two-pound bags of minced meat for you! And don't forget to tell him to keep a few nice tender pieces for himself and to tell nobody. Is that all right?'

He gave Dummy a thump on his arm. 'Listen, mutton chops, just fold the body up or squash it in somehow and down with you to Keef's in a flash, Okay?'

Dummy hadn't finished, however. 'How will we know which is which? I mean, when we go to retrieve the skeletons from the pot, how will we know them from the cows and sheep skeletons?' Luckily, we hadn't to answer as, and just in time for his sake, he came out with, 'Oh, I see. Sorry!' And that ended that for the time being.

Later, Redser, Nobby and I asked Conkers to extend his painting and baking endeavours to the two adjacent vaults beside the Saxe-Coburg one. One we would use as our office, the other for storage purposes. The Saxe-Coburg vault we would use down the line for entertaining clients once the business started to expand. Conkers even suggested selling decorated skulls and bones just like the ones he had already finished. We liked that idea immediately and told him to work away as fast as possible. He, too, was delighted and in no time, he had rearranged coffins, shelves, the recently evicted and started whitewashing the interior walls. Shortly afterwards we moved our scattered skeletons into the stockroom. For space saving and organisation purposes, Conkers had made wall-to-wall timber beams from coffins. We then folded the skeletons up, popped them into the skelly bags and hung them up on coat hangers attached to the beams or lay them on the shelves, all neat and tidy. We had little paths between the rows of skeletons so we would be able to fill orders fairly quickly.

Nobby also suggested displaying posters on the medical colleges' noticeboards advertising our business. We went into the office vault and sketched out some ideas such as 'Fresh from the Grave – Guaranteed Quality Skeletons', 'From the Grave to the Slab – Cut Price Skeletons', 'Skeletons Made to Measure', 'Skeletons for Students – Students for Skeletons' and, just in case, 'Spare Parts for Skeletons Readily Available'. Surprisingly, many of the students did need spare parts and we were glad to have a good selection in our stockroom. There was a good demand for spare ribs, tibia, fibula, fingers, toes and, of course, skulls. The students themselves liked dealing directly with us and we agreed that most of them seemed to have good coffin-side manners. Yes, we thought, we were making a good start in the strolling bones business.

An unexpected side-line to our business came about quite by accident when we found ourselves with lots of empty coffins, the former inhabitants having been put to work. Nobby suggested breaking them up to create extra space in our vaults. Redser felt we should get in one or two reliable ANCO lads who might be able to make some furniture pieces from the old wood.

'Wouldn't advise that, lads,' contradicted Morty. 'You might as well broadcast the whole set-up to the world! What we need is to borrow the Dustman's equipment from the Woodwork Room in school and try and do the job ourselves.' Morty did woodwork in school, so we had a ready-made furniture manufacturer with us. He, however, wanted to become a partner in the business. Morty was welcomed aboard the coffin ship when we reached an agreement after much arduous negotiations and not until after Nobby and I eased Redser's fulminations with the help of some 100-year-old whiskey from the Maxwell Redmond vault. He was good with his hands, it has to be said, and managed to make some small pieces of furniture for us, including lockers, small tables, desks and other bits and pieces.

'Looks all very distressed,' said John Jo, 'can't imagine anyone buying that stuff.' Then it struck me – why shouldn't we sell this battered and dusty-looking furniture and call it antique or 'distressed'? I asked Christy Bird for his views on the matter and he said that 'certain arty types' went in for that kind of decrepit furniture. We asked him if he could try to sell a few pieces for us, telling him that we only used genuine 150-year-old timber. He agreed and he sold.

As a result of our varying endeavours we did very well for the few years we were in business. Most importantly, I was able to help with Mum's finances, particularly useful at lean times when tenants were in short supply.

For much of the time when we were off school or at weekends, we just rambled around Mount Jerome and kicked football or, thanks to Morty, skull ball or 'skully' for short. One of us popped into the vault, collected the skully and away with us, back and forth along any of the many walks. At times the skull ball seemed to have a mind of its own, veering this way and that way, ignoring the rules of football. However, it was not nearly as bad as a rugby ball with its odd shape and even odder bounce. Some were of the mind that we should have a skully tournament with other local gangs, but it never came to anything.

If we tired of skully, we played bowls or croquet instead, using the same skull balls. We used to watch these games in the nearby Grosvenor Square clubs. For lawn bowls, we just wrapped a dozen or so skulls in different coloured socks to represent the different bowls. We usually had the jack in a white sock. We regarded our game as more skilful than the official game, as our skull bowls were at times inclined to deviate along the path rather than travelling along the planned curve. This was caused by the skull tripping over its nose en route. In croquet, we used discarded leg bones for mallets and pegs.

If a bone had a foot attached, it made the game much easier to play, but we weren't too choosy. Bowling was never a problem, with ready-made finger grips. At times, we used the Main Avenue in front of the Victorian Church. This had an ideal camber for our games and had a narrow lane at each side to catch the errant skulls.

The skulls came in very useful for another reason not too long afterwards. My Dad had been a great fan of the GAA for years and often took us to Croke Park. He also avidly listened to Michael O'Hehir on many a Sunday afternoon on Radio Éireann. He used to regale us with stories of the great Dublin teams of the 1950s and mentioned in particular Kevin Heffernan, known as 'Heffo'. In the 1970s, Heffo became manager of the Dublin football team and he seemed to have infused a new life into a county which had been in the doldrums since his playing days. Father Joe Kennedy of Mount Argus used to bring the locals from Mountain View to all the Dublin matches up and down the country. We were part of Heffo's Army and used to meet bright and early on a Sunday morning at Mount Argus and away with us on a hired coach. Dublin had won the All-Ireland in 1974 and were expected to win again the following year, but unfortunately lost to Kerry. This was a disaster and something magical was needed to pull the Dubs up.

I had a brainwave. Up I went to Heffo at a training session in Parnell Park. 'Howya Heffo!' I said. 'We need to work wonders if we are to have any hope of beating the Kingdom this year.'

'What do you have in mind?' he replied grumpily.

'A change of tactics and technique. Create anarchy amongst the team!' I suggested. He seemed a bit confused by all this anarchy business. 'What you need to do is inject some magic into the players' training,' I pointed out. 'Here, I have a solution just in my bag here.' I lifted out a skull ball and a regular O'Neill's football. 'Compare weights, now. Which is the heavier?' He seemed somewhat startled. 'Ah, sorry, lads, I have to go,' he went. The impression I got was that he didn't want to know, adding that he 'would bear it in mind', and off he ran like he was being chased by bulls. However, to this day I'm have no doubt he took up our suggestion with his back-room boys. All hush hush, of course.

The rest is history as Dublin went on to hammer Kerry for the Sam

Maguire Cup and repeated the performance the following year against Armagh. Even in the succeeding two years Dublin got to the final in Croke Park, thanks to the skull ball. I hoped Heffo would make sure that the players would never find out what they were playing with. 'Any complaints just tell them to give up the jar. Wrap it in leather like the usual ball,' I advised, the next time I saw him. 'And for heaven's sake, make sure those Kerrymen never find out! If they do, they will start using the puck goat's skull. Then we're really finished!' He just laughed.

Doubtless in recognition of our help with the Dub's success, Heffo sent a few of the team with the Sam Maguire up to the Greyhound Bar in Mountain View. We had a great chat with the winning lads. The owner of the establishment, Seán Flanagan, kindly filled the cup with punch. We were told the next day we had a great time.

24

BLACK BLOOMERS AND BLIND WINDOWS

W e did not confine our exploring and adventures to Mount Jerome or even town. We had much fun in the vicinity of Mountain View, but beyond its boundaries, and equally enjoyable, Dolphin's Barn, Portobello, Rathmines, Kimmage, Rathgar and Rathfarnham, had individual attractions unique to them. Dolphin's Barn was for years famous for its quarry and the yellow brick extracted which was used for decades in building some of Dublin's finest houses. In its heyday prior to the Second World War, there was extensive house-building in Dublin. The clay pits extended from Kimmage to the Grand Canal at Goldenbridge. Terenure was fine, particularly for passing through. The residents here always had a chip on their shoulders because they were not living in Rathgar. We usually nodded knowingly and sympathetically amongst ourselves passing Vaughan's Eagle Tavern at the crossroads, as it was the birthplace of James Joyce's mother, Mary Murray. Not that we were fans of Joyce, who we felt brought absolute disgrace on his family, what with him taking himself off up to Monto on a regular basis and then telling everyone afterwards about his adventures. Oh yes, we were on the side of poor Mrs Joyce. Although saying that, we did have a certain sympathy for James and all that schoolwork the Jesuits gave him when he was in Belvedere College. One would need a break from all that and if the girls in Monto were prepared to listen to all his complaints about his teachers, that was completely understandable.

Once one crossed Mountain View Bridge and the Grand Canal, going towards town ('An Lár' above the number on all the buses going in that direction), you were in Portobello. The name itself came from around the time of the War of Jenkins' Ear, fought between England and Spain, in the vicinity of Portobelo Colon on Panama's Caribbean coast. Poor Captain Jenkins had his ear chopped off by the Spanish and he showed it in Parliament to prove his point!

Because of the garrison barracks located on both sides of the canal, parts of Portobello developed a reputation for prostitution. So bad in fact, that the residents upgraded the names of some of the roads including Kingsland Park to Victoria Street, and an adjacent one to Windsor Terrace. Some of the houses along this road have carved images of the Queen's head over doorways to commemorate her visit to Dublin in 1900.

For a time in the early to middle twentieth century, it was known as 'Little Jerusalem' because of the concentration of Jews living and working there since the late 19th century. A future president of Israel, Chaim Herzog, grew up on Bloomfield Avenue. One of his playmates was a future president of Ireland, Cearbhall Ó'Dálaigh, who grew up around the corner on Portobello Road. They met again in 1985 at the opening of the Jewish Museum on Walworth Road. That road was where the famous Abbey and Hollywood actor Barry Fitzgerald was born. He starred in *The Quiet Man* with John Wayne and Maureen O'Hara. Another son of Portobello was the writer George Bernard Shaw, who was born and raised at number 33 Synge Street.

As young children, The Pixie shop with its Tipsy cake was our only contact with Portobello, yet we also knew of the 'slaughterhouse' at the bridge very well, particularly with all the cattle and sheep going there on a regular basis, past our house, and not coming back. Many times, on passing, we heard the squealing pigs, doubtlessly not wishing to be turned into sausages or bacon rashers. Mullin's scrap merchant was on the opposite side of the road and was useful at times in later years as he usually gave us a few bob for any old batteries, copper, lead and scrap we found and brought down to him. Next door was Gordon's Coal Merchants, lining the banks of the Grand Canal, and from there we hauled home a small bag of coal many times.

Caroline Records on South Richmond Street was a tiny ancient shop crammed with the latest LP's and tapes. That's where I bought Led Zeppelin's *Physical Graffiti* album and, after listening to it, I wanted to hitchhike to Kashmir. Christy Bird's second-hand furniture shop, Kilbride's Pawnbroker, the Bretzel Bakery sending its pleasant aromas around the neighbourhood since 1870, the Aprile Café, Gig's Place and the Manhattan takeaway, were often on our radar, particularly in our teen years. The latter was a favourite rendezvous spot for us on the way home from watching a late-night film – such as *Valdez is Coming* with Burt Lancaster – in the Plaza Cinerama. The service was unusual in that May, who worked behind the counter, was a former trapeze artist and juggler, and she imagined she was still in the circus. When she was busy, you would need to be razor sharp as she hurled your bag of chips or bottle of ketchup at you, a very sobering experience indeed. Nearby there were some excellent old pubs such as O'Connell's, the Lower Deck, the Bleeding Horse (aka the Falcon Inn) and Cassidy's. Another was called An Béal Bocht, a great place if you liked traditional Irish music, which we didn't for sure. Not then, anyway.

Rathmines had much to offer. It was widely known by outsiders as 'Flatland' with civil servants, students, nurses and the like travelling from the four corners of Ireland to reside in a bedsit there. The convenience for town made Rathmines ideal for anyone from the country coming to live in the city. Many of the fine big houses with steps leading up to their entrances had been vacated in the early twentieth century following Irish Independence, and the owners had either escaped the country or moved further afield. Some of the vacated grand properties were bought by developers and speculators and turned into numerous squalid bedsits and flats.

Consequently, Rathmines had a mixed pedigree and one it retains to some extent. 'Cosmopolitan' is the preferred word to describe the area today. The treasure trove of architectural gems of houses gave some indication of its history and heritage. The Cullenswood Massacre took place in the vicinity of Rathmines in c.1209, when the Gaelic clans descended from the Dublin Mountains to attack the residents of the walled city who had come out to the area for a day of celebrations and picnics. Rathmines was the site of one of the most important battles in Irish history – the 1649 Battle of Rathmines, which saw Oliver Cromwell defeat a combined force of Irish and Royalist forces and thereby gain a foothold in Ireland to pursue his 'To Hell or to Connaught' onslaught. The site of the battle was appropriately and subsequently called Bloody Fields, but in more refined but equally unenlightened times at the end of the nineteenth century it was renamed as Palmerston Park. This name came from Lord Palmerston, one-time Prime Minister of England, and of the Temple family who owned lots of land in the area. Lord Palmerston and the Cowper-Temple family had strong land-ownership links with Rathmines, going back hundreds of years to the time Sir William Temple was made the first Provost of Trinity College around 1600. He was given land to build a house nearby. A fashionable precedent was set and this led to reclamation of River Liffey shoreline land, the building of houses by famous adventurer families such as Crow, Eustace, Boyle, Anglesea, Crampton and Fownes, and the growth of what subsequently became Temple Bar, in the heart of Dublin.

Meanwhile, in Rathmines, the wealthy people lived in three- and four-storey mid-Victorian red-brick houses built from the early decades of the nineteenth century onwards. The calamity of the Irish Famine had resulted in hordes of the starving descending on Dublin and bringing their problems and diseases with them. Consequently, the Anglo-Irish Ascendancy, previously living in the fine Georgian houses near the city centre, quickly abandoned them and moved beyond the confines of the canals in the hope of finding peace and fresh air. They already had the prosperity. Their former dwellings had turned into slums and tenements by the end of the nineteenth century and some had evolved into areas such as Monto.

The impressive red-bricked Rathmines Town Hall, built at the junction of Rathmines Road and Leinster Road, in the very heart of the area and with a clock tower to be seen for miles, was built c. 1895/6. It was a deliberate reminder of the attitude of this Unionist and Protestant community that lived in an enclave in this part of the city – they wanted an independent Rathmines and Rathgar, free from the control of the Nationalist Dublin Corporation. They won this right to effectively govern themselves under a number of Township Acts passed in the middle of the nineteenth century. For decades, the Union Jack held sway over the Town Hall and later another flag, a distinctive Rathmines flag, joined it, asserting the residents' separate identity from the rest of the city and country. Here you find roads with names such as Palmerston, Cowper, Belgrave, Grosvenor, Bessborough and Temple. Interestingly, over the years the Town Hall clock acquired a name – the four-faced liar – as the various clocks gave different times!

The Fenian, John O'Leary, lived in Rathmines, as did James Stephens. In fact, it is quite surprising the number of prominent nationalists who had Rathmines connections in such a staunch Protestant Unionist community. Other names include Cathal Brugha, General Richard Mulcahy, the Gifford sisters (who married some of the 1916 Rising leaders), Francis Sheehy Skeffington and Darrell Figgis. Like Mountain View, it was a hotbed of intrigue.

As children, we often played with our bicycles in 'Lordy's' on Leinster Road, speeding and bouncing through the ruins and grounds of the former home of Lord and Lady Longford, whose mansion it had been until the early 1960s. Across the road, near the corner with Grosvenor Square, was Surrey House, the former home (during and after the 1916 Rising) of Countess Markievicz. This faced the home of the Haslams, pioneering suffragettes.

Whenever we went to the Stella cinema we would pop in beforehand to Harvey's Tobacconist next door and buy a couple of Orange Maids, a packet of Sobraine black Russian cigarettes, or a few Woodbines or Sweet Afton. Mr Nolan of Nolan's Butcher Shop a few doors up often gave us a job delivering messages to some of the grand houses on Palmerston Road. We loved this as it involved using his old messenger boy bike with a big wicker basket in front. He said the basket was made by the blind people in the craft shop, known as Blindcraft, facing the church.

Another area of the city that caught our attention was Rathgar, which bordered Rathmines and Mountain View. However, whereas Rathmines was slightly on the cosmopolitan and decadent side because of its 'Flatland' connotations, Rathgar was definitely not. Rathgar's image was solid, bourgeois and red-brick – cosy exclusiveness, which it stubbornly maintained. Rathgar was long regarded as being 'real posh' and famous for the Rathgar accent and upper-class pretensions. These reinforced the view of the area. It wasn't Dublin but was 'grand' or 'West Brit'. There was also the longstanding joke about Rathgar girls who thought 'sex' was what coalmen used to carry the coal in. There was even the new accent, with the 'th' emphasized. The common people usually referred to 'Ra'gar' or 'Ra'mines'. Saying that, many of the Rathgar people looked down on the Rathmines folk and their accent. They regarded Rathgar as far more exclusive, although they did begrudgingly acknowledge it.

Ireland's most famous comedian, actor and long-time Gaiety pantomime stalwart Jimmy O'Dea, created a popular catchphrase with 'Thank Heavens we are living in Rathgar' which preserved the well-heeled Rathgar image. It was written by his friend and colleague Harry O'Donovan. The song noted that in the days of agitators and dictatorships, schisms and isms (the world of the 1930s) one never knew who one was talking to. One might meet plumbers at golf dinners and at rugby dances and one's finer sensibilities would be shocked by vulgar glances. Consequently, the people of Rathgar were 'more danced against than dancing'. Luckily and despite all these challenges, the people of Rathgar had their evening dinners and where vulgar politics was never discussed. The song also bemoaned the fact that in places like Fairview in north-side Dublin, with their appalling accents, fellows played tennis in their braces and in Killester people ate cockles and, worse still, pig's knuckles! And not to mention all the kids in Kimmage! Luckily, these sorts of people never got beyond Rathmines Town Hall, so the residents of Rathgar were safe – thank heavens!

It always seemed to be quiet, with big four-storeyed red-brick Victorian houses towering into the sky along tree-lined roads. These were magnificent houses, many detached, such as on Orwell Road, Rostrevor Terrace, Orwell Park, Rathgar Road and Kenilworth. Rathgar Road and Winton Road also had numerous detached villas. Of course, Orwell Road was not always so-called, having originally been called Windmill Lane and with Washerwoman's Lane running off it in the village to the backs of the houses on Highfield Road. That name, however, 'just would not do' and so it was changed to Orwell Road. Most houses had impressive granite stepped entrances with ornate railings, magnificent chandeliered halls, sitting rooms and dining rooms, shiny hardwood floors, decorated plasterwork on ceilings and surroundings, huge marble fireplaces, and with servants to do your bidding. Of course, they had only the very best architects, including Beckett, Carson and Beaver, the latter who loved the area so much that he lived in five different houses on five different occasions. As was the case with Rathmines, many in the professional classes sought residences at a distance from the polluted, overcrowded city centre.

Many of the roads, houses, and villa names in Rathgar commemorated the British administration in Ireland – its heroes, the Royal Family, military heroes and battles, and Anglo-Irish landlords. Albert Villa, Victoria Road, Grosvenor Road, Malakoff Villas and Brighton Road are just some of the names. Kenilworth Road and Square recall the romantic historical novels of Sir Walter Scott. And, of course, many of the residents were part of that administration, and with the accents to go with it. So, if your servant was looking for an increase in wages, you would confide to your neighbour, 'Oh, how dreadfully awful! I do say, not quite pip, pip.' Well, matters got worse when the maids and servants had their own church built on Rathgar Road in the 1860s/70s, known by the established residents as 'the maids' church' or 'the servants' church'. When the foundation stone was laid in March 1860, the *Irish Times* warned that a 'Chapel' would depreciate the value of the property of the neighbourhood and drive the Protestant occupants from the place. This church had 'three blind windows' on its Leicester Avenue side so that the local residents would not have to witness the 'idolatry' and 'popery' going on inside.

Interestingly, the area was full of long lanes that were a feature of Rathgar and surrounding areas in the closing decades of the nineteenth century. Before the installation of toilets and bathrooms in these houses, the residents had to use outside facilities; a privy at the end of the back garden. At night time, the 'night soil' men would collect the contents of the chamber pots which the housemaid had emptied into a cesspit in the garden. The 'night men' would do their work via the back lanes of the houses. On no account would they enter through the front doors of houses. Many houses in Rathgar did not have indoor bathrooms until well into the 1890s. Not only that, but despite the advent of gas lighting, candles and oil lamps were still used in most houses until the early years of the twentieth century, and the demand even then was quite slow. And it was not until 1907–08 that residents of Rathgar, starting with Highfield Road, started to use gas for heating and cooking.

For us as children and young teenagers, the area had a certain magic and mystery to it. We used to sing the Jimmy O'Dea song on our trips to visit our relations on Grosvenor Avenue. We had heard it being sung in the Gaiety's Christmas pantomime. Across the road from aunt and uncle's house there were an array of houses with king's heads stuck over the entrances and just below the fanlights. Along Leicester Avenue was a real Hansel and Gretel-looking house that captured our imagination. That side of the road was called Leicester whereas the opposite side was called Kenilworth. Around the corner on the square were two houses, side by side, both number 1. The first was on Kenilworth Road, the second on Kenilworth Square. The square itself once belonged to Charles Eason, the bookseller, who lived in one of the houses overlooking it. Our aunt told us that another man in the book business also lived on the square and he and Mr Eason were always arguing over 'indecent' books and newspapers and what should be banned and not banned. She said his name was Mr Frank O'Reilly and he was in charge of the Catholic Truth Society of Ireland. She said that he was the man nobody ever heard of, yet he was the one that organised the 1932 Eucharistic Congress. We had vaguely heard of that congress from Mum, who used to tell us stories about coming up to Dublin as a teenager to attend and having white paint on her face.

That, for us, was part of the attraction of Rathgar. It's sheer eccentricity. Nothing was as it seemed. Take, for instance, the pleasant Monument Creamery shop in the village we popped into for ice cream on the way to the River Dodder, further along Orwell Road. The owner kindly told us that it was once a bomb despatch centre used by Michael Collins during the War of Independence. 'The bombs,' she said, 'were hidden in butter boxes and sent all over the country. You see, he was hiding out just off Rathgar Avenue and down from that bird stuffer Carleton's house.' Number 16 Airfield Road was where Collins hid while he loaded up the butter boxes with bombs, we learnt. While he was loading those boxes, he was also unloading eggboxes full of guns for the Volunteers. We told Mrs Ryan, who was serving us, that we had discovered a Second World War bomb shelter in the back garden of a house on Garville Avenue. We had been playing marbles and exploring Garville Lane, an ancient winding laneway behind the houses. Dummy had peeped in through a gap in some Mews gates and saw the beehive-shaped bomb shelter hidden in the long grass.

On another occasion we popped into the Monument for some wafers on the way to do some fishing by the River Dodder. The lady serving us the ice cream was in no hurry as we licked and licked. Neither were we on that hot summer afternoon; we liked listening to stories from the old days.

'This area was a hotbed of rebellion and intrigue in the good old days,' she said. It sounded as if little had changed to me. She continued. 'One of the great battles of Irish history took place near here. Do you know what it was?'

'Of course,' went Redser. He was with us and the lads on the way up to the Dodder. Like Freckles, our cousin, Redser always had an answer. 'The Battle of Rathmines,' said he with his smug face.

'Got you there, didn't I,' laughed the lady. 'It was the Battle of the Black Bloomers,' and Redser's face went even redder. 'Well I'll tell you now, it was that brazen hussy, Maud Gonne, one-time girlfriend of the poet Yeats, that caused the row with the police, so she did. What did she do? Only hanging a pole outside her window with her black bloomers on show for all to see. It was her way of protesting about the visit to Dublin of King Edward VII in 1903. You can well believe that not many were too pleased at these goings-on. Miss Gonne had an answer for them, however, saying it was out of sympathy for the death of the Pope who had only died recently. She was really trying to annoy her many royalist neighbours, there is no doubt about that. I can tell you for sure that she succeeded in creating uproar and the police were summoned when an apoplectic neighbour saw her underwear blowing in the breeze. Didn't her supporters arrive just then and tried to impede her arrest. This led to a stand-off which became known as the Battle of the Black Bloomers.'

The unexpected was always a feature of Rathgar for us. One day we went over to Brighton Square for a game of tennis. The park where we played had a white picket fence and was full of old chestnut trees. Just before he whacked the ball towards me, Four Eyes shouted that the square was in fact a triangle. Well, I did not care what it was when his lobby shot the ball over my head. I was completely distracted with his inane comment. Later on, he returned to the issue - why was a triangular-shaped park called a square? This puzzled us no end. We asked one of the residents who was sitting on a bench watching us playing. 'Ask Mr Joyce who lives over there,' he said, pointing to no. 41 across from the park. 'Oh, we have met a right smart aleck here,' sniggered Redser to us. 'Why's that?' asked Dummy. 'I don't mind; I'll go over and ask Mr Joyce.' Off he marched and we just didn't bother him. Later he came back and reported that Mr Joyce and his wife had moved to Glasnevin or some such resting place and had been there for quite a number of years. We decided to leave it at that all the while thinking that the young Mr Joyce must have turned out very strange indeed having been born in a house on a triangle which they called a square. 'Ah, his poor old mother,' sighed Markie, who always had a soft spot for mothers and old ladies.

25

FIG ROLLS AND RELATIONS IN THE ZOO

As the years drifted by and we had evolved into thoughtful, though at times thoughtless, teenagers, one luxury was added to the lack of luxuries we had in the house. Long before the tenant, called Milo, finally departed for good, he harangued Mum to get a television. She couldn't afford it, and anyway we watched TV lots of times with other obliging tenants. He eventually acquired a television himself, shortly after one of his return visits home from working in England. He was delighted at first, though he seemed to spend most of the time looking at the Telefís Éireann page full of coloured squares and with St Brigid's Cross or some such logo. At times he managed to view a screen filled with endless dancing black, white and silver dots. Yet he didn't really mind, because of the utter novelty of it for him as well as the comfort of a large bottle of Stowshus resting on the small table beside him. Eventually he gave up on the television, after kicking it. We discovered he had acquired it locally on the 'never, never'. This meant he would never own it and would never stop paying for it. 'Never here,' was Mum's riposte when the rental company called for arrears and back it went to TV land. Years later, when circumstances changed and improved, we got a television. As was the custom and because of the expense, it was similarly acquired on the 'never, never'.

Then Milo bought a very impressive second-hand bright green Humber Sceptre car. It also had a black roof and black leather upholstered seats, a wooden dashboard, and 'loads of extras', according to himself. He had bought it for £500 with the help of some of his 'winnings' in the bookies – P.J. Kilmartin's – the bookies with two entrances and two exits, but only two doors, and which linked Sackville Place with Lower Abbey Street. He parked it outside the house, half on the footpath and half on the road. He insisted we sit inside and admire all that he admired. We were told to 'feel this' but 'don't touch that'.

Eventually, and after much 'oohing' and 'aahing', mostly on his part, we moved back towards the front garden gate and watched as he sat in the driver's seat, adjusted the seat many times, tested the steering wheel, readjusted the mirrors inside and out, and only then turned on the engine. With a big smirk on his face he edged off the footpath onto the road and looked to his right and behind him to see if there was any traffic coming. With none on the horizon, and still looking to his right, he gave the engine an almighty rev and tore away. Too late did he see where he was going and he crashed into the lamp post straddling the edge of the footpath in front of where he had parked. The green pole swayed and light flickered on and off, and then remained on. Seriously ruffled, though uninjured, Milo jumped out of the car in a rage, rushed around to its front left side to see a crumpled wing and a bashed-in bonnet.

All the neighbours appeared from their houses on hearing the enormous crash. Not a word from him as he jumped back into the car, slammed his foot down and furiously drove off without a backward look. We just laughed and laughed. The next day a letter arrived for him from the Emerald Staff Agency in London offering him a job in a big insurance company. 'You're taking it,' said his wife, Deirdre, in a voice with an edge of finality about it. He never came back. She said she had a feeling there might be more stars in the sky the night of his departure to catch the mail boat. She remained with us.

From then onwards the house started to assume a certain sense of order, routine and normality. Mum was much more choosey with new tenants – making sure they had good permanent jobs and wouldn't be a source of trouble. Consequently, tenants were settled and staying longer, which was very important for stable finances and much else. We were able to get on with our school work, continue with our part-time jobs, meet our friends and basically get on with our lives. Mum started to reconnect with old friends and made new ones. She re-joined local groups and the Irish Widows Association, attended meetings and went on outings. She spent more time in her beloved back garden and on summer days while she was busy with her gladioli or geraniums I played some of her favourite tunes, including Simon and Garfunkel's 'I am a Rock' and 'Bridge over Troubled Waters'. I placed the stereo speakers out on the top windowsill at the back of the house for her to hear. So too could some of our neighbours, who weren't overly impressed. They never were anyway.

One beautiful summer's morning we took the bus across town with Mum to visit her cousin, who lived on Lindsay Road in Glasnevin. Afterwards we visited the Angel's Plot in Glasnevin cemetery, where her three lost children were buried. This plot was one of the few places in Ireland that allowed stillborn children to be buried in consecrated ground. Leaving the cemetery, we passed many monuments to the great including the O'Connell crypt and memorial which has a Round Tower on top. Many famous people in modern Irish history, including Charles Stewart Parnell and Michael Collins, are buried quite near the main gates to the cemetery.

Following this visit, we walked around the corner to the Botanic Gardens, where everything was in bloom. We used to call the gardens 'the bots' and had visited them with Dad many times as children. This time we visited the curvilinear range of glasshouses, saw the gigantic Amazon waterlily in the Aquatic House glasshouse, which, when introduced to the gardens in the 1850s, was seen as one of the wonders of the world. Even Queen Victoria on a trip to Dublin was brought to see it and Turner's world-renowned glasshouses. We liked the cacti and the Palm House range, whereas Mum preferred the rhododendrons. 'Often times,' she reminisced, 'your Dad and I drove out to the Rhododendron Gardens on Howth Head and shared a picnic there while enjoying the panoramic view of Dublin Bay.'

We then strolled through a double line of Yew trees, known as Addison's Walk, and Mum admired the Rockery at the end of the path. 'Always looking for ideas for Dad's rockery,' which was at the end of our garden at home, she said, smiling. As children, we had helped Dad build that rockery. We remembered hauling the white stones and placing them in various spots on the mound as it grew bigger and bigger. He used to say, 'Just dump them anywhere,' which suited us fine. Dad had acquired the stones from the well-known sculptor, his friend Mr Deghini, who also lived in Mountain View. Then on to the Rose Garden where we admired a special rose bush, 'The Last Rose of Summer', said to have inspired the great poet Thomas Moore to write a ballad with the same name.

On another day we decided to 'visit our relations in the zoo,' as Dad used to say. This was a nice warm day at the beginning of the summer holidays. We had to go into town to catch the bus to the Phoenix Park. Comrade Daisy was hoping to spend the summer working part-time in Wynn's Hotel and needed (wanted) to join the trade union, so we popped into Liberty Hall. We took the elevator to the top and could see for miles and miles with the Dublin Mountains in the distance. We could see the site where Nelson's Pillar used to stand before being blown up in 1966, just a few weeks after we had climbed it with our Dad. 'Gone, but not forgotten,' said Minnie, adding, 'Up went the GPO, and down came Nelson.' We hadn't forgotten how our legs had ached from the climb to the top. Liberty Hall was much better and we zoomed up to the top in an elevator.

Later we took the bus to the zoo, admired the Wellington Monument nearby, with a few of us testing our speed up and down the slanting steps. According to Daisy, some said of the Duke that he was born in a stable! Freckles said the sculptor of some of the famous battle scenes, including the Battle of Waterloo, depicted on the monument at the top of the steps, was Thomas Kirk. He was buried in an appropriately ornate tomb along the Main Avenue in Mount Jerome. Myself and the lads enjoyed cycling in the park, particularly racing around the steep slopes of the Furry Glen and the Corkscrew Bend. Oftentimes we cycled from there to the nearby, steeper still, Knockmaroon Hill and then down to the Strawberry Beds, by the banks of the River Liffey. Cruising along with the sun bouncing off the water into our faces, it felt magical. On the return journey, we might pop into the Angler's Rest for a ball of malt or a small bottle.

After saying goodbye to our relations in the zoo, we fitted in a visit to the Tearooms, near the entrance. While relaxing and chatting, we listened to the Army Number 1 Band playing on the bandstand in The Hollow. Mum loved the Army Band as it brought her back, as she said, 'through the corridors of time' to her days in the army during the Emergency. She told us that she cycled from Gardiner Place every day past the Magazine Fort and up to St Bricin's Military Hospital. She well remembered the huge stacks of stockpiled turf lining both sides of Chesterfield Avenue, which was used by many people as a cheaper alternative to coal when times were hard. It was good to see her retaining her *joie de vivre*.

When we came home for lunch during our Secondary School days, Mum was invariably busy around the house but also listening to one of her favourite programmes on Radio Éireann – *The Kennedys of Castleross*. She always quoted the line of one of the characters, 'someday I am going to be a millionaire!' This programme was followed once a week by a Jacob's Biscuits-sponsored programme – 'the people who make better biscuits better every day'. The programme opened with the music of Frank Sinatra singing 'Strangers in the Night' and was followed by a segment that the producers called 'Woman's Page'. This involved an agony aunt, Frankie Byrne, reading out listener's letters on marital and relationship problems and she started with the famous words, 'Dear Frankie,' and afterwards offered a possible solution. Other Frank Sinatra recordings were played during the course of the programme. Mum loved this programme, while I pretended not to listen by holding the newspaper in front of my face and turning the pages every so often.

We used the opportunity to take out some biscuits Mum had stashed away in a kitchen cupboard. These included our favourites such as Fig Rolls, Kimberley, Mikado and Coconut Creams. Dad had told us years previously, when passing by Jacob's Biscuit factory on Bishop Street, that the Kimberley name came from a diamond town of the same name in Australia. The Mikado name derived from the famous opera by Gilbert and Sullivan, which both Mum and Dad loved. Jacob's, he said, gave us our first cream cracker. I thought he was referring to Freckles and found it hilarious. We were not too bothered about cream crackers though, being more interested at the time in the Jim Figgerty mystery which lots of children in school and elsewhere were talking about. Apparently only Mr Figgerty knew the guarded secret as to how Jacob's got the figs into the fig rolls! Then, when we heard on the radio that he had gone missing, we were shocked. What a furore that caused, not only in our house, but all over Ireland! We never found out what happened to Mr Figgerty or how he got the figs into the fig rolls, but it didn't matter and we kept eating them and then going to the dentist for more laughing gas.

On one such visit down in Cornmarket, we were reminded of John's Lane Church nearby and the treasures it held. We were also faced with a similar conundrum as the Jim Figgerty mystery, but this time we wanted to know how to get ourselves into John's Lane church without being noticed for a particular task which had concentrated our minds of recent. This conundrum involved how to retrieve Mum's engagement ring out of the glass case in the church without being seen!

I discussed this dilemma with Redser, Four Eyes, Morty, John Jo, Nobby, Markie, Dummy, Conkers, Young Banjaxed and the rest of the lads. I knew they would have a solution, and rightly so.

'What do we have in common?' asked Dummy.

'You!' said Redser and we all nearly cracked up.

'Pray continue,' insisted Morty, already assuming the appearance of one of the Elder Conkers sitting around the Tree of Knowledge. He did. 'The reason why we are all here is that we grew up together all those years ago, didn't we? Have we lost that spirit we had then, now that we all took retirement from the same said occupation?' He has lost whatever remained of his marbles, I thought to myself. I changed my mind quickly, however, when he added: 'You remember that gung-ho spirit of Larry here and how everyone took the mickey out of him and all the while he was making lots of dung dough for his folks. And didn't he recruit us as barrow boys when his business expanded? And did we mind? No!' And what about the skelly business? Didn't we also make lots of dough from those heads in Mount Jerome and all the rest? And not forgetting his egg and jam businesses. Well that's the spirit we need again – we've got to go in there and grab the loot.'

Redser took the cue then. 'That's all very fine, Dummy, but we can't just go in there and grab the loot. We have to be somewhat subtle about it and that's why Larry needs us to figure out how to go about it. What you said, though, is bang on and fair play to you!'

What did we decide to do? We decided to do a daylight robbery! We would be seen but, most importantly, not noticed. To achieve this, we did what we knew best – we dressed up as latter day saintly altar boys. Of course, on over-hearing our plan, Daisy, Freckles and Minnie wanted to be in on the action, but Redser insisted that the lads always worked as a team and it would be best to continue that way. However, he agreed that the rest might come along and pretend to be devout members of the congregation, lighting candles, dropping coins into the poor boxes and praying at the statues for all the hopeless cases.

Meantime we, the lads, had agreed on our plan of action. We caught the 54A bus – nearly taking up the whole of the top deck – straight to Christ Church Cathedral and then walked up to a laneway at the back of John's Lane Church. There was a large, red-bricked old primary school on the corner. In we went, found an empty classroom and quickly changed into our altar boy gear, which most of us had found lying around our houses despite not being used for a couple of years. We looked like over-sized altar boys stuffed into undersized apparel. That is, except for Morty. He insisted on only wearing the long black soutane. With Morty leading us, we then marched procession-like in through the front entrance of the church and straight for the right-hand side altar, where there were half-a-dozen locked glass cases full of necklaces, bracelets, rings, watches and every kind of jewellery imaginable. On the way into the church I had noticed two words, 'Tolle Lege', written on the mosaic floor in the porch. I whispered to Nobby to ask if he knew the meaning.

He hesitated for a second. 'Eh, yes. Take ... something,' he replied, though not sounding too sure.

Young Banjaxed chipped in. 'It means "take and leg it",' he laughed.

'Very charitable indeed,' I replied. 'That's exactly what I intend to do!'

Most of the glass cases were in the sanctuary, behind the altar rails and quite inaccessible. They were also attached to the walls and quite high up, for obvious reasons. A ladder would have been needed to get at them. Luckily for us – and we had got Daisy to check this out previously – Mum's damaged engagement ring was in the glass case attached to the wall, quite high up and between a confession box and a pillar, but outside the altar rails. The slim case, about two inches deep, had two sections, top and bottom with two panes of glass, a gold-coloured frame, and with a dark blue velvet or baize material at the back. Hooks were screwed in through this material into the back of the case with rings, watches and other items dangling from them. The items in this case, we imagined, would not have been as valuable as the jewellery in the other cases.

Out came our cleaning rags and brushes and we started looking busy. As expected, despite there being many people in the church praying and walking around and doing the usual things people do in churches, nobody noticed us even though they saw us. Four Eyes started quietly singing 'Tantum Ergo' and 'Adeste Fidelis', 'for atmosphere,' he said. Morty, on the other hand, opted for T. Rex's 'Children of the Revolution' and sang on about not getting fooled. Four Eyes was practicing to become the next Pope and Morty was singing and swaying like one of the Hare Krishna's. Redser hissed at them to 'shut the bleedin' racket.'

I, meanwhile, had climbed up on the brass-topped altar rail with my cleaning rag. I had one foot resting on it, the other on an outcrop of a pillar beside the case. One hand held the upper part of the pillar for support, while the other held the cleaning rag. Quick as a flash, I reached over and started vigorously cleaning the glass. I slowed down near the case's lock and covered it as if I was shining it. I then prised open the lock with the Stanley knife that was hidden in the rag. In went my chubby fingers and I grabbed Mum's engagement ring. Then I replaced it with a Lucky Bag ring and popped hers into the bag. 'Fair exchange,' I said to myself and locked the door again before dropping down onto the floor. The lads continued cleaning around the candle stand for a few minutes and then we gave each other the nod and marched out of the church. Job done!

Minnie said afterwards that Daisy nearly gave the game away by starting to cackle at the back of the church. She wondered why I didn't do some window cleaning at home and then started laughing at her own joke. Minnie had to stuff her hanky into Daisy' mouth to stop her giving the game away.

Redser, Four Eyes and I popped into O'Connor's jewellery warehouse on Hell's Lane, a few doors from the House of Geraniums, once we got back. We knew one of the staff there from school who was serving his apprenticeship. O'Connor's said they would repair, reset and polish the burnt ring, which they did.

Didn't we give Mum a big surprise on her birthday a few weeks later. She said she never thought she would ever wear it again. We presented it to her in one of her favourite parks, St Stephen's Green, while she was sitting on her favourite seat, the one with her name on it – Annie Haslam.

The days, months and years passed quickly from then onwards. Daisy became a fashion guru going around wearing bell bottoms and listening to Leonard Cohen, the Chieftains and Clannad. She read, or so she said, Camus, Kafka, Gibran and Solzhenitsyn and had 'gulags' and 'cancer wards' for breakfast, dinner and tea. Then she talked about Bacon, Egg and Freud. Not to mention Blue Nuns and Black Round Towers. She and some friends became involved in the Irish Anti-Apartheid Movement and the Irish Women's Liberation

Movement. Then they took the train to Belfast with the Four Mary's on some sort of protest about women's rights. They also brought home yucky yoghurts. They adopted a more aloof manner with myself and my pals. Even Daisy's voice had changed. Completely gone was the last hint of a country accent and in its place was a grandiose tone directed at Minnie and I as if we were riff-raff. Moreover, she reverted to her real name, Elizabeth, saying it was more suitable in her 'social circle'. After ten years of living in Dublin, she had changed from West of Ireland to West Brit. She and her pals, prancing around the house, really seemed to have lost the run of themselves – chatting endlessly about bicycle regulators, someone's doll's house, tennis-playing girls scratching their bums, Mrs Warren's forthcoming profession, sex kittens, *Sticky Fingers* and Nancy Sinatra's boots.

Daisy later went to work for the Summer holidays in a kibbutz in Israel, where she met Moshe Dayan, hero of many wars. 'We are a small nation, but strong', he said. She 'understood only too well', was her reply. 'We too are a small nation, but proud! The sun has set upon an Empire.' Very taken with her, he regaled her as 'the Second Coming of Countess Markievicz!' From there she travelled to France but always regretted being too late for the students' protests. So did we. 'I'm attached to the Sorbonne,' she wrote home in a haughty tone, having persuaded the powers-that-be that they needed her '*savoir faire*' to run the university properly. She was right, however, and soon became its President!

Freckles, the hands-on one in the family, got a job drilling for oil in Alaska. Everyone laughed at the idea – until he struck liquid gold! Minnie got a job running the NHS in the UK. As a side-line, she set up a consultancy company called Aching Heads' Aftercare (Aha!), which was involved in education in the palliative care sphere. She also brought her experience of checking for signs of life in the corpses in the hospice morgue to great advantage.

After leaving school, I got a job in Barclays Bank in England. I don't know how or why. On my application form under 'hobbies' I included horse-racing to fill in a space. At the interview in the Hibernian Hotel, I was queried about this. 'Did I own a horse? Was I involved in horse breeding?'

Dublin Be Damned!

'No,' I said. 'I'm a regular in P.J. Kilmartin's. I like gambling on horse-racing.'

'At least you don't keep any skeletons in your cupboards,' said she. I laughed and thanked her inwardly for reminding me to get on to Redser and Nobby to ensure the next consignment went down to UCD at the weekend. 'And do you ever win?' asked the very attractive interviewer with a gorgeous English accent. She reminded me of Sally.

'All the time, I absolutely clean up,' said I, winking at her. Her eyes seemed to dance. Very strange. It was as if I had hypnotised her. She winked back and I got the job. Barclay James Harvest's song, 'Everyone is Everybody Else', sprang to mind.

I left the hotel door and bounded down the steps onto Dawson Street, sun shining on the world, trees in perfect bloom, good cheer everywhere. The aroma of geraniums and lavender suffused the air. I knew that money didn't always make the world go around. No, I realised, but Argent does, and I started humming 'Hold your head up! Hold your head up! Dunk, dunk, dunk. Didi, dunk, dunk, dunk. Hold your head high!'

I thought of the words of some famous character from the past, John Charles or maybe JFK Redmond? – 'Ask not what your country can do for you. Ask to go wherever the firing line extends!' Okay, fair enough, I thought. Dublin be damned! I'm off!

Na, na, na, na, na, na, na, na, hey, hey, hey! Goodbye! Na, na, na, na, hey, hey, hey! Goodbye! Na, na, na, na, hey, hey, hey! Goodbye!